Hutcheson Macaulay Posnett

Comparative literature

Hutcheson Macaulay Posnett
Comparative literature
ISBN/EAN: 9783337204945

Printed in Europe, USA, Canada, Australia, Japan

Cover: Foto ©Paul-Georg Meister /pixelio.de

More available books at **www.hansebooks.com**

COMPARATIVE LITERATURE

BY

HUTCHESON MACAULAY POSNETT

M.A., LL.D., F.L.S.

BARRISTER-AT-LAW; PROFESSOR OF CLASSICS AND ENGLISH LITERATURE
UNIVERSITY COLLEGE, AUCKLAND, NEW ZEALAND

AUTHOR OF "THE HISTORICAL METHOD," ETC.

LONDON
KEGAN PAUL, TRENCH & CO., 1, PATERNOSTER SQUARE
1886

PREFACE.

To assume a position on the border-lands of Science and Literature is perhaps to provoke the hostility of both the great parties into which our modern thinkers and educationists may be divided. The men of Literature may declare that we have fallen into the hands of the Philistines, and that the mere attempt to explain literary development by scientific principles is worthy of none but a Philistine. The men of Science may be inclined to underrate the value of a study which the unveiled presence of that mysterious element, imagination, makes apparently less definite than their own. In a word, our position may arouse hostility and fail to secure friendship. What, then, is our apology for assuming it?

To our friends, the men of Science, we would say that the culture of imagination is of the utmost service alike in the discovery of new truths and in the diffusion of truths already known; that the supposed hostility of Science to Literature, by discrediting this faculty, tends to lower our attainments alike in Science and Literature; and that the study on which we now propose to enter affords a splendid field for the exercise at once of analysis and of imagination.

To our friends, the men of Literature, we would say that nothing has contributed more largely to lower the value of their studies in the eyes of thinking men than the old-fashioned worship of imagination, not merely as containing an element of mystery, but as altogether superior to conditions of space and time; that, under the auspices of this irrational worship, the study of Literature tends to become a blind idolatry of the Unknown, with a priesthood of textual pedants who would sacrifice to verbalism the very deity they affect to worship; but that the comparative study of Literature not only opens an immense field of fruitful labour but tends to foster creative imagination.

Mr. Matthew Arnold in his *Discourses in America* has recently discussed this supposed conflict between Science and Literature; and, though his treatment of the definition of Literature—a subject to which we shall presently refer—is by no means satisfactory, few will refuse to join with him in the hope that Literature may some day be "studied more rationally"[*] than it is at present. To such rational study this volume is intended as a contribution, however slight—an effort, it may be feeble, to treat Literature as something of higher import to man than elegant dilettantism or, what is possibly worse, pedantry devoted to the worship of words.

Should the present application of historical science to Literature meet with general approval, the establishment

[*] *Discourses in America*, p. 136.

of chairs in Comparative Literature at the leading Universities of Great Britain, America, and the Australian Colonies would do much to secure the steady progress of this vast study, which must depend on the co-operation of many scholars. The harvest truly is plenteous; but the labourers, as yet, are few.

The translations which this volume contains are, for the most part, the author's workmanship. Many illustrations, however, which he had placed in his manuscript have been left out from want of space, even an entire chapter, on the development of Greek prose, having been omitted for the same reason. These illustrations may be added on some future occasion, or published in another volume. Meanwhile, indulgent readers will kindly attribute any apparent dearth of evidence to this want of space.

Should errors of print or matter have escaped the author's notice, he would also beg his readers to remember that this work was passing through the press just as he was on the eve of leaving this country for New Zealand.

24, TRINITY COLLEGE, DUBLIN,
January 14, 1886.

CONTENTS.

BOOK I.
INTRODUCTION.

CHAPTER		PAGE
I. What is Literature?		3
II. Relativity of Literature		21
III. The Principle of Literary Growth		57
IV. The Comparative Method and Literature		73

BOOK II.
CLAN LITERATURE.

I. The Clan Group		89
II. Early Choral Song		99
III. Personal Clan Poetry		130
IV. The Clan and Nature		162

BOOK III.
THE CITY COMMONWEALTH.

I. The City Commonwealth Group		171
II. Clan Survivals in the City Commonwealth		177
III. Poetry of the City Commonwealth		198

BOOK IV.
WORLD-LITERATURE.

CHAPTER	PAGE
I. What is World-Literature?	235
II. The Individual Spirit in World-Literature	242
III. The Social Spirit in World-Literature	269
IV. World-Literature in India and China	288

BOOK V.
NATIONAL LITERATURE.

I. What is National Literature?	339
II. Man in National Literature	347
III. Nature in National Literature	374
Conclusion	390
Index	393

BOOK I.
INTRODUCTION.

COMPARATIVE LITERATURE.

CHAPTER I.

WHAT IS LITERATURE?

§ 1. CHARLES LAMB in one of his essays speaks of " books which are no books " as a catalogue including calendars and directories, scientific treatises and the statutes at large, the works of Hume and Gibbon, the histories of Flavius Josephus ("that learned Jew"), Paley's Moral Philosophy, almanacks, and draught-boards bound and lettered on the back. It moved the spleen of Elia "to see these *things in books' clothing* perched upon shelves, like false saints, usurpers of true shrines—to reach down a well-bound semblance of a volume and to come bolt on a withering Population Essay—to expect a Steele or a Farquhar and find Adam Smith." But, humorous and capricious as it is, this catalogue gives us a glimpse of problems which since the days of Elia have gradually assumed defined shape and serious significance :—How shall we distinguish the various classes of writing which social evolution produces ; how shall we separate specialized scientific studies from the works of creative imagination—the latter apparently Elia's ideal " books ; "

what, in fact, as distinct from scientific treatises and all other "things in books' clothing," is "literature"?

The unfortunate word has indeed been sadly abused. In popular usage it has come to resemble an old bag stuffed out and burst in a hundred places by all kinds of contents, so that we hardly know whether it could not be made to hold anything "written," from to-day's newspaper or the latest law reports, to Assyrian inscriptions, the picture-writings of the Aztecs, or the hieroglyphics of Egypt. Even professed scholars have contributed little towards the prevention of this cruelty to words. For example, Sismondi, one of the pioneers of literary history, though starting in his *Littérature du Midi de l'Europe* (1813) with the suggestive promise that he intended "above all to illustrate the reciprocal influence of the peoples' history, political and religious, on their literature, and of their literature on their character," vitiates from the outset any scientific treatment of his subject by leaving its nature unexplained. It is the same with Hallam. Shirking any effort to define the meaning of "literature," or even indicate the necessary difficulties in any such definition, Hallam uses the word (as he tells us in the preface to his *Literature of Europe*) "in the most general sense for the knowledge imparted through books;" and so treats it as a common, and apparently useless, label for a perfect farrago of subjects—logic, astronomy, the drama, philology, political economy, jurisprudence, theology, medicine. Even immense improvements in the extent and depth of historical studies have done little to redeem the use of the word "literature," the origin of languages having for the most part diverted attention from that of the forms of writing as dependent on social evolution. Hence, such excellent scholars as J. J. Ampère, Littré, Villemain, Patin, Sainte-

Beauve, Taine, in France; G. G. Gervinus, Koberstein, Hettner, Scherer, and the authors of "culture-histories"— Grün, Riehl, Kremer, and others—in Germany, have by no means clarified European ideas of "literature" so thoroughly as might have been expected. No doubt we would not now, with Hallam, apologize for neglecting such "departments of *literature*" as books on agriculture or English law; still we have by no means reached any settled ideal of "literature" such as Hallam himself obscurely outlined by excluding history, save where it "had been written with peculiar beauty of language or philosophical spirit," from his *Literature of Europe*. Must we, then, surrender the word to the abuse alike of the learned and unlearned at the peril of some such caprice as that of Lamb—caprice not to be enjoyed as a freak of humour, but rather despised as the miscarriage of sober, possibly prosaic, inquiry? If we review the causes which have produced the abuse we shall at least understand the difficulties to which any definition of "literature" must be exposed.

§ 2. The word *literatura* even among the Romans had no settled meaning. Tacitus uses the phrase *literatura Græca* to express "the shapes of the Greek alphabet;" Quintilian calls grammar *literatura*; and Cicero uses the word in the general sense of "learning" or "erudition." Accordingly, when scholars of the Renaissance began to use the word they did not intend to convey ideas which it now readily suggests. They did not intend to convey the idea of a body of writings representing the life of a given people; much less did they purpose by using the word to draw distinctions between one class of such writings and another. Borrowing the word in its Latin significations, they did not stop to dream of days when modern nations would possess their own bodies of writings, just as they did not stop to inquire whether Greek or Latin ideas of the lyric, the epic, the drama, were suited or unsuited to the new life of Europe they saw around them. Greece and Rome, though rich in terms for special branches of poetry, oratory, or philosophy, had not in fact needed a word to express the general body of their writings as representing a *national* development. Greece had not needed such a word because she never was at one with herself, never attained to permanent national unity. Rome had not needed such a word partially because she passed, as if at one bound, from municipality to world-empire without halting to become a nation, partially because the cultured few who were the makers of her writings worked day and night upon Greek models. It was only when bodies of national writings, such as those of England and France, had been long enough in existence to attract reflection, it was only when the spread of democratic ideas in the eighteenth century began to make men regard the writings of their countrymen as something more than elegant copies of antique models made under the patronage of courts and princes, as in truth the fruits of the nation's historic past, that the word "literature" became useful to mark an idea peculiar to the nations of modern Europe. But the word in which the new idea was embodied served rather to conceal than to disclose any conceptions of national authorship. "Literature," long a mere generalization for letters or the knowledge of letters, classical or modern, was ill adapted to express the idea of a definite national growth.

§ 3. One cause of the indefiniteness of "literature" we have thus found in the source from which the word has reached us; another and more interesting cause we shall find in the development of social life. Karl Otfried Müller tells us how we may trace the three different stages of civilisation among the Greeks in the three grand divisions of their poetry; how the epic belongs to a period of monarchical institutions when men's minds were impregnated and swayed by legends handed down from antiquity; how the elegiac, iambic, and lyric poetry arise in more agitated times and accompany the growth of republican governments; and how the drama represents the prime of Athenian power and freedom. But this is only one out of a host of such examples. Take any branch of verse or prose composition, and you soon find that directly or indirectly its existence implies certain conditions of social life. The oratory of the Athenian Ekklêsia or the Roman Forum, of the English Parliament or the French Pulpit; the hymns of the Indian or Hebrew priests; the rythmical prose of Hebrew or Arab poets; the songs of the Homeric *aoidos* or the Saxon *scôp*; the chorus of the *Khorovod* in the Russian *Mir* or village-commune; Athenian, Roman, Sanskrit, Chinese, Japanese, English, French, and German dramas; —all result from and reflect the action, thought, and speech peculiar to the particular places and particular times at which they appear. But this dependence on limited spheres of social life is concealed by the vague word "literature." Containing a generalization, and as such suggesting some abstract unity unconditioned by time and space, the word leads us to expect identity in the form and spirit of writing whenever and wherever it appears—an identity which does not strike us as false until repeated comparisons and contrasts have forced upon us the recognition of the falsity. We can easily understand how the enthusiastic study of classical models contributed to disseminate in modern Europe the idea of this uniformity, and the belief that archetypes of "literature" had been fixed once for all in the brilliant ages of Pericles and Augustus. We can easily understand how the universal claims of medieval theology and philosophy directly or indirectly contributed to strengthen this belief in universal exemplars which threatened for a time to make the masterpieces of Athens and Rome idols of literary imitation as unquestionable, if not as sacred, as the Qur'ân. But it is not so easy to grasp the facts that "literature," far from enshrining universal forms and ideas of beauty, owes both its creative and critical works to the development of social life ; that familiar general or special conceptions suggested by the word drop off one by one as we retrace the steps of such development; and that all our subtle literary distinctions finally disappear in the songs of those isolated clans and tribes whose fusion produced the people and the language of future art and criticism. We may be sure that it is difficult to keep the varying relations of social development to literary growth steadily in view when we find a scholar like Mr. J. A. Symonds speaking of Athenian literature as "National," or an antiquary like Herr Ten Brink applying the phrase "National Epos" to days when the Saxons were merely a loose federation of tribes.

Indeed, we have only to watch the beginnings of national history in order to see how readily the actual development of literature is obscured, how hardly it is to be recovered. Nations, like individuals, have been always disposed from interest or vanity to forget their day of small things; like individuals, too, they have been always unwilling to isolate their origins from the great ones who have gone before. Some Æneas will connect the pedigrees of Ilium and Rome, some Brute the Trojan will serve as an aristocratic eponymous ancestor for the wild tribes of Britain. Thus, at the price of much confusion in language and thought, the interlacing of national histories reproduces on an enlarged scale the interlacing of clan traditions which has everywhere accompanied the fusion of clans into larger social groups. Thus, too, chronological standards, which can never carry us beyond the adult and self-conscious age of some particular group, are so applied as to raise the most confused impressions of relative antiquity in institutions and thought; and languages, customs, ideas, come to be reckoned old or young by measurements taken from the First Olympiad, or A.U.C., or B.C., or from the Flight. Hence, *within* the group, social development is obscured by inability or dislike to look back to times when national language and ideas could not exist; *without* the group, it is obscured by imitation of peoples who have attained to higher grades of social progress; and so the conception of national literature, as well as that of national history, becomes a medley of confusion in which differences of time and place, of social and individual character, are obliterated. Nothing but historical reflection can restore the real order of development out of this chaos; and historical reflection, as a work of science, is only the tardy product of the present century. How recent are its applications to the domain of literature we may judge from two facts. Hallam, in 1838, could truthfully say that "France has no work of any sort, even an indifferent one, on the universal history of her literature; nor can we (Englishmen) claim for ourselves a single attempt of the most superficial kind." Donaldson, in his "Translator's Preface" to the first volume of Müller's *Literature of Ancient Greece*, observed, in January, 1840, that "before the publication of the present work no history of Greek literature had been published in the English language."

§ 4. But if it be hard for the popular mind to avoid confusing early and adult conceptions of literature, the critical mind, from causes peculiar to itself, is exposed to a similar confusion. If the facts of social development have been almost unavoidably overlooked by average intelligence, they have been deliberately set aside by the professed critic. When men first began to ask themselves why it was that the poet's works pleased them, they sought to find the cause not in human senses, emotions, intellect, but in analyses of the works themselves. Thus the *Poetics*, attributed to Aristotle, mark an effort to extract general principles of dramatic creation from the practice of the Athenian masters, Sophocles in particular. Few questions are asked about the development of the Athenian drama. The literary influences of Athenian life, contrasted with the life celebrated by the early epic and lyric poets of Greece, are ignored. No attempt is made to compare the drama of Athens with that of other Greek cities, much less to discover whether " barbarians " possessed any similar spectacles. Thus, by neglecting the influences of social life on literature, Greek criticism fostered the deadly theories that literature is essentially an imitation of masterpieces, that its ideals are not progressive but permanent, that they have no dependence on particular conditions of human character, on the nature of that social instrument language, on circumscribed spheres of time and place. In the imitative workmanship of Roman artists the principles of the Greek only gathered strength ; and, transmitted through Rome to the peoples of modern Europe, they everywhere more or less checked the growth of truly national literature. While the more vigorous life of England and Spain developed new forms of the drama, Italy and France accepted the classical models, Germany following their example. It is true that at length the learning of Germany revolted from a bondage in which it recognised a hybrid monster of Greek, Roman, and French extraction. It is true that France herself, especially after the Revolution had thrown her back on older memories than those of Richelieu's centralism or Henri Quatre, came to learn the literary value of her own early history. But, in spite of these successes of the national against the classical spirit, one strong survival of classical influences lingered, and still lingers, in the critical mind of Europe. If men like Goethe and Victor Hugo could cast off the bondage of Greek models, and appeal triumphantly to the art of Shakspere and Calderon, criticism was still far from giving up those universal ideas which, logically enough, had accompanied the conception of literature as the imitation of universal models. Thus, for example, the main purpose of A. W. Schlegel's defence of the "Romantic School" was to reconcile the conflicting principles of "Romantic" and classical art in universal ideas common to and underlying both; and Coleridge upholds the universal claims of Shakspere's art with as much enthusiasm as any classical critic ever upheld those of the ancient masters.

The truth is that the "Romantic School" represented reformers imperfectly conscious of the purport of their reforms. These dissidents from an ancient creed of critical dogma failed to see that if literary art is something better than an imitation of models, if these models are admitted to be out of place when carried into social conditions markedly different from those under which they were produced, then the dependence of literary ideals on limited spheres of human association follows as a matter of course, and "Romantic" pretenders to universal rights are caught in the act of self-contradiction. Failure to observe this self-contradiction need not surprise any student of the social sciences. Political economists, for example, have based their science on assumptions of personal freedom, social classification, and human character which possess a very limited application even within the recent history of the English people; yet such facts as medieval serfage, the different social classification of different countries and ages, or the impossibility of action from self-interest in communal life, have only within the last few years prevented our economists from claiming universality for their theories. Again, English jurisprudence for a time did not hesitate to advance similar claims, although its leading idea of a central government, from which the commands, obligations, and sanctions of law shall issue, is in the political life of early communities as clearly out of place as the literary ideals of Athens, Rome, or Paris would have been among the early Arab clans. If we find fault with the shortcomings of "Romantic" criticism we must remember that nothing is more difficult than to see an ideal without expanding it into universality even in the prosaic accuracy of scientific reasoning, how much more in works peculiarly belonging to the imagination—works in which the consciousness of thinking within limits is a fatal damper to the enthusiasm which creates without reflecting on the nature of its materials, and is paralysed when it attempts to critically retrace the steps of the creative process. Yet, unless we limit the range to which our criticism shall apply, we may find ourselves applying the standards of the Athenian to the Japanese drama, or those of the Greek lyric to the *Shih King* of ancient China. Clearly such limitless criticism has done much to obscure all ideas of literary development, and consequently to make the conception of literature the medley we have found it.

§ 5. But there are obstacles to the definition of literature which arise not from the origin of the word, nor from unhistorical ideas of the learned or the unlearned, but from the different and even conflicting aims of writing in different states of social life and the different means adopted to secure such aims. "By literature," says Mr. Stopford Brooke, "we mean the written thoughts and feelings of intelligent men and women arranged in a way which will give pleasure to the reader;" and the same admirable critic adds that "prose is not literature unless it have style and character and be written with curious care." Without pausing to ask whether Mr. Brooke would extend his ideal of "prose" so as to cover the rythmical cadence of Al-Harîrî, or the Chinese *Tsze* in which rimes are repeated at the end of lines of indeterminate length, without raising any questions about the development of prose, and allowing one ideal end of literature as opposed to science to be pleasure, not discovery or instruction, we find that the pleasure imparted by literature and the means of imparting it have in different states of social life varied surprisingly. For example, from our modern standpoint Professor Jebb is perhaps right in saying that "there can be no literature without writing; for literature implies fixed form; and, though memory may do great feats, a merely oral tradition cannot guarantee fixed form." Yet we cannot forget that even at the zenith of Greek civilization music and dancing (to say nothing of acting) formed an integral part of certain literary pleasures to a degree which our modern familiarity with printed books renders almost inconceivable. Not only have the pleasures of literature varied with the average character of the men and women it addressed—from communal villagers singing their harvest hymn to the courtly audience of Boileau—but the means to secure such pleasures have likewise varied from wild combinations of gesture, music, dance, and song, in which the words were of the least importance, to printed letters as the main instrument of the literary artist. Compare, for example, the so-called "Pindaric" odes of Gray with those of the Greek master himself, and nothing but our modern idea of literary art, as mainly an appeal to the eye and ear through print, can hide the grotesque absurdity of *strophe* and *antistrophe* reappearing like fleshless skeletons two thousand years after the dance and song that gave them life have died away.

As the means so also the ideal ends of literary production have varied remarkably under different conditions of social life. The prevalent belief that the proper ends of science are discovery and instruction, but that of literature pleasure, the greatest pleasure of the greatest number in the given national group,* is due to developments in social organisation and thought which have democratically expanded the audience of literature, specialised the pursuits of science, and established rather superficial distinctions between experience and its students on the one side and imagination and its votaries on the other. Some of these ideas would have been sadly out of place in days when the cultured few (as in Athens or Rome) reposed upon the labours of a mass of slaves; others, in days when science and literature were so closely intertwined as in the science-poetry of Empedocles or even the dialogues of Plato, would have been too con-

* Mr. Palgrave (*Songs and Sonnets of Shakespere*, p. 237) tells us that "pleasure is the object of poetry; and the best fulfilment of its task is the greatest pleasure of the greatest number." They who still fancy that literature in an age of democracy can remain the monopoly of a cultured Cloud-cuckoo-town will shrink from this use of a Philistine formula and resent the expression of poetry's ideal end in an echo of Benthamism. But art and criticism, if they are living, must reflect contemporary life and current thought.

fused to supply distinctions. In fact, the differentiation of literature from science, however "natural" it may now look to us, was a process of slow and fitful evolution dependent not only on individual intelligence but on social development. The dependence of the ideal ends of literature on such development might be illustrated from the writings of every people, every social group, which has produced a literature of its own. If it may be seen from Spenser's introductory letter to his *Faerie Queene* that our modern democratic conceptions of literature have no place in his knightly theory of poetry as intended "to fashion a gentleman or noble person in virtuous and gentle discipline," similar contrasts might be easily discovered between the early and modern ideals of song in France, or Germany, or Spain. But we need not confine our examples to European nations. The paternal government of China and the sentiments of family life which form the striking social characteristic of that vast empire have left their marks upon the ideals of Chinese literature in general and upon that of the Chinese drama in particular. "Chinese poetry," says M. Bazin (introduction to his *Théatre Chinois*, p. xxvii.), "requires every dramatic work to have a moral end or meaning. For example, the moral purpose of the play called *Tchao-meï-hiang*, or *A Maid's Intrigues*, discovers itself in the words addressed by the lady Han to her daughter, 'Know you not that now, as in ancient times, the marriage of husband and wife needs to be consecrated by rites and ceremonies?' The *dénoûment* is the triumph of virtue. Any play without a moral purpose is in Chinese eyes only a ridiculous work in which one can find no meaning. According to Chinese authors the object aimed at in a serious drama is to present the noblest lessons of history to the ignorant who know not how to read; and, according to the Chinese penal code, the end of theatrical representations is 'to exhibit true or imaginary pictures of just and good men, chaste women, and loving and dutiful children—characters likely to lead the spectators to the practice of virtue.' Obscenity is a crime; and composers of obscene plays, says a Chinese writer quoted by Morrison, shall be severely punished in the abode of expiations, *ming-fou*, and their torment shall last as long as their plays remain on the earth."

Contrasting this aim of the Chinese drama with that of the æsthetic Athenian—for, in spite of the famous definition in the *Poetics*, we can scarcely speak of Attic tragedy, much less comedy, as possessing a moral purpose—critics who refuse to separate their ideals of literature from those of human conduct will probably agree with M. Bazin in placing the Attic sense of the beautiful below the didactic morality of the Celestial. Aristophanes, it is to be feared, stands condemned by Chinese judgment to a very lengthy experience of *ming-fou*; and as for such dramatists as Wycherley and Vanbrugh, their only hopes must depend on the rather dusty condition of their volumes nowadays. It may be true that the Chinese ideal is higher than that of our modern European dramas, which would limit itself to the truthful imitation of human character and custom in contemporary life. It may be that the Chinese is superior to the Indian dramatic ideal laid down in the prologue of the *Málati and Mádhava*,* and clearly expressing the dramatic taste of a cultured class such as the Bráhmans of India are known

---

* "Again," says this prologue, "what avails it to boast a knowledge of the Yoga, the Sankhya, the Upanishads, or the Vedas? Such knowledge is of no use for dramatic composition. Fertility of imagination, harmony of style, richness of invention—these are the qualities which mark education and genius in this kind of writing. Such is the drama written by our venerable friend Bhavabhúti."

to have been. But our object is not to canvass the merits of this or that dramatic ideal; it is simply to show how widely such ideals have differed in different conditions of social life, and to illustrate by their conflict the difficulty, or rather impossibility, of reconciling such contradictions in any universal definition of literature which, be it remembered, must also include, many branches of verse and prose not to be found in the drama.

§ 6. We have now reviewed four causes of the obscurity overhanging the word "literature"—the source from which it has reached us, unhistorical ideas about it entertained by the learned and the unlearned, the subtle changes in the means and the no less subtle changes in the ends of literary workmanship. In short, we have found what was to have been expected wherever the dependence of written upon living thought and of the latter upon social and physical conditions is overlooked —confused views of the present nature, the past, and the ideal future of literature. Other causes contributing to the same confusion might easily be added. For example, many problems properly belonging to any scientific treatment of literature are hidden away in more or less cognate studies. Thus, the origins of metres, if discussed at all, are generally treated as the worthless *peculium* of that broken-down philosopher, the grammarian; and rhetoric absorbs much of the interest which might be well bestowed on a subject so attractive as the developments of prose in different languages and social groups. But we need not extend our search for the causes of an obscurity which average thinking and cultured taste concurred to render unavoidable.

Definite ideas of literature have, in truth, been impeded by two grand facts which theory may affect to conceal but cannot really banish—the fact that all literatures, even to some degree those wrought by the hand of mere imitators like the Romans, depend upon conditions of social life, and, if not stationary or decaying, constantly throw out new forms of vitality, constantly enter new phases of art and criticism; and the fact that, in spite of this constant movement in each separate literature, in all literatures viewed together as productions of humanity, definition implies, and must at least provisionally assume, a degree of *permanence* which is too often secured off-hand by violently declaring selected ideas to be universal and independent, not only of social life in its myriad shapes, but even of space and time. Hereafter we shall have other opportunities for discussing these obstacles to the scientific study of literature—obstacles, it must be remembered, common to all the social sciences, political economy, jurisprudence, even logic, so far as the laws of thought are dependent on social evolution. At present, however, we shall be satisfied with two principles which may serve to guide our efforts to reach defined ideas of literature. (1) Our definition cannot cover an unlimited range of human life save at the expense of confusing perceptions of sense, emotions, thoughts, not only belonging to widely diverse social and physical conditions, but often directly conflicting in the form and spirit of their literary expression. (2) We must be ever prepared to forego our limited definitions of literature, or any species of literature, when we pass out of the conditions to which they are properly confined.

Bearing these principles in mind, we may be content to set out with a rough definition of literature, as consisting of works which, whether in verse or prose, are the handicraft of imagination rather than reflection, aim at the pleasure of the greatest possible number of the nation rather than instruction and practical effects,* and appeal to general rather than specialised knowledge. Every element of this definition clearly depends on limited spheres of social and mental evolution—the separation of imagination from experience, of didactic purpose from æsthetic pleasure, and that specialisation of knowledge which is so largely due to the economic development known as "division of labour." In truth, our definition will carry us, and is intended to carry us, a very short way satisfactorily—perhaps no distance at all beyond conditions of art and science under which we live, or similar to these. If the student has expected something better, let him reflect that breadth of definition is only to be purchased by flagrant violations of the facts but just stated. He can, indeed, have no better introduction to the scientific study of literature than a definition which shall bring home one of the great lessons to be learned from this and every other science, the limited truth of human ideas.

We have spoken of our study as a "science;" let us

* M. Victor de Laprade (*La Sentiment de la Nature chez les Modernes*," pp. 312-322), while discussing Goethe's efforts to combine science with poetry, raises the question whether didactic poetry is at the present day a legitimate form of poetic art. In doing so he draws a careful distinction between the didactic poetry of Greece or India, and that of days in which "science has left the path of hypothesis and imagination, has become possessed of fixed methods and knows its proper limits." In these latter conditions M. Laprade decides that didactic poetry is "un genre bâtard, dangereux, à peu près impossible;" that it is poetry at all only "in proportion as it withdraws itself from science to enter into the imagination." Goethe's *Faust* may contain geology, optics, chemistry; his *Wilhelm Meister*, scientific discussions and demonstrations; but in his *Elective Affinities* there appears that "fatalistic conception" of scientific law before which human liberty, master-maker of literary art, would seem to disappear. But M. Laprade has scarcely touched the true cause of that dissatisfaction which the metaphysical as well as the didactic poetry of modern times can hardly fail to produce. This cause is to be found in the fact that poetry and literature in general are expected to address the average mind in average, not specialised, language; whereas science pursues its studies and expresses its truths in the technical language it requires.

state at the outset the meaning we intend to convey by that term. It must be evident from what we have already said that by "science" we cannot mean a body of universal truths, that the very evolution of literature is fatal *per se* to any such literary "science." But by the use of the term we mean to imply that limited truths discoverable in the various phases of literature may, nay, in order to be understood even as limited truths, *must* be grouped round certain central facts of comparatively permanent influence. Such facts are the climate, soil, animal and plant life of different countries; such also is the principle of evolution from communal to individual life which we shall hereafter explain at length. The former may be called the statical influences to which literature has been everywhere exposed; the latter may be called the dynamical principle of literature's progress and decay. But before we attempt to explain this principle we shall illustrate the dependence of literature on social conditions, and the consequent relativity, or necessary limitation, alike of its creative art and criticism.

CHAPTER II.

RELATIVITY OF LITERATURE.

§ 7. LITERATURE, however rude, however cultured, expresses the feelings and thoughts of men and women on physical nature, on animal life, on their own social communion, on their individual existence. It is incumbent, therefore, on the champions of universal literary ideas to discover the existence of some universal human nature which, unaffected by differences of language, social organisation, sex, climate, and similar causes, has been at all times and in all places the keystone of literary architecture. Is there one universal type of human character embracing and reconciling all the conflicting differences of human types in the living world and in its historic or prehistoric past? Can really scientific reasons be advanced in support of the sentimental belief in that colossal personage called "man," whose abstract unity is allowed to put on new phases of external form, but whose "essence" is declared to remain unaltered? Unfortunately any such scientific inquiry has been generally supplanted by explosive or pathetic assertions of dogma. Yet the relativity of literature may not unaptly be illustrated by the dogmatic assertions of its opponents.

Kingsley, in his address on "the limits of exact science as applied to history," reminded his audience that "if they wished to understand history they must try to understand men and women. For history is the history of men and women, and nothing else. If you should ask me how to study history I should answer, Take by all means biographies, wheresoever possible, autobiographies, and study them. Fill your minds with live human figures. Without doubt, history obeys and always has obeyed in the long run certain laws. But these laws assert themselves, and are to be discovered not in things but in persons, in the actions of human beings; and just in proportion as we understand human beings shall we understand the laws which they have obeyed or which have avenged themselves on their disobedience. This may seem a truism; if it be such, it is one which we cannot too often repeat to ourselves just now, when the rapid progress of science is tempting us to look at human beings rather as things than as persons, and at abstractions under the name of laws rather as persons than as things." Kingsley's confusion in this passage of physical, social, and political "laws"—orderly successions of the forces in physical nature and of cause and effect in social organisation with those commands of a person or body of persons which do indeed require to "assert themselves" and depend on the "obedience" of "human beings"— cannot easily escape detection. But with this confusion we are not at present particularly concerned. We prefer to observe how Kingsley has here expressed that side of history with which creative art finds itself most at home. Why? Because clear-cut personality, individual being without any touch of the collective and impersonal, is evidently capable of more concentrated interest, of more artistic treatment, than the hazy outline of a multitude or an impalpable abstraction. How, indeed, can an artist conceive the conduct of his hero or heroine as the expression of an impersonal "law," of an order of events to which innumerable social and physical causes have contributed? It is the work of creative art to bring before us "live human figures;" and an artist's view of literary and every other kind of history is best conceived from this strongly individual standpoint. But requirements of art are one thing, truths of science another; and a little reflection will convince us that Kingsley's idea of character-history is far less truthful than artistic.

§ 8. To understand history we must understand men and women. True; but men and women are exceedingly complex units, and their treatment as purely isolated units would not only fail to contribute to the understanding of history, but would tend to resolve all human knowledge into a mass of disconnected atoms among which all general principles and even thought itself would perish. In order to understand either ourselves or history we must therefore combine and compare these personal units with each other, with the rest of the animal world, with physical nature. The bodies of men and women consist of components which may be chemically resolved into the vegetable and mineral elements of other animals and of physical nature. Their unreflecting emotions seem to be a current of sense-life not greatly different from that of other animals. But their social sympathies vary from a sense of obligation as narrow as that of clan-ties to one as wide as universal brotherhood; and their individual reason varies from the weakest sense of personal existence to the most profound depths of subjective philosophy. So far as the elements of each individual man or woman are shared with other animals and physical nature, we have certainly not reached the sphere of biographies or autobiographies. But when we have reached the sphere within which differences make their appearance not merely between human beings and physical nature, between human beings and other animals, but between different groups of men and women and different individuals composing these groups, it is a matter of little importance whether with Kingsley we use the concrete phrase "men and women," or prefer to sum up varieties of group or individual in the highly abstract term "man," provided we never forget that our abstract groups as well as our individual "men and women" depend for their character on space and time, on conditions of social organisation, on physical influences, geographical, climatic, and the like.

To select one out of many examples of the dependence of human character on social development, look at the different manner in which different literatures, or different periods of the same literature, have treated the characters of women. The status of women in different conditions of social life has left its marks in literary pictures of their character amazingly different. Simonides of Amorgos, in a very famous poem, contrasted different types of female character by comparing them with a hog and a fox, a dog and an ass, a weasel, an ape, and a bee; but if we were to search through the various likenesses of female character in literatures of the East and West, we might not only increase at will this uncomplimentary catalogue, but discover how profoundly female liberty or tutelage, public freedom or private seclusion, have affected the general and particular characters of women in different ages and countries. The women of Indian, Chinese, and Japanese dramas are, as we would anticipate, different enough from those of Attic tragedy and comedy, or from those of our modern European theatres. But such differences are by no means confined to countries so far removed from each other in social and physical circumstances. The careful study of any literature possessing a history sufficiently long reveals the most diverse treatment of female character within its own limits. Even in the "stationary" East the heroines of the classical Indian dramas possess a degree of independence impossible under the system of seclusion which has followed the Mohammedan conquest of India; and those of the early Chinese drama likewise contrast with the domestic prisoners of modern China described by the Abbé Grosier and others. But in the "progressive" West the evolution of female character may be more readily illustrated. Thus, Mr. Mahaffy has the merit of being among our earliest critics in contrasting the various conditions of women at different stages of social life in ancient Greece. The women of the *Iliad* and *Odyssey*—Helen, Andromache, Nausicaa—bring before us social relations very different from those of Aristophanes' women. Elsewhere like contrasts may be seen. The songs of Miriam and Deborah, even the witch of Endor, carry us back to days of Hebrew social life when the woman possessed a status far higher than one of her lord's harem. Again, the Roman women of the early republic, under the perpetual tutelage of their fathers, husbands, sons, or guardians, could have supplied no such rumours of ill fame as Juvenal voices, and, deprived of that freedom which permits at once the development and the display of character, might have realized the Periclean ideal of the sex. But the lesson which comparative literature must draw from such contrasts is something more than the dependence of human character on social conditions; it is also the impossibility of exact historic truth in the workmanship of literary art. In this impossibility lies one of the great facts which our phrase "relativity of literature" is intended to mark. . We shall, accordingly, illustrate its nature and bearing on the scientific treatment of literature. But let us first understand the full meaning of historical propriety by contrasting it with the universal assumptions of unhistoric criticism.

§ 9. Macaulay, commenting on some of Dryden's plays (*Aurungzebe,* the *Indian Emperor,* and the *Conquest of Granada*), observes that the sentiments put into the mouths of certain *dramatis personæ* violate all historical propriety; that, in fact, "nothing similar was ever even affected except by the cavaliers of Europe. The truth of character is the first object, the truth of place and time is to be considered only in the second place. We blame Dryden, not because his characters are not Moors or Americans, but because they are not men and women—not because love as he represents it could not exist in a harem or a wigwam, but because it could not exist anywhere." This is a moderate estimate of historical propriety, allowing, as it does, certain universal characteristics of all men and women while assigning a subordinate position to those differences of time, place, and social life which it is the part of the historical artist to indicate. But our Shaksperian critics of the subjective school will have nothing to do with such limitations of art. Shakspere's characters are to their minds true for all space and all time; nay, they rise above time and space, being apparently conceived, if not worked out, in an altogether Platonic world. Shakspere, says Coleridge, will not, like Plautus or Molière, draw for us the character of a miser because such a character is not "*permanent;*" and Shakspere's characters "must be *permanent,* permanent while men continue men, because they stand on what is absolutely necessary to our existence." Certainly of *permanence,* in one sense, we have enough and to spare in Shakspere's plays; for his chivalrous and Christian men and women of the Elizabethan age, the clergy, the clowns, and even the London artisans, are *permanent* enough to find a place in the Rome of Coriolanus and of Julius Cæsar impartially; and if the dramatist had undertaken to depict the contemporary life of Russia, Hindustan, or China, we cannot doubt that the conditions of his art would have demanded a similar display of "universal ideas," and that the scenery of Warwick or some other English county would, if required, have done excellent duty in the country of Romanoff or of Shah Jehan as the physical background for English men and women in something like (or perhaps not at all like) Russian or Indian dress.

We do not honour Shakspere by ignoring such truths; we merely display our ignorance of the necessary limitations of dramatic art which result from its social nature; we merely impose upon ourselves the penalty of ignorance —self-contradiction. If we wish to see the contradictions into which the subjective school of criticism is perpetually betrayed by its anxiety to raise a human idol above the sphere of human associations, we need only compare different passages of Coleridge or Carlyle *inter se*. Unwilling to find in the Elizabethan age the models of Shakspere's characters, looking upon them as " creatures of his meditation," " fragments of the divine mind that drew them," Coleridge, in spite of his ultra-idealism, cannot avoid self-contradiction; and his twofold defence of Shakspere's " conceits " is a *reductio ad absurdum* of itself. " If people would in idea throw themselves back a couple of centuries," he says, " they would find that conceits and puns were very allowable because very natural. We are not to forget that at the time Shakspere lived there was an attempt at, and an affectation of, quaintness and adornment, which emanated from the court, and against which satire was directed by Shakspere in the character of Osric in *Hamlet*." So much for the critic's admission of Shakspere's dependence on the associations of his age, with which of course we have no fault to find save its inadequacy. In treating the matter thus, Coleridge is aware that he is "only palliating the practice of Shakspere; he ought to have had nothing to do with merely temporary peculiarities; he wrote not for his own only, but for all ages." So far his conceits must be regarded as defects; "they detract sometimes from his *universality as to time, person, and situation*." * But the critic has already made the conceits and puns of Shakspere "natural" † or universally proper; the latter, he tells us, "often arise out of a mingled sense of injury, and contempt of the person inflicting it, and as it seems to me, it is a *natural* way of expressing that mixed feeling." Self-contradiction is likewise the fate of Carlyle's Platonism; he, too, in spite of a display of the mystic universal worthy of Novalis, is compelled to admit, for example, that "Dante knows accurately and well what lies close to him; but in such a time, without printed books or free intercourse, he could not know well what was distant." Miserable fall! for one who writes above space and time to depend on the printer's "devil" or the telegraph-clerk. But even the author of *Heroes and Hero-Worship* allows that "Dante does not come before us as a large Catholic mind, rather as a narrow and even sectarian mind," and that this narrowness is at least "partly the fruit of his age and position"—an opinion which any one who compares the social life of Italy in the thirteenth and fourteenth centuries with the *Divina Commedia* will heartily endorse.

* *Lectures and Notes on Shakespere* (ed. T. Ashe), p. 93.
† *Ib.*, p. 73.

If we are determined to lay down the dogma that Shakspere, or Dante, or any other poet wrote above space and time, above the social and physical conditions under which he lived, we really exclude historical propriety by a creed of literary inspiration which has been frequently asserted, if not believed in, with theological assurance. We imitate the criticism of the Arabs and make a literary Qur'ân out of our Shakspere or Dante. "Were we to examine the Qur'ân," says Baron de Slane,* "by the rules of rhetoric and criticism as they are taught in Moslem schools, we should be obliged to acknowledge that it is the perfection of thought and precision—an inevitable result, as the Moslems drew their principles of rhetoric from this very book." Reasoning in circles can supply as good foundations for a literary as for a theological creed, and save both a good many historical troubles. Yet it is remarkable that, in spite of their anti-historical dogma, our subjective critics are always anxious to show not only that Shakspere's characters are, in Macaulay's phrase, "men and women," but that they are *the* men and *the* women of the particular time and place which the poet represents on his stage. In the Rome of Coriolanus appear English drums and doublets, coals and bowls, and the Devil, English "gentlemen," "testy magistrates" from the Puritan Corporation of London, "divines" and "bare heads in a congregation" (*Cor.* iii. 2), while the servants of an English household take the place of slaves; and in the streets and Forum "Hob and Dick" (*Cor.* ii. 3), and the London trades oust by the rights of a free *bourgeoisie* the slaves and freemen of the Eternal City. But is it not pedantry to be careful about these things? And if an English clock strikes in the Rome of Julius Cæsar, or rime is there spoken of, or a proper English

* Preface to translation of Ibn Khallikân's Biographical Dictionary.

clown appears in Cleopatra's Alexandria, why not dismiss the anachronism with a smile? Because to do so would be to accept false views of human nature and of dramatic art; because the historical critic cannot forget that he who mistakes the social life of a group must misinterpret the characters of its individual units, that he who Londonises the public life of the Roman plebs is sure to Christianise or feudalise the private relations, feelings, thoughts of the Roman wife and mother and son and father. We are told by critics who should know better that "Shakspere is profoundly faithful to Roman life and character;" and the most accurate historian will scarcely dislodge the notion that the great dramatist's English "histories" are altogether correct descriptions of the individual and social characters of their times and places. But this shallow universalism is merely a last resource of subjective critics whose method—at least in the hands of such an extremist as Coleridge—is almost as fatal to true historical science as the Moslem belief that the language and ideas of their Bible came direct from God Himself. In opposition to all such critics, we are prepared to maintain not only that Shakspere's historical characters are often highly inaccurate, but that attempts of the kind, if they are to be dramatically successful, *must* be inaccurate; that the inaccuracy results from the most profound truth about literary and all human ideas—their limitation or relativity; and that the subjective critics are not only mistaken in their views of individual character, through overlooking the social, but that they have failed to grasp the real conditions of dramatic art.

§ 10. The dramatist draws his characters of men and women not for himself, not to be visible only to his own eyes, or to eyes as penetrating as his own, but to live and move and have their being in the sympathies and antipathies, in the senses and emotions, in the imaginations and intellect of his audience. This is the reason why the drama discloses in some respects better than any other branch of literature the average character of the age.* Orestes on the stage is driven to crime and madness by the effects of a long descent of inherited sin, but the feelings and beliefs which make his story tragic are in the heads and hearts of the Athenian audience.

The Ali or Hosein of the Persian passion-plays are figures splendidly and tragically beautiful, not as the æsthetic workmanship of any writer, but because they are seen through mists of religious faith by the devout audience of the *tekya*. The sensuality of a Vanbrugh lived in the hearts of his audience before it walked his stage. The refined intrigue of a Molière or Sheridan was performed to the life in courtly circles before it was dramatised. This is why the Roman plays of Ben Jonson were a failure, while those of Shakspere succeeded. What mattered it whether the Catiline of Sallust or the Sejanus of Tacitus were presented to Elizabethan men and

* M. Bazin (*Théâtre Chinois*, introduction, p. li.) makes some observations on literature in general, and the drama in particular, as reflecting the forms of social life, which may be here translated. "We have already remarked that literary productions initiate us more rapidly and sometimes more accurately in the secrets of social institutions than works apparently more serious ; and we do not fear to maintain that probably not a single Chinese play exists which does not throw light on some facts altogether ignored. Thus, the comedy translated by Davis has determined the true position of the legal concubine contrasted with the legitimate wife. Before the publication of that comedy the oblations of the Chinese at the tombs of their parents were often mentioned ; but did we know the prayers which they recite in these mournful ceremonies or the terms of the ritual they employ ? Does not the first drama of this (M. Bazin's own) collection furnish an example of marriage brought about by order of the emperor, and for the celebration of which the couple and the parents are freed from the formalities prescribed by custom and the rites ? The piece called *The Singer* similarly presents us with the formula of contract-of-sale in the case of a child; moreover, we find in it a scene which, as far as the evidence goes, proves that the sale was simply a mode of adoption. Such facts, it must be admitted, were at least very obscure points in Chinese character and custom."

women? They had to live in Elizabethan feelings or they were dead, long since dead, and, worst of all, not buried out of sight. He who, as Walt Whitman says, "drags the dead out of their coffins and stands them again on their feet," who "says to the past, Rise and walk before me that I may realize you," is the truly great dramatist; but to do this the puppets of the show must move along many a subtle wire which the feelings of the audience have supplied, but which their intellect shall not detect. The tribute of the heart must be paid to the past much as the Chinese offer their oblations to living persons representing their deceased ancestors; and no culture of the intellect must be allowed to destroy the fiction. So the "Romans" of Shakspere might not be historical Romans, might not even belong to the social life of Rome at all, but they were living human figures for the men and women of the Elizabethan theatre because they resembled themselves. The women of Shakspere's "Roman" dramas—Portia, Calphurnia, Volumnia, Virgilia—are not really pagans; they are Christian women, married by Christian marriage, and standing towards their sons and husbands in the Christian and chivalrous relations of family life. Volumnia enjoys a position which perpetual tutelage could not have tolerated; and the public freedom of the Roman woman is conceived in a thoroughly Elizabethan, or rather Elizabethan-London spirit. So, too, the men of Shakspere's Roman plays are as free from any sentiments of the Roman family as Elizabethan London can make them; and if in the Rome of Coriolanus we have clergy, and Christian clergy too, ("Hang 'em! I would they would forget me, like the virtues which our divines lose by 'em." *Cor.* ii. 3), Coriolanus himself is more a medieval knight than a Roman citizen.

All this is historically inaccurate; but it is so just because no dramatic or other poet is universal in his conceptions of character any more than in his conceptions of plants, or animals, or scenery. It is so because the social and individual developments of character prevent historical accuracy save at the expense of that conscious contrast between our own and different social and physical environments in which science delights but art perishes. It is so because historical accuracy is banished by the conditions of language and thought under which the dramatist writes, and through which his art must work. It is so because the dramatist's similes and metaphors, as well as his men and women, are not derived from "airy nothing," nor from an equally airy everything, but from a limited sphere of human associations, of animal and plant life, of physical nature. If a contemporary people, differing from ourselves in language and customs, should supply our stage with characters or incidents, strict accuracy is for similar reasons impossible. Thus the *Persians* of Æschylus, though the Athenians must have known a good deal about the would-be conquerors of Greece, are to a considerable degree Persians in Attic dress; and when Shakspere merely reminds us that we are in France by an occasional phrase like the Dauphin's "cheval volant," or by the mixture of French and English in the scene between Katharine and Alice, he displays a far deeper acquaintance with dramatic art, than Plautus, who in his *Pœnulus* makes the Carthaginian Hanno deliver a speech in Phœnician which, for the benefit of the audience, he is compelled immediately to translate into Latin. So closely is the dramatist bound within the limited sphere of his audience's thoughts and feelings, so completely does he depend on their average associations and the degree of social evolution they have

D

attained. If the *autos sacramentales* of Calderon, with their abstract and allegorical personages, and their intense feelings of Roman Catholicism, would fail to awaken profound sympathy save in a devoutly religious people like the Spaniards of the sixteenth and seventeenth centuries —a people among whom the average feelings and intelligence of men and women would give life even to such personages in the sacred spectacle—the mysteries of medieval England would be something worse than a farce in the England of to-day. Turn where we may, we shall meet the relativity of dramatic art wherever a drama of any description has been developed.

§ 11. But the critical as well as the creative spirit of the drama serves to illustrate that limitation of literary art which results from the development of social and individual character. Such an illustration, for example, is supplied by the three famous unities over which so much angry and dogmatic discussion has been expended. The unities of time, place, and action have been very differently understood and derived. A. W. Schlegel has been at some trouble to show that they are not found in the *Poetics*—at least in the form which French criticism had fathered upon Aristotle. Coleridge sees in them the results of the Greek chorus, the centre of the Athenian drama, not to be easily moved from place to place, or from time to time. Others have regarded them as resulting from the architectural arrangements of the Greek theatre. Every one knows how differently they have been discussed and valued in different ages of European literature. Victor Hugo, for example, tells us that if we imprison the drama in a classical unity of place, "we only see the elbows of the action; its hands are elsewhere."[*] Shall we reduce our dramatic time to twenty-

[*] Preface to *Cromwell* (p. 24).

four hours? The same poet and critic reminds us that every action has its own duration, that to apply the same time-measurements to every action would be to act like a shoemaker who could make only one size of shoe for all sizes of feet. Moreover, it is easy to show that "unity of action" is a very indefinite phrase, which might mean harmony of character with conditions of place and time, or harmony of events with the central incident of the drama, or both of these combined and confused. But it would be a serious error to rise from the study of conflicting opinions on the nature and origin of the unities with a self-satisfied belief that, whatever the classic rules may owe to the theatres of Athens and Paris, we may now rest in a broad declaration that we hold with the "Romantic School," and that the unities have no significance beyond the ancient drama and its modern imitators. The truth is that under an aspect conventional, pedantic, and therefore repulsive alike to creative and critical freedom, the unities conceal an attempt to solve certain problems involving the highest efforts of philosophic inquiry. The need of dramatic limitation in space, time, and action is no mere whim of critical fancy. It rests on truths which the evolution of man, socially and individually, establishes, and which his animal and physical environments amply confirm.

The drama is a picture of individual character, social life, and, to some degree—in Indian, Chinese, and Japanese plays to a considerable degree—physical nature. If its characters and social life are patchworks of different ages—sentiments of blood-revenge blended with courtly refinement, associations of Elizabethan London in the Rome of Cæsar or the Athens of Alcibiades—we only enjoy the medley seriously so long as we are unconscious of the historical contrasts which, to the eyes of those who can see them, cannot but lend the most solemn tragedy a look of caricature. In this way scientific knowledge may incapacitate us for pleasures which depend on limited vision. This will be seen from a case which Mr. E. B. Tylor, in his *Anthropology*, incidentally notices. "The negro," says Mr. Tylor, "in spite of his name, is not black, but deep brown, and even this darkest hue does not appear at the beginning of life, for the newborn negro child is reddish brown, soon becoming slaty grey, and then darkening. Nor does the darkest tint ever extend over the negro's whole body, but the soles and palms are brown. When Blumenbach, the anthropologist, saw Kemble play Othello (made up, in the usual way, with blackened face and black gloves, to represent a negro), he complained that the whole illusion was spoilt for him when the actor opened his hands." Descriptions of impossible scenery and animal life in which the *flora* and *fauna* of India and Iceland, England and China, should be indiscriminately confused, will not strike the listener or onlooker as ridiculous if he knows nothing of such distinctions. So also with human character and customs. A play to be performed before an audience of antiquaries would need to reach their standard of accuracy; and every one sees how different this standard would be from that of an ordinary audience. But every one does not see that the difference between the scientific few and the unscientific many is only on a smaller scale the difference between an uncivilised and a civilised audience; that the degrees of accuracy demanded increase with the widening ranges of experience, with an expanding sphere of comparison and contrast. Still less does every one see that in social and individual character there are limits to this accuracy resulting from the direct conflict between feelings and ideas of very limited evolution, and those of one far more advanced. It is just in such widening spheres of social development—clan, city, nation—and this impossibility of representing certain species of human character save as contrasts to our own, that the relativity of literature peculiarly discloses itself.

Social circumstances, it may be added, possibly produced the local limitations of the Athenian tragedy quite as much as the chorus or the architecture of the theatre. We have seen how differences of custom and language give rise to a conflict between what can and what cannot be dramatically represented through the medium of the spectators' speech, and thoughts, and feelings; and in the practice (not the merely critical rules) of the unities, especially that of place, it is possible that we have an unconscious feeling of such a conflict. But, it will be asked, how could Greeks, so slow to compare "barbarian" manners and customs with their own, so disdainful of everything beyond their own Greek associations, acquire any sense of social contrasts as affecting dramatic art? By the striking social and political contrasts of their little city commonwealths, contrasts to which the intellectual energy of Greece was so largely due. Here were opportunities for the recognition of relativity in miniature. What was true of individualised life at Athens was by no means true in the corporate organisation and sentiments of Sparta; the men and women of the Asiatic Ionians differed in many respects from those of Thessaly or Bœotia; and differences of dialect helped to emphasise those of social and political life. When we remember how largely these contrasts contributed to create the comparative thinking of the Sophists, and (by force of repulsion) the universal ethic of Socrates and the universal metaphysic of Plato, we cannot help believing that Greek contrasts, social and political, within the narrowest local limits, may have affected Athenian tragedy and limited its spheres of local propriety. The local differences of feudalism and the medieval towns were far indeed from producing any such limitations in the mysteries and miracle-plays. But why? Because a world-creed had in the mean time supplied Europe with a vision of the world's past and future before which all local and temporal distinctions appeared to vanish. But in the little commonwealths of early Greece, local differences formed the very life-blood of local character and patriotism; and it was not until the days of Isokrates and Alexander that the Greek ceased to be a citizen in order to become a cultured cosmopolitan.

§ 12. But the drama is far from being the only branch of literature from which literary relativity may be illustrated. The lyric—to use a vague but necessary generalisation—will supply the student of comparative literature with many evidences of its dependence on social and individual evolution. Mr. Palgrave (in the preface to his *Golden Treasury of English Lyrics*) has attempted to define the meaning of "lyric," but, as he himself admits, with no very remarkable success. Lyrical, he holds, " essentially implies that each poem shall turn on some single thought, feeling, or situation; " "narrative, descriptive, and didactic poems have been excluded; " so, too, " humorous poetry, except where a truly poetical tone pervades the whole; " and " blank verse, the ten-syllable couplet, with all pieces markedly dramatic, have been rejected as alien from what is commonly understood by song, and rarely conforming to lyrical conditions in treatment." We must be struck by the variety of elements on which this definition depends—elements of spirit, such as thoughts and feelings, and elements of form, such as the metres employed; and yet this is little more than an effort to define the *English* " lyric." Turn to Dr. Buchreim's *Deutsche Lyrik*, and we shall find even greater varieties of spirit (the *Volksleid*, the *Kirchenlied*, songs of the *Göttingen Hainbund*, of Goethe, of the War of Liberation, of personal *Weltschmerz*) and of form (from the metres of Luther to those of Heine) in the development of the German "lyric." If, moreover, we were to examine the songs of France or Spain, of Italy or Russia—to say nothing of the literatures of the East— we should find many other and conflicting varieties of form and spirit summed up in the generalisation " lyric." Reverting, then, to Mr. Palgrave's attempted definition, it would be easy to prove that the lyrical idea it expresses can claim only limited truth even within the literary evolution of England. But students of comparative literature should rather thank Mr. Palgrave for an anthology exquisitely illustrating "the natural growth and evolution of our poetry" than find fault with a definition to which that evolution necessarily allows only limited accuracy.

The truth is that "lyric" poetry has changed prodigiously both in form and spirit, not only with differences of language and nationality, but with the alterations which social and individual character undergo in the development of any given community. If in the songs of the *Shih King* we find the sentiments of the Chinese family and its ancestor-worship, if in the hymns of the *Rig-Veda* we discover the spirit of the early Indian communities and their nature-worship, the song of the Saxon Scôp with its appeal to clan feelings, of the Norman troubadour with its feudal chivalry, of the English minstrel on *Chevy Chace* or Robin Hood, remind us that each country has its own "lyrical" developments expressing the changes of its social life. The "lyric" has varied from sacred or magical hymns and odes of priest-bards, only fulfilling their purpose when sung, and perhaps never consigned to writing at all, down to written expressions of individual feeling from which all accompaniments of dance or music have been severed, and nothing remains but such melody as printed verse can convey, and the eye or ear of the individual reader detect. In the rude beginnings of literature among loosely federated clans we find the communal "lyric" reflecting the corporate organisms and ideas of contemporary life. Even in Pindar, the communal, as opposed to the individual characteristics of the "lyric," are still visible, the victor of the games being often merely a centre round which the achievements of his clan or city are grouped. But as the old communal brotherhoods break up before the powers of the chiefs' families, as even family life is in its turn weakened in city democracies, the "lyric" becomes more and more an expression of individual feelings. No doubt we have excellent specimens of communal "lyrics" on a colossal scale at the present day—the sea-songs of England, the war-songs of France, the German *Freiheits- und Vaterlandslieder*—and whenever any great movement sets masses of our modern men on foot, we may be sure that a Campbell or a Körner will be ready to sound its reveille in song. But the development of individualism has left its marks deep upon the modern "lyric." The span-life of the individual contrasted with the corporate existence of social groups and of the human species, contrasted still more regretfully with the apparent eternity of physical nature, becomes a recurring theme in social conditions which thrust the life of the individual into vivid consciousness of itself, its brevity, and its littleness. It is this individualism which invests with such intense feeling our "lyric" poetry of youth and age, which lingers over personal associations within the limits of its own time and space with a sadness almost inexpressible in the language of any group, and which watches the withering of its own passions and emotions with the conviction that "there's not a joy the world can give like that it takes away."

"Dewdrops are the gems of morning,
But the tears of mournful eve."

§ 13. Formal distinctions in literature often survive in the language of criticism into conditions totally different from those among which they arose. Our European criticism has in this way inherited from the Greeks such words as "epic," "lyric," "dramatic," which we have learned to bandy to and fro with astonishing facility. But though these words are so constantly on our lips that we have come to regard the ideas they generalise as not only permanent, but almost sufficiently concrete to be touched and handled, we rarely remember that the conceptions they denoted for Greeks differ greatly from those which we denote by the same names, that their meanings varied among the Greeks themselves at different stages of their civilisation, that among Greeks, as among ourselves, there were days when none of these literary forms existed, much less were distinguished *inter se*, and that there have been and are states of social life in which only some or even none of them have been either developed or named.* As rarely is it remembered that other peoples

* Mr. Matthew Arnold (preface to his edition of Wordsworth's Poems) has observed with justice that Wordsworth's method of classifying his own poetry as belonging to "fancy," "imagination," and the like sources —that is, classifying by "a supposed unity of mental origin"—is "ingenious but far-fetched." But when Mr. Arnold proceeds to maintain that "the tact of the Greeks in matters of this kind was infallible, that their categories of epic, dramatic, lyric, and so forth, have a *natural*

(ourselves included) have produced literary forms unknown to the Greeks, or that countries widely removed from European culture possess such forms as no European language can correctly express, because among no European people have they been developed. Our *à priori* notions of "epic," "lyric," "dramatic," can only be dispelled by such comparisons; and not until we have taken the trouble to trace the rise of different species of literature in different countries, and have thus learned the more or less different general and special ideas of literature entertained in each, can we hope to rise above the gross errors to which such *à priori* notions must expose us.

We have already seen the weakness of searching for universal conceptions of the "lyric;" let us now turn for illustrations of a similar weakness to the "epic." When Hallam contrasts *Paradise Lost* in choice of subject with the *Iliad, Odyssey, Æneid, Pharsalia, Thebaid, Jerusalem Delivered*, he implies that all these poems belong to a common species which he calls "heroic poetry;" and, according to Macaulay, in his comparison of Milton with Dante, this is "the highest class of human compositions." Now, whether we use the name "epic" or "heroic" is, of course, a verbal matter; the important point is that we declare certain poems of very different ages and countries to possess certain common characteristics, and to approach some universal model. Of such a model Coleridge was evidently thinking when he said

propriety and should be adhered to," we cannot help refusing our assent, not because we have any objections to urge against the Greek classifications of their own poetry, or the various uses to which modern critics have applied them, but because neither the art nor the criticism of the Greeks (or any other people) can possess that infallibility and "natural" propriety which Mr. Arnold would admire. If we find a certain propriety in Greek classifications, it is not because they possess any universal "nature," but because, shorn of many ideas they conveyed to the Greek mind, they fall in with modern modes of thought and conceptions of life similar in some respects to those of the Greeks, especially the Alexandrian Greeks.

that an "epic" poem "must either be national or common to all mankind." Such common characteristics M. Géruzez seeks when, criticising Voltaire (*Histoire de la Littérature Française*, vol. ii. p. 410), he says that "scenes depicted with vigour, portraits sketched by an artist powerful and ingenious, some beautiful lines, some noble ideas well expressed, are not enough to make an epic; there must be varied characters, personages full of action and heroic life, communion between heaven and earth, in fine, unity of action and interest—vital conditions which are not observed in the *Henriade*." These marks of an "epic," evidently collected from Homer and Vergil, do not carry us much farther than Johnson, who praised the "universal" interest of *Paradise Lost* and the "integrity" (or unity) of its design. Possibly M. Géruzez did not mean to say more than that the "epics" of Greece and Rome are models of such compositions; and we can hardly object to the harmless assertion that persons or poems are models of themselves. But when Johnson tells us that the question "whether the poem (*Paradise Lost*) can be properly termed heroic is raised by such readers as draw their principles of judgment rather from books than from reason," we may see that he at least, like Schlegel and Coleridge, is thinking of some universal model not to be discovered in the *Iliad* or other epics, but innate in the human heart or intellect as a kind of literary conscience. If our subjective critics would only stop to ask how far their literary conscience extends, to what countries, or ages, or social groups it belongs or does not belong, we should soon hear no more of universal ideas of the "epic" or any other species of literature. But it is much easier, much more showy, to talk and, if possible, to think in the free and splendid language of universals than to accept the awkward consciousness of a prisoner confined within the necessary limitations of human thought. We may judge, however, from these examples of the "epic" *idea*—the *word* "epos"* simply takes us back to the rise of poetical recitation without musical accompaniment, and suggests the Arab Reciter—the necessity of insisting on the relativity of literary growth to social evolution as opposed, on the one hand, to the treatment of literature as the mere imitation of arbitrary models; and, on the other hand, to *à priori* conceptions alike of the genus literature and of its species.

§ 14. We shall now seek the signs of literary relativity, not in the comparison of different species of literature, nor in the different characters of men and women in various stages of social life, but in that effort to transfer the thoughts expressed in the language of one social group into that of another, which we call *translation*. How far is accuracy of translation possible? It is clear that both in prose and verse there are difficulties in the way of the translator sometimes insurmountable. Even in prose translation objects such as animals or plants nameless in the translator's language, or customs and institutions unknown to his group, or ideas, political, religious, philosophic, similarly nameless, may present such obstacles. But in verse, besides these difficulties, there is the close connection between sounds and ideas which in every language is more or less recognisable. For example, in the Chinese drama *Ho-han-*

---

* "Epos" (root *vep*, cf. Latin *vox*) seems at an early period of Greek life to have been used especially of an oracular "saying." These "sayings" were given in verse (the development of metre and music being in early Greece, as elsewhere, partly in priestly hands), and so "epos" came to mean "a verse." When lyric songs set to music, "melê," as the Greeks called them, came to be distinguished from merely *spoken* verses, the "epos" or "recited poetry" was separated from the "melos" or "poetry of song." (Cf. the recurring invocation, ἔσπετε μοι, Μοῦσαι, "recite for me, ye Muses," and the root σεπ-.)

chan, Tchang-i's delight at the falling snow is expressed by changing the regular stanza, apparently reserved for dignified monologues and solemn descriptions, into the irregular or free measure which frees itself from the rule which subjects Chinese verse to the double yoke of cæsura and alliteration; in short, as M. Bazin says, "we must be able to read the verses in the original to gain an idea of the harmony which subsists between the style and the situation of the personage." How can this harmony be retained in the process of translating into any European language? If an effort were made to reproduce the Chinese metres in English, for example, the result would look ridiculous, even if it were not a complete failure; but that it would be a complete failure is clear from the fact which another Chinese scholar (Sir John Francis Davis) observes, viz. "that every word in Chinese poetry, instead of being regarded as a mere syllable, may more properly be regarded as corresponding to a metrical foot in other languages." Hence, one of the striking characteristics of Chinese verse is its parallelism in sound and sense, which has been compared with the parallelism of Hebrew poetry so carefully discussed by Lowth. Suppose, then, we were to translate a stanza of Chinese parallelism into Hebrew, would the result convey the Chinese form without alterations due to the Semitic dress? Far from it. The formations of the Semitic verb, noun, and particle are so different from the monosyllabic Chinese, that nothing like the Chinese parallelism could be produced either in Hebrew or Arabic. Here, then, is a case to illustrate the dependence of that harmony of sound and idea which we call "verse" upon the different sound-structures of languages, sound-structures which must be attributed to the varying appreciation of sounds possessed by the peoples whose social developments made the languages, and which may be as untransferable into a given Semitic or Aryan speech as certain barbarous notes of music into our European system of musical notation. Moreover, this Chinese example is only adopted because it is peculiarly striking. The same relativity of linguistic sounds to the group by which the language is spoken may be illustrated by contrasting, say, Arabic sounds and metres with Sanskrit, or Italian with English, or Russian with German, or by observing the loss of the hexameter, and the appearance of a new form of verse with the rise of modern Greek in the eleventh century. We may, indeed, gauge to some degree the progress of discrimination in sounds by contrasting the ruder forms and metres in a given people's language with the more advanced—the confused union of syllabic and metrical scansion in Plautus with the Pope-like smoothness of Vergil, a similar confusion in Chaucer with the machine-like regularity of the ten-syllable couplet, the monotonous repetition of rimes in the *Chansons de Geste* * with the Alexandrine of modern France, or (to take two examples from prose) the harsh antitheses of Thucydides with the delicate perceptions of sound in Isokrates, and the clumsy sentences of Milton with the modulated harmony of Ruskin. Such progress

---

* The rudeness of this versification, says M. Géruzez (*Hist. de la Litt. Fran.*, vol. i. p. 27), is marked by monorimes, of indeterminate length, which only stop when the trouvère, having exhausted his final consonants or assonants, thinks fit to continue his psalmody on another rime till it, too, is in its turn exhausted. In the *Kasida* of the Arabs (to which we shall elsewhere refer) the same rime is, likewise, repeated, only in this case at the end of every verse throughout the entire poem, and the *ráwi*, or "*bindfast*" letter, which remains the same throughout, may be compared to a rivet driven through the verses and holding them together. (Cf. Wright's *Arabic Grammar*, vol. ii. pp. 378, 379, and the European and Arab authorities cited by Dr. Wright on p. 377.) In ages when writing was either unknown or the monopoly of a few, it is clear that this repetition of the same rime would have supplied a powerful prop for the memory. But on this subject we shall have something to say presently.

in the appreciation of sounds explains, indeed, the failure of attempts to modernise early poetry, such as those of Dryden and Pope. In such cases we expect the old harmony between earlier sounds and ideas to be kept up by the moderniser, whose ideas and sounds are both more or less different, and consequently the harmony into which he transforms the old verse. Our expectation is, of course, disappointed; it overlooks at once the subtle progress we have observed, and the peculiar fitness of certain sounds for certain ideas—a fitness which the poet of any age, just in proportion as he is a poet, is sure to detect and to express for him who has the ears to hear.

If there ever lived a poet who was likely to clearly express these very subtle relations of sound, speech, and thought, and their effects on translation, that poet was Shelley; and, though it often happens that a man who himself knows how to produce an effect has not reflected upon his powers so as to rationally explain their operation, we may see from the following quotation that Shelley was not unconscious of the process by which his own exquisite harmonies of word and thought were produced, and the impossibility of transferring them from one language to another, which must needs be a different sound-instrument. "Sounds, as well as thoughts," says Shelley, in his *Defence of Poetry*, "have relations both between each other and towards that which they represent; and a perception of the order of these relations has always been found connected with a perception of the order of the relations of thought. Hence, the language of poets has ever affected a sort of uniform and harmonious recurrence of sound, without which it were not poetry, and which is scarcely less indispensable to the communication of its influence than the words themselves without reference to that particular order. Hence the vanity of translation; it were as wise to cast a violet into a crucible that you might discover the formal principle of its colour and odour, as seek to transfuse from one language into another the creation of a poet." The Aramaic expression for translating (*targêm*, from which our "dragoman" is descended) conveys the figure of "throwing a bundle over a river;" and the truth is that in the translation process the bundle never arrives at the other side exactly as it was before starting. Language, in fact, is a sound-catalogue of all the objects and thoughts familiar to the community to which it belongs, be that community ever so small or ever so large, be it an African tribe or the widespread speakers of English or Arabic, be its average senses—sight, hearing, touch, taste—as sharp, but unæsthetic, as those of an American Indian, or as æsthetically appreciative, though perhaps physically inferior, as those of the most cultured people. With the contents of this catalogue the individual makers of a group's literature must be content. Beyond it they cannot pass. To modify it to any appreciable degree they cannot hope. Their work, so far as the sound-materials they use, is one of arrangement not of creation, and, in one sense, they are the servants of the language they employ. If that language is full and melodious, such is their treasury of expression. If it is poor and rude, they can only hope to make the best use of materials which have been made for them, not by them.* Even the intensely developed individualism of

---

* The relative influences of inflectional and analytic languages on metre are subjects deserving careful attention. The most superficial observer cannot fail to remark that the former, allowing greater freedom of position to words, tend to foster metrical scansion such as the poetry of Greece and Rome presents, while the latter, allowing far less freedom of position, tend to prefer the less stringent systems of rime or assonance.

Greek literature could not overlook this truth. For example, Professor Jebb, in his admirable account of the "Attic Orators," observes that one of the leading contrasts between Athenian and modern eloquence, such as that of Pitt or Burke, is to be found in the artistic feeling of the Greek orators, who, having once discovered a combination of words peculiarly fitted to convey a certain combination of ideas, do not hesitate to repeat such a sentence or phrase; whereas the modern orator, from whom at least the appearance of an *extempore* speech is expected, carefully avoids such repetitions. These relations of sound to idea may, moreover, partially explain two facts exceedingly interesting in the development of literature, the growth of poetic diction and the decadence of poetry in an age of analytic thought—facts in which we shall find further illustrations of the relativity of literature to social life.

§ 15. We are all familiar with Wordsworth's conception of "poetic diction" as an "unnatural" growth. The early poets of all nations, he tells us, wrote generally from passions excited by real events; they wrote "naturally," and so their language was daring and figurative in the highest degree. But succeeding poets mechanically adopted such language, applied it "to feelings and thoughts with which it had no *natural* connection whatsoever," and insensibly produced a language "differing materially from the real language of men in *any* situation." This conception of "poetic diction" as a "distorted language," gradually separated from that of real life, is only true of certain literary epochs which may be

It is no mere accident that the Greek and Latin metres admit of easy imitation in German, with its comparatively strong inflections, while in English, the language of lost inflections, efforts such as those of Tennyson, Longfellow, A. H. Clough, contrast feebly with those of Schiller and Goethe.

called epochs of classical imitation. It would be easy to show that some of the grandest specimens of poetry in the world (Greek and Indian epics, for example) offer many a mark of stereotyped diction in repeated epithets. Partially, such epithets may be attributed to an early and inartistic age in which the dependence of memory on the verse—writing being yet unknown—must have tended to stereotype many a striking epithet as a kind of resting-place for the memory. So far, "poetic diction" would seem to be the common property of poetic guilds, religious or secular, common aids to the memory of bard-clans like the Homêridæ. But partially, also, "poetic diction" may be attributed to a very real feeling of art, the feeling that made the Greek orator rest assured that an exquisite turn of phrase, when once discovered, was the most artistic combination of thought and sound of which his language was capable, and should be repeated in preference to any search for variety. "Form," says Victor Hugo,* "is something much more fixed than people suppose. It is an error, for example, to think that one and the same thought can be written in many ways, that one and the same idea can have many forms. One idea has never more than one form peculiarly its own, excellent, complete, rigorous, essential, the form preferred by it, and which always springs *en bloc* with it from the brain of the man of genius. Hence in the great poets nothing is more inseparable, nothing more united, nothing more consubstantial, than the idea and the expression of the idea. Kill the form and you nearly always kill the idea." Here is a conception of "poetic diction" which is neither that of lifeless imitation nor that of antique epithets stereotyped as aids for the memory, one by no means peculiar to Victor Hugo, but which, wherever we find it,

* *Littérature et Philosophie*, vol. i. p. xxiv.

derives its significance from the figure of an artistic *individual* author gathering with free hand in the garden of his country's language such words as shall blend with his ideas in a beautiful harmony of thought and speech. Days without writing when poetic guilds were the great conservators of human tradition—days of courtly imitators crowning their brows with the withered roses of buried poets—days of democratic art when he who has the living spirit is free to choose its proper embodiment— so various are the epochs of social life and literature to which "poetic diction" may belong, so different are the facts and the ideas which it may express.

But, it will be asked, how does the decadence of poetry in an age of analytic thought illustrate the dependence of literature on social conditions? Can we find any connecting links between analytic thought and social conditions, and between both of these and the spirit and form of poetry? We have seen how closely related are the idea and its embodiment, the thought and the language, of poetry, and how different are the harmonies in which they may be combined in different societies or in different ages of the same society. Sever such relations between sound and idea by the separate consideration of each in scientific analysis, and you reach the inartistic or analytic conception of prose as the proper instrument of reflection and totally unconnected with poetic form—you *Aristotelise* your prose; and poetry, so far as it depends on the harmony of sound and idea, vanishes before a "philosophic" contempt which would ridicule or deny altogether the subtle relations of sound and idea in the languages of social groups. But, however analytic thinkers may deride such relations, the forms of poetry, and even of prose to some degree,* prove by the

* "The constructional parallelism of sentences," says Sir J. F. Davis

best of human proofs—evidences unconsciously given—the existence of harmonies between idea and sound varying in different states of language and social life. Still, it may be asked, where is the connection between analytic or individualising thought and social conditions? How is the desire to see the individual object in preference to the general idea connected with social evolution? Let social life be decomposed into individual units, let men's sympathies be narrowed into the sphere of self, in a word, let the group be individualised, and we shall find that men's imagination is impaired, that it ceases to pass spontaneously beyond self, that it too becomes individualised. Such imagination may be wondrously inspired by nature, but hardly by human life. Thus the individualising process in social life which thrusts analytic thinking to the front, not only impairs the sympathetic imagination—and there is little imagination without sympathy—but undermines the belief in those harmonies of sound and thought of which poetry so largely consists. We may, therefore, find a very profound relation between what are called "prosaic" ages and individualism in social life, as well as between "poetical" ages and such social conditions as foster imagination by their vigorous sympathies, and do not affect to break the harmony of sound and idea by refined analysis.

But if we turn from men and their languages and life to animal and physical nature, we shall not only find the rela-

(Chinese Poetry, p. 26), extends to prose composition, and is very frequent in what is called *Wan-chang* or "fine writing"—a measured prose, though not written line beside line, like poetry. Other examples of rhythmical prose (or the recognition of harmony between sound and idea in prose), such as the Hebrew and Arabic, are well known; and it is to be remembered that such prose manifested itself among peoples unaccustomed to that analytic thought which carved out of Greek, Latin, and modern languages prose instruments for itself. Mr. Ruskin is certainly not an analytic thinker; so much the better for the delicate rhythm of his prose.

tivity of literature in the different kinds of animals and plants and scenery it depicts—the physical, or, as we formerly called it statical, relativity of literature—but even discover new aspects of its social relativity already discussed.

§ 16. The mere presence of a beautiful physical environment can do little towards the creation of a beautiful literature if social life moves under conditions adverse to sentiments of sympathy with nature. This man who, like Wordsworth's *Wanderer*, has lived among the wildest and grandest scenery earth can offer, is moved by none but petty motives, and reflects in his spirit neither the dignity nor the beauty of his native mountains. Another, who has passed his life in the grimy atmosphere of an English factory, surveys with boundless delight the ice-field of a glacier or the dizzy dangers of an Alpine pass. The sturdy, narrow-minded mountaineer is callous to sights and sounds of nature, whose gigantic features have not merely lost their interest for him from their constant presence, but have always been associated in his mind with very real hardships. Such common cases as these warn us against rashly inferring any sense of natural beauty or any deep sympathy with nature in consequence of her companionship with man, no matter how beautiful the dress she may wear. From under the rainbow arch of the cataract rises the witch of the Alps— but for whom? For Manfred, or rather for Byron's shadow called "Manfred," for one whose intense feeling of self has turned away from man to nature for poetic inspiration. What cares the chamois-hunter for witch or cataract? Search the pages of Greek poets and orators, and you will rarely find a picture of the varying forms of nature such as our town-begotten literatures of modern Europe present with rather monotonous frequency. And yet the literature of Athens, in a far deeper sense than that of modern England, France, or Germany, is town-begotten. Whence comes the contrast? From the different aspects not only of physical, but much more of social, life. The isolated city commonwealths of Greece saw beyond their own walls little but the work-fields of their slaves, or an exposed borderland which war and brigandage were perpetually devastating; where roads, if they existed at all, were as often the highways of enemies as the conductors of friends, and where the best of nature's favours would be a network of impassable rocks, to be valued for their practical defence, not admired for any beauty of their scenery. So, too, with the expanding town-sovereignty of Rome. Into the wilderness of nature and men uncivilised she throws her outposts of armed towns, and views with infinitely deeper sympathy the tiresome regularity of her military roads than all the splendid scenery of lake and mountain coming within the widening horizon of her empire. This is the march of human force armed *cap-a-pie;* before it nature is good for growing corn, raising men and cattle, for the soldier's ambuscade or the evolutions of horse and foot—and that is all. If the Roman poet turns his face away for a moment from the Forum and the city-folk to nature, it is (like Vergil) to nature *humanised* as the agricultural mainstay of man's life, or (like Lucretius) to nature *humanised* for the purposes of social theory. In the same way different social conditions in contemporary life may be observed to affect the aspects of nature; the same physical circumstances summon up different associations for the bards of the Homeric princes and for Hesiod, the singer of the people; the country life wears a different look for the medieval burgher and the medieval knight. Schiller tells us * that the sun of Homer still shines on

---

* "Und die Sonne Homers, siehe! sie lächelt auch uns."
(*Der Spazicrgang.*)

us; but, though the sunshine be the same, nature has changed her looks since the days of Homer, of Athens, of Rome, not only because our vision of the world has been greatly widened and corrected by discovery, but even more on account of changed conditions in social life.

If such effects attended municipal life in ancient Greece and Italy, if men under such social conditions could not feel the life of nature till it was *humanised*—as it was even by Theocritus—we shall be prepared to find a very different aspect of nature in the literature of a social life widely removed from that of Athens or Rome. Sanskrit poetry, as readers of such a poem as the "Indian Song of Songs" need hardly be reminded, is full of adoring reverence for nature and her elements. Moreover, contrary to European ideas of dramatic propriety, the Indian drama delights in lengthy and vivid descriptions of nature. Thus in *Mrichchhakati*, or "The Toy-Cart," we have a description of the Indian rainy season which we shall elsewhere quote; and the splendid forest-scene in *Vikramórvasi* completely subordinates man to nature. This strong sentiment of nature cannot be attributed to Indian scenery and climate alone. The Greek, too, was surrounded by splendid scenery; yet, as Schiller says, nature appealed to his understanding rather than his feelings, and while his few descriptions of nature are faithful and circumstantial, they exhibit only such warmth of sympathy as the embroidery of a garment or the workmanship of a shield might arouse. To understand the contrasts of Indian and Greek sympathy with nature, we must remember the Indian village community and the Greek city as well as the scenery by which they were each surrounded. Nor is the explanation to be found solely in the village and agricultural life of India contrasted with the city communities of Greece.

The system of caste, with its corporate and impersonal conceptions of human being, could not humanise nature in at all the same manner as that strongly-developed individualism which meets us in the cities of Greece. Ideas of human existence more or less impersonal are found in all early communities where, as in the clan, the individual is morally merged in the corporate being of his group; and the weak sense of personality in such social conditions is readily transferred to the phenomena of nature. Indeed, one of the main results of that development of *personal* consciousness which everywhere accompanies that of individual independence from communal restraints, is to see nature no longer clothed in the confused and confusing garb of man's early personality, but in clear contrast with a profound consciousness of each man's individual being.

But we have now illustrated the social and physical relativity of literature at sufficient length. It is time for us to ask what use the scientific student of literature can make of such relativity. Over and above the influences of climate and scenery, plant-life and animal-life, can we discover any tolerably permanent principle of social evolution round which the facts of literary growth and decay may be grouped? And, assuming that some such principle has been discovered, what is the proper method by which the collection of facts and their reference to this central principle shall proceed? It is to these questions that we now propose to turn; and first to the problem whether the growth and decay of literature contain any such guiding principle in spite of their apparent chaos of limited causes and effects.

CHAPTER III.

THE PRINCIPLE OF LITERARY GROWTH.

§ 17. SIR WALTER SCOTT, in his preface to the *Bridal of Triermain*, published in 1813, offered some remarks "on what has been called romantic poetry." Though the main object of these remarks was to deprecate the practice of selecting "epic" subjects after the Homeric model, they contain a passage which, apparently without any conception of this particular bearing on the author's part, touches a most profound problem, not only of literature, but of all human thought. The passage is as follows: "Two or three figures, well grouped, suit the artist better than a crowd, for whatever purpose assembled. For the same reason, a scene immediately presented to the imagination and directly brought home to the feelings, though involving the fate of but one or two persons, is more favourable for poetry than the political struggles and convulsions which influence the fate of kingdoms. The former are within the reach and comprehension of all, and, if depicted with vigour, seldom fail to fix attention; the other, if more sublime, are more vague and distant, less capable of being distinctly understood, and infinitely less capable of exciting the sentiments which it is the very purpose of poetry to inspire. *To generalise is always to destroy effect.*

We would, for example, be more interested in the fate of an *individual* soldier in combat than in the grand events of a general action; in the happiness of two lovers raised from misery and anxiety to peace and union than in the successful exertions of a whole nation. From what causes this may originate is a separate and *obviously immaterial consideration*. Before ascribing this peculiarity to causes decidedly and odiously selfish, it is proper to recollect that while men see only a limited space, and while their affections and conduct are regulated, not by aspiring at an universal good, but by exerting their power of making themselves and others happy within the limited scale allotted to each individual, so long will *individual history and individual virtue* be the readier and more accessible road to general interest and attention; and perhaps we may add that it is the more useful, as well as the more accessible, inasmuch as it affords an example capable of being easily imitated."

The limited range of living human sympathy is, no doubt, a key to many secrets of our modern literature; but it is not true that individual character has always been the centre of human interest, or that generalisation in all states of society "destroys effect." The individualism on which Sir Walter Scott bases his theory of poetry has been evolved from conditions under which men and women were more deeply interested in social action and communal sympathies than in any emotions or thoughts of personal being. If we compare the early dramas of Athens, England, France, we discover certain points of similarity which cannot be attributed to imitation; and the most striking of these resemblances is the absence or weakness of individual character. In the medieval mysteries and morality-plays, as is well known, the so-called "characters" introduced are either divine or allegorical—God and His angels, Satan and his devils, Justice, Mercy, and the like. We are accustomed to regard these abstract or general personages as the handiwork of the monks and medieval religion. We are accustomed to credit these spectacles as well as the scholastic lovers of abstractions with a profound desire to express the invisible and the infinite in their art and philosophy. But let us not confuse the idealism of a Plato or a Berkeley with the average thought of peoples saturated with superstitions grossly materialistic and narrowly limited in their intellectual and social views— men and women who forgot limitations of space and time in feudalised pictures of Hebrew, or Greek, or Roman antiquity, not because of their "universal" ideas, but because they were incapable of apprehending even very limited ideas correctly; who could only see the crucifixion through the associations of knights or burghers, and who reduced divinity with an almost savage confidence to the compass of their human senses and the little sphere of their sensual wit. Such men, such women, can have possessed no real conceptions of the infinite, can be credited with no true efforts to express it. The "realism" of the Middle Ages—which shines out as clearly in their dramas and allegorical "epic" poetry as in their formulated philosophy—is but a weak power of abstraction seeking to prop its steps on every kind of external object. Far from indicating a lofty feeling for the invisible and infinite, it shows how short a distance the human mind could then travel without perpetual returns to the visible. This "realism," as well as the allegorical and abstract characters of the medieval mysteries and moralities, reflects a weak sense of personality which is found in all early stages of social life, and to which the social organisations of medieval Europe contributed in a manner to be hereafter discussed. But let us pause to note certain evidences of the same weakness in the early drama of Athens.

The weakness of character-drawing in the early Athenian drama cannot escape the most superficial student of Athenian literature. Thus in the *Prometheus* of Æschylus we have Violence (Βία) and Force (Κράτος) executing the will of Zeus against Forethought (Προμηθεύς); and, as Æschylean critics have often observed, the chorus, and not the individual characters, may be seen to predominate in the dramas of Æschylus. Far from the Athenians of the Æschylean age being, in Sir Walter Scott's phrase, "more interested in the fate of an individual soldier than in the grand events of a general action," the *Suppliants* (the earliest Greek play extant) turns entirely on the action and character of its chorus—the fifty daughters of Danaus; the *Persians* derives its name from the chorus of twelve Persian elders, and is far less individual than social in its interest; and the *Eumenides* centres in the action and character of the Furies who form its chorus, supply its name, and make the allegorical personifications of the inherited curse—a conception of impersonal ethics with difficulty harmonised in the later Athenian drama with freedom of personal character. Moreover, when we follow the developments of the ancient and modern dramas, we find a striking similarity in their progressive treatment of character. By degrees the divine, saintly, or allegorical personages of our medieval stage give way to human character in its contemporary individualities, and the tragedy or comedy of real life is reached. So, also, in the Athenian drama. The chorus, dominant, as we noticed, in Æschylus, is by Sophocles subordinated to individual character, and by Euripides is finally converted.

into a mere spectator. Heroic personages are, indeed, retained,¶ but only as the external clothing, the stage "properties," under which varieties of individual character may be put forward. Allegorical personages, like Dêmos and Eirênê, "The People," and ." The Peace," walk the stage side by side with living celebrities, just as in the ".Miracle du Saint Guillaume du Desert." *
Saint Bernard, the famous Abbé de Clairvaux, figures beside Beelzebub and the rest. And, at length, the open introduction of everyday life banishes or altogether subordinates the mythical heroes and allegorical characters of old Athenian tragedy and comedy. It will not, of course, be supposed that individual character in the Athens of Æschylus was as weakly developed as in the French *Communes* of the twelfth century or the early German town-guilds, much less that the social life of Athens at the time of Euripides did not differ in many respects from that of England and Spain, of Italy, France, and Germany, at the appearance of the legitimate drama in modern Europe. But they who will remember how inherited sin supplied the pivot conception of theatrical ethics in Athens, and how a grossly sensual view of vicarious punishment supplied the ethical doctrine of the mystery-plays, will admit that weak ideas of individual responsibility and character imparted as much interest to early Athenian tragedy as to the medieval spectacles. Wherein do we find the causes of such similarity ? The answer to this question discloses that principle of literary growth to which in preceding pages we have incidentally referred.

§ 18. The development of individual character is at the outset confused by certain facts which tend to mis-

* See *Miracles de Nostre Dame*, edited for the Ancient French Texts Society, by MM. Gaston Paris and Ulysse Robert.

lead both the makers and the critics of literature. It is easy to forget that the very existence of a literature implies a considerable degree of social and linguistic unity, and that such unity involves the break-up, more or less, of those miniature communities, clans, and tribes in whose corporate and unindividualised ideas we find the roots of early religion, law, and literature. Thanks to such scholars as Von Maurer and Nasse, Emile de Laveleye and Sir Henry Maine, we now know more of these little circles of kinship than we ever did before. We know that, with more or less modification, they are to be found in every part of the East and West, and that wherever they have perished survivals of their existence have been left in human action or thought. But we too often forget that in literature, in the productions which states of social communion on a much larger scale than that of clan or tribe have thought worthy of transmission, we must view any survivals from these early communities through the medium of much later associations. Hence it is easy to be deceived by the prominence of individual life in the *Iliad*, or *Beowulf*, or the *Nibelungenlied*. Yet this prominence is readily enough explained. The clan communities, whose impersonal conceptions of ownership, contract, crime, have only been recovered because at the birth of central government they forced themselves on the recognition of a weak authority, were in the process of their decomposition into larger groups (such as tribal federations) subordinated to military and religious chiefs; and it was only when this process had reached a considerably advanced stage that writing began to be employed, and, in the interests of the widening social groups, legends of clans once isolated were combined and centred round this or that eponymous ancestor, this or that individual hero. Literature, therefore, *apparently*

THE PRINCIPLE OF LITERARY GROWTH. 63

begins in some countries with the prominence of the individual. But we must remember that this early individualism is something very different from that to which our modern associations are accustomed. The chief of clan or tribe *represents* his group. Such personifications of the group we are liable to confuse with individual character in the modern sense. We are liable to forget that personality in an age of even weakened communal life means something quite different from personality in an age when individual independence—feudal or democratic—has been developed. Some leading ideas of clan life will sufficiently illustrate not only the differences which set a gulf between primitive and highly-evolved personality, but also the hopelessness of attempting to understand the nature of social evolution without attending to such differences.

The clan, as such, knows nothing of personal responsibility in a future state, for its corporate view of life needs no such individual sanction for morality. The Hades of the clan, therefore, like that of the *Odyssey* or like the Hebrew *She'ôl*, is merely a subterranean gathering-place of buried kinsmen whose life is a pale reflection of their life on earth. Reward and punishment, the terrors or consolations of an individualism not yet developed, have here no place, and for a reason easy enough to understand. This reason is that each clan, as a corporation which "never dies," suffers, or is liable to suffer, for the sins committed by any of its members as long as atonement is not made. Hence the place of *personal* reward or punishment in a future state is taken by *corporate* responsibility in the present life. Just as among the Bedâwi the rights and liabilities of *Thâr* or Blood-Revenge extend to the fifth generation, so in all clan communities responsibility is more or less an impersonal matter. Hence, too, there is nothing illogical to the clan mind in the sacrifice of an innocent man as a compensation for the sin of a guilty member or of the group; such a sacrifice only becomes illogical when the idea of individual intention and personal responsibility is clearly realised. Hence, also, as the clans lose their communal character (for example, by their land ceasing to be common property, and their ties of kinship being weakened by artificial expansion) and are broken down into their component families and individuals, ideas of inherited guilt survive into the new social conditions, and are misapplied to purely individual life in a manner which can only issue in a conflict between personal intention and corporate responsibility. It is by this kind of survival that we find inherited guilt the leading ethical doctrine of the Athenian drama in its earlier period—for example, in the *Seven against Thebes*, in the Orestian trilogy, in *Œdipous Tyrannus*. It has been observed that the subtle Greek gradually altered the old and gross conception of inherited guilt into a personal liability to commit fresh offences, and so to incur divine vengeance. In this way his growing individualism avoided such a direct repudiation of inherited sin as the less subtle Hebrew found himself compelled to utter. But even conceptions of impersonal responsibility so considerably removed from the oldest and purest life of the clan as the ethics of the early Athenian drama are enough to show the gulf which separates our modern analyses of intention, and consequently our ideas of personal character, from days in which the individual was morally merged in his group. Indeed, the survival of such conceptions in the highly-intellectual atmosphere of Athens is altogether a more remarkable fact than the condemnation of belief in inherited guilt, the ethics of the Decalogue, by Ezekiel (ch. xviii.). If the latter proves that in Ezekiel's age the communal sympathies of the old Hebrew clans (*mishpâchôth*) had dwindled into an individuality with which inherited guilt came into direct collision, the former should prepare us for survivals from the impersonal view of human character in any state of social life, however civilised, however favourable to individual independence.

§ 19. Impersonal ideas of human character, mainly resulting from certain forms of social organisation, are thus the source of the similarity we have observed between the early dramas of Athens and modern Europe. If such ideas are in Athens survivals from the corporate life of the clan, a life gradually expanded into the entire dêmos of the city commonwealth and at the same time narrowed into an evolution of individual culture, they are in medieval Europe due to a resurrection of corporate life in the towns whose rise everywhere marked the decadence of feudal individualism. If clan communities have been in literature more or less concealed from view by the fact that only during their absorption into larger groups and their decomposition into individualised life has literature to any considerable extent made its appearance, if they were fused into cities and nations, the town communities of the Middle Ages likewise lost their corporate sentiments by becoming the local organs of monarchical centres, and neither the literature of feudal castles nor that of kingly courts could sympathise with their corporate life. But we must here remember another cause of the darkness which hangs between us and really archaic conceptions of human character. In any comparison of the classical and modern literatures of Europe in their early developments we must be ready to allow for the influence of a world-religion (as well as a world-language) on barbaric and medieval imagination and intellect. Christianity, like the eagle wounded by an arrow which a feather of its own had winged, is to-day attacked by social and physical theories which claim to rule a wider empire of time and space; but at the Christianising of Europe, this majestic world-religion must have opened up such visions of human unity as the barbarians would have needed centuries of internal conflict, civilisation, and philosophy to approximate. To the Europe of the barbarian hordes Christianity came as a ready-made philosophy—a philosophy, moreover, not too refined to touch certain deep feelings of clan life; indeed, two leading conceptions of the new faith were identical with conceptions long familiar to such life, viz. inherited sin and vicarious punishment. So far as these doctrines were concerned, Christianity did not introduce new ideas; it simply extended ideas already existing, within small circles, to a range apparently boundless. How, then, it may be asked, did the Christian world-religion contribute to throw ideas of clan life and impersonal character into the background?

The Christian conceptions of personal immortality, personal reward or punishment in a future state, must have contrasted curiously with the usual doctrines of clan ethics. We cannot here attempt to trace at any length the influence of this individualism on barbarian feelings; we need only observe how largely it must have contributed to strengthen such sentiments of personal independence as had been developed among the tribal chiefs before Christianity became known to them. As in the two social lives of early Greece brought before us by the contrast of Homer with Hesiod—the life of the chiefs splendid with heroic ideals and personal prowess, the life of the villagers oppressed with poverty and toil—we find among the barbarians of the fifth and sixth centuries marked differences between the independence of the chiefs and that of the common clansmen. But the difference does not assume Homeric proportions until the barbarian conquerors have settled down, and the *comitatus* or *gefolge* of the chief changes into the retainers of a feudal lord, while the body of clansmen sink into villagers over whose common lands the seigneur alternately extends his protection and his domain. Then a striking contrast to the social life of Athens and Rome begins to disclose itself. Instead of the life and the ideas of the city, we find men passing their days in isolated groups under the shadow of the seigneur's castle, serfs dependent on a master whom there is no public opinion and little public force to keep in check, serfs who hardly know of any world beyond their village and their lord's retainers, and who bear in ruined harvests or devastated homes the marks of that knightly independence to which Europe for a season offered a romantic field for individual caprice or chivalry. In such ages literature had no resting-place save in the lord's hall or in the monk's cell; and it is not surprising that some centuries of this feudal individualism did much to destroy recollections of the clan and its social character. In such ages the very notion of "the people"—that abstraction which the social conditions of our modern life have made so significant—did not exist; for the isolated groups of villagers had, until the rise of towns, no bond of social communion save through their lords. Hence, in feudal, as in Homeric, literature, personal character, aggressive and isolating, overshadows all corporate bonds of social unity. To create such bonds was the work of new groups whose rise in Spain, Italy, Germany, France, England, makes the most memorable chapters of modern social history. With the rise of the modern towns—so different at once from the early clan communities and from the municipal systems of Greece and Rome—began a twofold process; the subordination of individual to collective interests accompanied by a development of individual liberty within limits prescribed by law. It is in the earlier growth of this town life, when feudal enemies kept the *commune* and its corporate interests uppermost in the burghers' minds, that we find the social source of likeness between the early dramas of Athens and modern Europe. How much of this resemblance was due to survivals from the clan age in Athens and medieval Europe we need not now inquire. It is enough to observe how great must be our difficulties in tracing the evolution of personal out of impersonal character when Homeric bards, feudal trouvères and troubadours, or monks deeply imbued with the universal humanity of a world-religion and the personal ideas of Christianity, were in the course of social progress our early makers, and witnesses to the making, of literature.

But there is another cause of our difficulties in realising the evolution of individual character. Living in communities highly individualised, which have derived so much of their art from Athens and Rome—communities themselves highly individualised—adult ideas of personality have long formed for us the centre of all our creative art, of all our criticism. The corporate life of men in groups has only found admittance in our modern literatures since industrial development began to create a new social and impersonal spirit. Marks of this corporate life on creative art we may, for example, discover in *Faust*, with its allegorical personages recalling the medieval mystery, in the *Légende des Siècles*, with its vision of the social changes through which humanity has passed, or in the poems of Walt Whitman, in which, as it has been well said, each individual suggests a group, each group a multitude, and the poet manifests a recurring tendency to become a catalogue-maker of persons and things. The impersonal laws of science have also contributed to aid the corporate spirit of our industrial life and modern democracy in producing a creative art of corresponding nature; witness the reign of law, physical and social, in the works of many contemporary makers of literature, whose feelings of personality sometimes seem to die within them at the vast vision of social and physical causes and effects—

"On n'est plus qu'une ombre qui passe,
Une âme dans l'immensité."

But such conceptions are of comparatively recent origin. Corporate life had little place in the masterpieces of earlier European poetry—little in the song of Dante full of the note of Italian individualism, more perhaps in the character-types and allegories of Chaucer, but little in the drama of Shakspere in which the "people," seldom noticed, appear only as a fickle and irrational mob, now huzzaing for Cade and now for the King, now siding with Brutus and now with Antony. Nor need we feel any surprise at this predominance of the individual in modern European literature till the middle of the last century. "The people" at the time when Shakspere wrote was scarcely in existence in England, or France, or Germany; towns there were, indeed, with their local patriotism, their parochial politics, their hostility to the seigneurs and to each other; but "the people," in the sense familiar to our modern industrial communities, in which the steam-engine and the telegraph have done so much to destroy local distinctions, was then and for a long time afterwards, in Mr. Dowden's excellent phrase, like Milton's half-created animals, still pawing to get free its hinder parts from the mire.* Hence the progress of literary art under the patronage of courts, as previously under that of seigneurs, moved in a groove of individual thought and feeling to which the influence of classical imitation only confined it more strictly. Hence, too, the language of criticism which expressed or analysed this literary progress was altogether conceived from the individual standpoint, and can with difficulty be employed by the socialising spirit of the present day. To take one example of the influence of these individual associations, we may refer to the unfinished essay of Montesquieu on Taste. In his famous *Spirit of the Laws*, Montesquieu, after starting, indeed, with abstract principles not much superior to the usual imitations of Plato and Aristotle, had struck into the true path of social and physical causation; yet, when he afterwards came to discuss the theory of Taste, there rose before his mind the figure of an individual, dependent indeed for his conceptions of the beautiful on his senses and liable to have such conceptions altered by the sharpening or blunting of his senses, the increase or diminution of their number, but still an individual with whose *statical* nature questions of æsthetic development as depending on social life or physical environment have little to do. So hard was it even for such an intellect as that of Montesquieu to rise above ideas of individuality which the art and criticism of classical antiquity and modern civilization had combined to create.

§ 20. Anticipating evidences to be adduced elsewhere, we may here lay down the principle that in the movement of civilisation—a movement by no means regular, but often spasmodic, back and forward, forward and back, though on the whole forward—personal character comes

* *Shakspere: his Mind and Art*, p. 320.

to stand out more and more distinctly from the general crowd. But this evolution of personal character—under which we include the actions, instincts, emotions, reason, imagination of the individual unit—must not be viewed apart from the extent to which it prevails, that is, the number of units in any social group who may be regarded as having attained a given standard of such evolution. The highest evolution of character is where every individual in the entire group stands out in clear-cut personality—it cannot be found in a sprinkling of individuals, as in the priestly culture of the East, nor in an educated few supported by masses of slaves, as in Athens and Rome, nor in a few seigneurs towering like their castles among herds of serfs, nor in the poets and orators of European courts. To use a phrase of logic, we must not only regard the *comprehension* but also the *extension* of individuality; and only as both of these go hand in hand can we say that permanent personal progress is being made. Walt Whitman, whose three leading ideas are clearly democracy, American nationality, and personality, seems to keenly appreciate this truth. The American bard, who will content himself with "no class of persons, nor one or two out of the strata of interests," sees "eternity in men and women—he does not see men or women as dreams or dots." * How immense is the difference between this conception of a multitudinous people composed of perfectly distinct personalities, and the little groups of common kinship in which personality was almost unknown ! How vast and intricate this twofold process of individuality deepening in the separate units while expanding in the number of units it includes ! Now, it is this *twofold* process which we mean by "the principle of literary growth." Only when depth and

* Preface to *Leaves of Grass*.

extent of individuality are concurrently developed can we feel confidence in the permanence of such growth; witness the rapid withering of Athenian literature. In a well-known canon Sir Henry Maine has expressed one aspect of this individual evolution when he says that the movement of progressive societies has been from status to contract, or, to translate the legal into everyday language, from the restraints of the communal group to personal freedom of action and thought. But the extent to which this free individuality prevails is an aspect of such evolution no less important than its degree or depth. If any one doubts this, let him remember that average character, on which the reasoning of sociological science is based, means simply the extent to which any given individuality prevails.

We accept, then, as the principle of literary growth, the progressive deepening and widening of personality. We shall find in the course of our inquiries that not only have the depth and extent of personality varied in different conditions of social life to an astonishing degree, not only have they left upon diverse literatures the most diverse marks, but that the animal and physical worlds have assumed new aspects under new phases of personal being. At present, however, we turn to a question which more immediately concerns us, viz. : What is the method by which the discovery and illustration of our principle may be best conducted?

CHAPTER IV.

THE COMPARATIVE METHOD AND LITERATURE.

§ 21. THE comparative method of acquiring or communicating knowledge is in one sense as old as thought itself, in another the peculiar glory of our nineteenth century. All reason, all imagination, operate subjectively, and pass from man to man objectively, by aid of comparisons and differences. The most colourless proposition of the logician is either the assertion of a comparison, A is B, or the denial of a comparison, A is not B; and any student of Greek thought will remember how the confusion of this simple process by mistakes about the nature of the copula (ἐστι) produced a flood of so-called "essences" (οὐσίαι) which have done more to mislead both ancient and modern philosophy than can be easily estimated. But not only the colourless propositions of logic, even the highest and most brilliant flights of oratorical eloquence or poetic fancy are sustained by this rudimentary structure of comparison and difference, this primary scaffolding, as we may call it, of human thought. If sober experience works out scientific truths in propositions affirming or denying comparison, imagination even in the richest colours works under the same elementary forms. Athenian intellect and Alexandrian reflection failed to perceive this fundamental truth, and the failure is attributable in the main to certain social characteristics of the Greeks. Groups, like individuals, need to project themselves beyond the circle of their own associations if they wish to understand their own nature; but the great highway which has since led to comparative philosophy was closed against the Greek by his contempt for any language but his own. At the same time, his comparisons of his own social life, in widely different stages, were narrowed partially by want of monuments of his past, much more by contempt for the less civilised Greeks, such as the Macedonians, and especially by a mass of myth long too sacred to be touched by science, and then too tangled to be profitably loosed by the hands of impatient sceptics. Thus, deprived of the historical study of their own past and circumscribed within the comparisons and distinctions their own adult language permitted, it is not surprising that the Greeks made poor progress in comparative thinking, as a matter not merely of unconscious action but of conscious reflection. This conscious reflection has been the growth of European thought during the past five centuries, at first indeed a weakling, but, from causes of recent origin, now flourishing in healthy vigour.

When Dante wrote *De Eloquio Vulgari* he marked the starting-point of our modern comparative science— the nature of language, a problem not to be lightly overlooked by the peoples of modern Europe inheriting, unlike Greek or Hebrew, a literature written in a tongue whose decomposition had plainly gone to make up the elements of their own living speech. The Latin, followed at an interval by the Greek, Renaissance laid the foundations of comparative reflection in the mind of modern Europe. Meanwhile the rise of European nationalities was creating new standpoints, new materials, for comparison in modern institutions and modes of thought or sentiment. The discovery of the New World brought this new European civilisation face to face with primitive life, and awakened men to contrasts with their own associations more striking than Byzantine or even Saracen could offer. Commerce, too, was now bringing the rising nations of Europe into rivalry with, and knowledge of, each other, and, more than this, giving a greater degree of personal freedom to the townsmen of the West than they had ever possessed before. Accompanying the increase of wealth and freedom came an awakening of individual opinion among men, even an uprising of it against authority which has since been called the Reformation, but an uprising which, in days of feudal, monarchical, and "popular" conflict, in days when education was the expensive luxury of the few, and even the communication of work-a-day ideas was as slow and irregular as bad roads and worse banditti could make it, was easily checked even in countries where it was supposed to have done great things. Individual inquiry, and with it comparative thinking, checked within the domain of social life by constant collisions with theological dogma, turned to the material world, began to build up the vast stores of modern material knowledge, and only in later days of freedom began to construct from this physical side secular views of human origin and destiny which on the social side had been previously curbed by dogma. Meanwhile European knowledge of man's social life in its myriad varieties was attaining proportions such as neither Bacon nor Locke had contemplated. Christian missionaries were bringing home the life and literature of China so vividly to Europeans that neither the art nor the scepticism of Voltaire disdained to borrow from the Jesuit Prémare's translation of a

Chinese drama published in 1735. Then Englishmen in India learned of that ancient language which Sir William Jones, toward the close of the eighteenth century, introduced to European scholars; and soon the points of resemblance between this language and the languages of Greeks and Italians, Teutons and Celts, were observed, and used like so many stepping-stones upon which men passed in imagination over the flood of time which separates the old Aryans from their modern offshoots in the West. Since those days the method of comparison has been applied to many subjects besides language; and many new influences have combined to make the mind of Europe more ready to compare and to contrast than it ever was before. The steam-engine, telegraph, daily press, now bring the local and central, the popular and the cultured, life of each European country and the general actions of the entire world face to face; and habits of comparison have arisen such as never before prevailed so widely and so vigorously. But, while we may call *consciously* comparative thinking the great glory of our nineteenth century, let us not forget that such thinking is largely due to mechanical improvements, and that long before our comparative philologists, jurists, economists, and the rest, scholars like Reuchlin used the same method less consciously, less accurately, yet in a manner from the first foreshadowing a vast outlook instead of the exclusive views of Greek criticism. Here, then, is a rapid sketch of comparative thought in its European history. How is such thought, how is its method, connected with our subject, "Literature"?

§ 22. It has been observed that imagination no less than experience works through the medium of comparisons; but it is too often forgotten that the range of these comparisons is far from being unlimited in space and time, in social life and physical environment. If scientific imagination, such as Professor Tyndall once explained and illustrated, is strictly bound by the laws of hypothesis, the magic of the literary artist which looks so free is as strictly bound within the range of ideas already marked out by the language of his group. Unlike the man of science, the man of literature cannot coin words for a currency of new ideas; for his verse or prose, unlike the discoveries of the man of science, must reach average, not specialised, intelligence. Words must pass from special into general use before they can be used by him; and, just in proportion as special kinds of knowledge (legal, commercial, mechanical, and the like) are developed, the more striking is the difference between the language of literature and that of science the language and ideas of the community contrasted with those of its specialised parts. If we trace the rise of any civilised community out of isolated clans or tribes, we may observe a twofold development closely connected with the language and ideas of literature—expansion of the group outwards, a process attended by expansions of thought and sentiment; and specialisation of activities within, a process upon which depends the rise of a leisure-enjoying literary class, priestly or secular. The latter is the process familiar to economists as division of labour, the former that familiar to antiquaries as the fusion of smaller into larger social groups. While the range of comparison widens from clan to national and even world-wide associations and sympathies, the specialising process separates ideas, words, and forms of writing from the proper domain of literature. Thus, in the Homeric age the speech in the Agora has nothing professional or specialised about it, and is a proper subject of poetry; but in the days of professional Athenian oratory the speech is out of keeping with the drama, and smacks too much of the rhêtor's school. Arabic poets of the "Ignorance" sing of their clan life; Spenser glows with warmly national feelings; Goethe and Victor Hugo rise above thoughts of even national destiny. It is due to these two processes of expansion and specialisation that the language and ideas of literature gradually shade off from the special language and special ideas of certain classes in any highly developed community, and literature comes to differ from science not only by its imaginative character, but by the fact that its language and ideas belong to no special class. In fact, whenever literary language and ideas cease to be in a manner common property, literature tends either towards imitation work or to become specialised, to become science in a literary dress—as not a little of our metaphysical poetry has been of late. Such facts as these bring out prominently the relation of comparative thinking and of the comparative method to literature. Is the circle of common speech and thought, the circle of the group's comparative thinking, as narrow as a tribal league? Or, have many such circles combined into a national group? Are the offices of priest and singer still combined in a kind of magic ritual? Or, have professions and trades been developed, each, so to speak, with its own technical dialect for practical purposes? Then we must remember that these external and internal evolutions of social life, take place often unconsciously, making comparisons and distinctions without reflecting on their nature or limits; we must remember that it is the business of reflective comparison, of the comparative method, to retrace this development *consciously,* and to seek the causes which have produced it. Let us now look at the literary use of such comparison in a less abstract, a more lifelike form.

When Mr. Matthew Arnold defines the function of criticism as "a disinterested endeavour to learn and propagate the best that is known and thought in the world," he is careful to add that much of this best knowledge and thought is not of English but foreign growth. The English critic in these times of international literature must deal largely with foreign fruit and flower, and thorn-pieces sometimes. He cannot rest content with the products of his own country's culture, though they may vary from the wild fruits of the Saxon wilderness to the rude plenty of the Elizabethan age, from the courtly neatness of Pope to the democratic tastes of to-day. M. Demogeot has lately published an interesting study * of the influences exerted by Italy, Spain, England, and Germany on the literature of France; our English critic must do likewise for the literature of his own country. At every stage in the progress of his country's literature he is, in fact, forced to look more or less beyond her sea-washed shores. Does he accompany Chaucer on his pilgrimage and listen to the pilgrims' tales? The scents of the lands of the South fill the atmosphere of the Tabard Inn, and on the road to Canterbury waft him in thought to the Italy of Dante and of Petrarch and Boccaccio. Does he watch the hardy crews of Drake and Frobisher unload in English port the wealth of Spanish prize, and listen to the talk of great sea-captains full of phrases learned from the gallant subjects of Philip II.? The Spain of Cervantes and Lope de Vega rises before his eyes, and the new physical and mental wealth of Elizabethan England bears him on the wings of commerce or of fancy to the noisy port of Cadiz and the palaces of Spanish grandees. Through the narrow and dirty streets of Elizabethan London fine gentlemen, with Spanish

* *Histoire des Littératures étrangères* (Paris, 1880).

rapiers at their sides and Spanish phrases in their mouths, pass to and fro in the dress admired by Spanish taste. The rude theatres resound with Spanish allusions. And, were it not for the deadly strife of Englishman and Spaniard on the seas, and the English dread of Spain as the champion of Papal interference, England's Helicon might forget the setting sun of the Italian republics to enjoy the full sunshine of Spanish influences. But now our critic stands in the Whitehall of Charles II., or lounges at Will's Coffee-House, or enters the theatres whose recent restoration cuts to the heart his Puritan friends. Everywhere it is the same. Spanish phrases and manners have been forgotten. At the court, Buckingham and the rest perfume their licentious wit with French *bouquet*. At Will's, Dryden glorifies the rimed tragedies of Racine; and theatres, gaudy with scenic contrivances unknown to Shakspere, are filled with audiences who in the intervals chatter French criticism, and applaud with equal fervour outrageous indecencies and formal symmetry. Soon the English Boileau will carry the culture of French exotics as far as the English hothouse will allow; soon that scepticism which the refined immorality of the court, the judges, and the Parliament renders fashionable among the few who as yet guide the destinies of the English nation, shall pass from Bolingbroke to Voltaire, and from Voltaire to the Revolutionists. We need not accompany our critic to Weimar, nor seek with him some sources of German influence on England in English antipathies to France and her revolution. He has proved that the history of our country's literature cannot be explained by English causes alone, any more than the origin of the English language or people can be so explained. He has proved that each national literature is a centre towards which not only national but also international forces gravitate. We thank him for this glimpse of a growth so wide, so varying, so full of intricate interaction; it is an aspect of literature studied comparatively, but, in spite of its apparent width, it is only one aspect. National literature has been developed from within as well as influenced from without; and the comparative study of this internal development is of far greater interest than that of the external, because the former is less a matter of imitation and more an evolution directly dependent on social and physical causes.

§ 23. To the internal sources of national development, social or physical, and the effect of different phases of this development on literature, the student will therefore turn as the true field of scientific study. He will watch the expansion of social life from narrow circles of clans or tribal communities, possessed of such sentiments and thoughts as could live within such narrow spheres, and expressing in their rude poetry their intense feelings of brotherhood, their weak conceptions of personality. He will watch the deepening of personal sentiments in the isolated life of feudalism which ousts the communism of the clan, the reflection of such sentiments in songs of personal heroism, and the new aspects which the life of man, and of nature, and of animals—the horse, the hound, the hawk in feudal poetry, for example—assumes under this change in social organisation. Then he will mark the beginnings of a new kind of corporate life in the cities, in whose streets sentiments of clan exclusiveness are to perish, the prodigious importance of feudal personality is to disappear, new forms of individual and collective character are to make their appearance, and the drama is to take the place of the early communal chant or the song of the chieftain's hall.

Next, the scene will change into the courts of monarchy. Here the feelings of the cities and of the seigneurs are being focussed; here the imitation of classical models supplements the influences of growing national union; here literature, reflecting a more expanded society, a deeper sense of individuality, than it ever did before, produces its master-pieces under the patronage of an Elizabeth or a Louis Quatorze. Nor, in observing such effects of social evolution on literature, will the student by any means confine his view to this or that country. He will find that if England had her clan age, so also had Europe in general; that if France had her feudal poetry, so also had Germany, and Spain, and England; that though the rise of the towns affected literature in diverse ways throughout Europe, yet there are general features common to their influences; and that the same may be said of centralism in our European nations. Trace the influence of the Christian pulpit, or that of judicial institutions, or that of the popular assembly, on the growth of prose in different European countries, and you soon find how similarly internal social evolution has reflected itself in the word and thought of literature; how essential it is that any accurate study of literature should pass from language into the causes which allowed language and thought to reach conditions capable of supporting a literature; and how profoundly this study must be one of comparison and contrast. But we must not underrate our difficulties in tracing the effects of such internal evolution on a people's verse and prose. We must rather admit at the outset that such evolution is liable to be obscured or altogether concealed by the imitation of foreign models. To an example of such imitation we shall now turn.

The cases of Rome and Russia are enough to prove

that external influences, carried beyond a certain point, may convert literature from the outgrowth of the group to which it belongs into a mere exotic, deserving of scientific study only as an artificial production indirectly dependent on social life. Let an instrument of speech be formed, a social centre established, an opportunity for the rise of a literary class able to depend upon its handiwork be given, and only a strong current of national ideas, or absolute ignorance of foreign and ancient models, can prevent the production of imitative work whose materials and arrangement, no matter how unlike those characteristic of the group, may be borrowed from climates the most diverse, social conditions the most opposite, and conceptions of personal character belonging to totally different epochs. Especially likely is something of this kind to occur when the cultured few of a people comparatively uncivilised become acquainted with the literary models of men who have already passed through many grades of civilisation, and who can, as it seems, save them the time and trouble of nationally repeating the same laborious ascent. The imitative literature of Rome is a familiar example of such borrowing; and that of Russia looked for a time as if it were fated to follow French models almost as closely as Rome once followed the Greek. How certain this imitation of French models was to conceal the true national spirit of Russian life, to throw a veil of contemptuous ignorance over her barbarous past, and to displace in her literature the development of the nation by the caprice of a Russo-Gallic clique, none can fail to perceive. In a country whose social life was, and is, so largely based on the communal organisation of the *Mir*, or village community, the strongly-individualised literature of France became such a favourite source of imitation as to throw into the background altogether those folk-songs which the reviving spirit of national literature in Russia, and that of social study in Europe generally, are at length beginning to examine. This Russian imitation of France may be illustrated by the works of Prince Kantemir (1709-1743), who has been called "the first writer of Russia," the friend of Montesquieu, and the imitator of Boileau and Horace in his epistles and satires; by those of Lomonossoff (1711-1765), "the first classical writer of Russia," the pupil of Wolf, the founder of the University of Moscow, the reformer of the Russian language, who by academical *Panegyrics* on Peter the Great and Elizabeth sought to supply the want of that truly oratorical prose which only free assemblies can foster, attempted an epic *Petreid* in honour of the great Tsar, and modelled his odes on the French lyric poets and Pindar;* or by those of Soumarokoff, who, for the theatre of St. Petersburg established by Elizabeth, adapted or translated Corneille, Racine, Voltaire, much as Plautus and Terence had introduced the Athenian drama at Rome. As in Rome there had set in a conflict between old Roman family sentiments and the individualising spirit of the Greeks, as in Rome nobles of light and leading had been delighted to exchange archaic sentiments of family life and archaic measures like the Saturnian for the cultured thought and harmonious metres of Greece, so in Russia there set in a conflict between French individualism, dear to the court and nobles, and the social feelings of the Russian commune and family. The most ancient monuments of Russian thought—the Chronicle of the monk Nestor (1056-1116) and the *Song of Igor*—were as unlikely to

* The son of the fisherman of Archangel did much, no doubt, to create national literature, especially by his severance of the old Slavon of the Church from the spoken language; but his works contain evidences of French influence in spite of his national predilections.

attract the attention of such imitators as the *Builinas* and the folk-songs; and among a people who had never experienced the Western feudalism with its chivalrous poetry, to whom the Renaissance and Reformation had been unknown, came an imitation of Western progress which threatened for a time to prove as fatal to national literature as the imitation of Greek ideas had proved in Rome. In this European China, as Russia, with her family sentiments and filial devotion to the Tsar, has been called, French, and afterwards German and English, influences clearly illustrate the difficulties to which a scientific student of literature is exposed by imitative work out of keeping with social life; but the growing triumph of Russian national life as the true spring of Russian literature marks the want of real vitality in any literature dependent upon such foreign imitation.

§ 24. These internal and external aspects of literary growth are thus objects of comparative inquiry, because literatures are not Aladdin's palaces raised by unseen hands in the twinkling of an eye, but the substantial results of causes which can be specified and described. The theory that literature is the detached life-work of individuals who are to be worshipped like images fallen down from heaven, not known as workers in the language and ideas of their age and place, and the kindred theory that imagination transcends the associations of space and time, have done much to conceal the relation of science to literature and to injure the works of both. But the "great-man theory" is really suicidal; for, while breaking up history and literature into biographies and thus preventing the recognition of any lines of orderly development, it would logically reduce not only what is known as "exceptional genius," but all men and women, so far as they possess personality at all, to the unknown, the causeless—in fact, would issue in a sheer denial of human knowledge, limited or unlimited. On the other hand, the theory that imagination works out of space and time (Coleridge, for example, telling us that "Shakspere is as much out of time as Spenser out of space") must not be repelled by any equally dogmatic assertion that it is limited by human experience, but is only to be refuted or established by such comparative studies as those on which we are about to enter.

The central point of these studies is the relation of the individual to the group. In the orderly changes through which this relation has passed, as revealed by the comparison of literatures belonging to different social states, we find our main reasons for treating literature as capable of scientific explanation. There are, indeed, other standpoints, profoundly interesting, from which the art and criticism of literature may also be explained—that of physical nature, that of animal life. But from these alone we shall not see far into the secrets of literary workmanship. We therefore adopt, with a modification hereafter to be noticed, the gradual expansion of social life, from clan to city, from city to nation, from both of these to cosmopolitan humanity, as the proper order of our studies in comparative literature.

BOOK II.
CLAN LITERATURE.

CHAPTER I.

THE CLAN GROUP.

§ 25. CHATEAUBRIAND, in a remarkable chapter of *Le Génie du Christianisme*, maintains that "unbelief is the principal cause of the decadence of taste and genius. When people believed nothing at Athens and Rome, talents disappeared with the gods, and the Muses gave up to barbarism those who had ceased to have faith in them." If we put the word "sympathy" where Chateaubriand would have used "belief," and maintain that the decay of sympathy between man and man is one cause of the decay of literature, just as its deepening and expansion immensely contribute to literary progress, we shall exchange a vague theory of dogma for a fact which the social history of the world abundantly illustrates. The prospect of being heard with sympathy or indifference must profoundly affect the makers of verse or prose, the literary artist and even the scientific inquirer; and it would be an interesting question to ask whether the supposed decay of imagination in civilised progress (a favourite theory with Macaulay) does not mark that temporary break-up of sympathy which constantly accompanies the transition from one social stage to another. Whatever pleasure the scientist may derive from his solitary study—and even this generally finds its source in some prospective audience for his achievements—there can be no doubt that literature, whether its form be verse or prose, whether its spirit be intensely individual or social, cannot live apart from some kind of sympathetic group. Hence the gradual extension of social sympathy is a leading feature of literary development. Sensations and emotions, moral and intellectual ideas, widen in their range as smaller groups merge into larger; and this progressive merger underlies the development of institutions and language, and is largely a maker of myth, the interlacing of group traditions (easily illustrated by early Arab history) creating eponymous myths of every variety.

But it is not to be supposed that the social groups, or their progressive merger into widening circles, admit of exact definition. We cannot select any exact point and say, "Here the clan breaks up and the city succeeds." We cannot deny the existence of clan associations in days when the leading features of clan life have been obliterated—nay, it is often only because such survivals have taken place, owing to the progress of different parts of society at different rates, that we can recover the past at all. We can draw no hard-and-fast lines limiting the idea of "clan" absolutely, or denying its concrete existence save where our ideal definition is exactly realised. And the reason of this apparent vagueness is the best of all possible reasons—viz., the absence of any such definite lines in social phenomena not abstractly sketched on paper, but as living and moving realities. The jurist does not attempt to minutely define the Roman *familia*, or give the exact dates at which the marked features of that social unit faded away. The economist, with all his masses of statistical information, cannot distinguish his capitalist and labouring groups save by broad distinctions which in concrete life insensibly fade into each other; nor would he fix the decade in which English landlords, or capitalists, or labourers became sufficiently free from medieval restraints to allow his ideal groups some semblance of truth. In fine, no competent judge will deny that these and all social scientists must ideally construct definitions which concrete facts only temporarily and indistinctly contain—unless, indeed, we are content to look in despair on that vast moving mass which we call "social life" and give up the attempt to understand and explain it altogether. The search after minute distinctions in social classification and minute time-marks in social evolution is in fact an *eidolon tribûs*. An image of the individual's life is insensibly transferred to the action of men in groups, and the distinctness of an individual's personality and career is required from social classifications the very essence of which is their immunity from that defined birth and death which give to individual life its clear-cut limits. The concrete existence of the individual in space is, likewise, sought in group life, and we perpetually forget that, even in the simplest cases, a group is essentially an abstraction drawing up an immense detail of individualities into an apex of common points which are found in actual life diverging into many degrees of diversity. While we thus erroneously seek the unity and personality of the individual in groups, the common standards of chronology are likewise applied by universal consent to the life of groups as to that of individuals. Let the first year of our social memory be once settled, and, whether it be an Egyptian dynasty or the first celebration of public games, or the birth or the death or the flight of a prophet, we are ready to measure back by year and day to this arbitrary terminus the lives of individuals and of groups alike. The observer of organic nature knows by what insensible grades the individuals of his various classes, plants or animals, fade into each other, yet his distinctions, however faint at the outline, are clear enough in the colour. So, too, the observer of inorganic nature must assume the lines which nature does not draw. Least of all should the observer of social life expect minute exactness in those abstract classifications by which he attempts to overcome difficulties peculiarly great in his subject—to stop ideally the constant motion of social life in a kind of instantaneous photograph of its facts, and then to offer an explanation of these facts and a series of pictures detailing social life in progress and explaining its complicated motion. In nature, as A. W. Schlegel has pointedly remarked, the boundaries of objects run into one another; surely it will not be supposed that any magic of science can banish this natural indistinctness of outline?

§ 26. When, therefore, we say that the "clan" is a social classification, we need not be ashamed to admit the ideal character of our abstract term, or our inability to state precisely the points at which its communal career begins and ends. But we must know the leading facts which this abstract term idealises, the wide domain of human history which clan life has dominated, the significant truth that this form of social organisation, under a great variety of names and a considerable variety of features, is the most archaic to which historical science enables us to ascend with confidence. We shall, therefore, explain our ideal of clan life and the nature of the archaic universality it claims so far as anything human can claim that proud title. But first we have something to say about the practical and theoretic conditions which have turned men's attention to the clan organisation.

The importance which the clan has assumed in recent

speculation is due to a variety of associations, partly incidental to the ordinary activities of our nineteenth-century life, partly peculiar to the character of our modern thought. The everyday life of Europe in general and of England in particular is now habituated to social contrasts greater than ever before fell within the positive range of human knowledge. While civilised nations stand face to face by aid of press, telegraph, steam-engine, their differences, once thought so considerable, have almost ceased to attract attention compared with the countless grades of Eastern and Western barbarism which adventure, commerce, or missionary zeal have brought home to us as living realities. At the same time, the historical faculty, in which Macaulay rightly places the great superiority of modern over ancient culture, enlarged by new ranges of comparison and contrast, has since the Renaissance and Reformation cast off the shackles which impeded its freedom in Athens and Rome. The overweening contempt for foreigners, which in the Greek and his imitative conqueror despised the lights of comparative inquiry lying all round their march of conquest, was impossible among the variety of nationalities and languages which rose out of the ruins of the Roman empire. The recovery of Greek literature, even while it diverted national literatures into imitations of itself, fostered this growth of conscious comparison. And, after the individual had dared to question the authority of creed with a freedom which Greece and Rome ventured to apply to their myths only when their vitality had perished, the fruits of historical criticism (untimely in the sneering nihilism of Voltaire and Gibbon) needed little but improved knowledge of India and the East in general to ripen into an abundant harvest. It is this harvest which the nineteenth century now reaps in language, in law, in political economy; in fine, in the most accurate and most extended knowledge of history which the world has ever known. Science, like a hundred-handed Briareus, working in many a field, yet watching with the eyes of an Argus all the richly varied ingathering, has learned how to probe among the very roots of social thought, and speech, and action. The hands of the mighty Titan have found the clan ideas, the clan facts, at the roots of property and political institutions, of legal rights, religious doctrines, and moral principles. Are we not justified in the belief that we shall find them also at the roots of literature?

What is a "clan"? As already observed, we are not to suppose that all clans are exactly alike. Trades-unions and co-operative associations are called by their respective common names, yet even with our abundant means of contemporary information we are content to merge individual differences in our general notions of the one and the other. The ancient clan groups—not a whit the less ancient because they coexist with the most advanced civilisation as at the present day—differ widely from trades-unions and co-operative societies in being for the most part of natural, not artificial, growth. They are groups not made with hands, not planned with a set purpose, not supplied with defined rules which can be printed and exhibited in the rooms of a club, but intensely united by bonds of common thought and feeling compared with which the deepest sentiments of Christian communion can hardly be regarded as other than artificial. This bond of unity is common kinship, common ancestry. Not realised as an idea of the intellect, not reflected upon as an emotion of the heart, but profoundly felt to be the centre of social life, this common kinship is as real as though it could be touched in the person of that communal ancestor from whose loins the group is sprung or thought to be sprung, whose imaginary presence sanctifies every festival of common joys, whose favour is to be propitiated in every common affliction, and to whom, in company with others long since gathered to their fathers, it is the destiny of the clansman, sooner or later, to return. Unformulated in any doctrine, but not on that account less real, unwritten in any code, but not on that account less lasting, this unity of blood is the central conception of clan life, the central point to and from which sets the current of the clansmen's deepest feelings.

The outward marks of this common kinship are numerous. Common religious rites, or *sacra gentilicia*, bind the clansmen in a fellowship of ancestral worship and the village community to its eponymous ancestor. Reciprocal obligations of defence and vengeance unite the brotherhood, whether it consists of Hebrew or Arab Semites, of Greek or German Aryans, of kinsmen in Central Asia or in the wilds of the New World. Rights or obligations of marriage within the clan everywhere attest the same communal exclusiveness; and some forms of clan life would even lead us to believe that the brotherhood once lived under a common roof, and shared not only their sacred festivals but even their ordinary meals. Conspicuous, however, among these signs of communal kinship is an economic feature of the settled clan which living scholars have investigated with equal patience and learning—the common ownership of land. This feature M. de Laveleye, for example, in his *Primitive Property*, and Sir Henry Maine, in his *Village Communities* and *Early History of Institutions*, have illustrated by examples taken from every quarter of the globe—from India and Russia, from the Germanic Mark, and from the agrarian communities of the Celts and the Arabs. No doubt such common ownership of land is not always a mark of clanship. No doubt it marks sometimes the desire to get as much as possible out of the soil by a kind of agricultural co-operation. But, allowing for such economic motives, and admitting the existence of village communities, which are signs of economic rather than clan organisation, we are amply justified in treating common property as an ordinary and prominent feature of clan life.

More interesting, however, than outward signs of clan communion is the inward spirit of these communities. On this moral side the intense social unity of the group expresses itself in notions of right and wrong which curiously conflict with those of civilised nations. Individual responsibility is conceived most obscurely; personal intention, if seen at all, is visible only through mists of communal sentiment; and the corporate responsibility of the group is vividly realised. Inherited guilt, vicarious punishment, the absence of belief in a future state of *personal* reward or retribution—such are some of the most interesting signs of this clan spirit. It is easy to see how these three characteristics of the clan spirit follow with an unconscious logic from corporate responsibility. The clansman has done wrong, and, until that wrong is atoned for, any member of the offending group is liable to punishment, a liability nowise altered by the birth or death of the individuals composing the group. In the eyes of the clan the inheritance of such responsibility seems not a whit less reasonable than the acquisition of rights in the common lands by birth. In the eyes of the clan the selection of this or that person for punishment seems as reasonable as the escape of others by death from the only known sphere of punishment—

human clan life. Indeed, this corporate liability for sins is the only possible moral sanction so long as the individual's intention is left out of sight, his personal being dimly realised, and his personal share in a future life but vaguely felt. And so the communal rites of burial, which form the closing scene in the clansman's career, are but the appropriate dismissal of a comrade to a shadow-world in which reward and punishment for things done in the light of the sun have no place.

§ 27. It will be at once observed that such a group must have prodigiously influenced the beginnings of literature. From it, for example, come the sentiments of blood-revenge so common in early Arab and Saxon poetry. From it come those feelings of duty to kindred which permeate all early poetry, even when it belongs to the chief's hall and *gefolge* much more than to clan life. But it is not to be supposed that any literature of any country or age does, or could, contain an exact reflection of clan life in its purity. Such purely communal life is clearly impossible save within narrow limits; and the very narrowness of such limits prevents the development of action, thought, or language capable of supporting a literature. It is true that the wild festivals of Indian tribes supplied observers a century ago (such as Dr. Brown, whose *History of the Rise of Poetry*, noticed approvingly by Percy, deserves more attention than it has hitherto received) with curious combinations of dance, music, song, and gesticulation, in which, as comparative evidences have since proved, they were right in discovering the primary sources of literature. But until some fusion of clans has developed wider sympathies and opened the way for religious centralisation with its ritual of choral song, until bards who can depend upon their art for subsistence have found their patrons in chiefs

H

whom war and property have raised above the group, few of the materials requisite for literature can be said to exist. When these points of social progress have been attained, the development of literature parts into two remarkably different directions, which the literature of the Hebrews on the one hand, and the early poetry of Greece on the other, aptly illustrate. The literature of the Hebrews passed into the hands of a central priesthood; the early poetry of the Greeks is the song of bards possessing local independence. The social and hereditary spirit of the clan predominates in the former; the individual spirit of the chief lives and moves in the latter. There is, no doubt, a strong bond of connection between these early forms of literature in the individual character which decomposing clan life tends to create— a character in which sentiments of devotion to the chief supplant the old ties of communal kinship; and elsewhere we may return to this connection between communal and feudal life and literature. At present, however, we shall devote our main attention to the corporate character of clan literature.

CHAPTER II.

EARLY CHORAL SONG.

§ 28. FROM the subordinate position of the commonalty (dêmus) in the Homeric poems, a position not much superior to that of the serfs as compared with the kings and chiefs, it might not be supposed that song in Greece, as elsewhere, was in its beginnings neither the making of royal minstrels like Demodokus, nor the celebration of princely heroes like Achilles and Ulysses. But the width of sympathy between Greeks of many tribes and cities in the Homeric poems, no less than the common knowledge they imply of heroic and divine myths, and even special tales of epic character,* are enough to prove that behind the *Iliad* and *Odyssey* existed poetry of local sympathies and songs of local sentiment long before the genius of one master-bard, or of many, built up the Greek epics into the forms in which they have reached us. As has frequently been observed, the picture of social life in the Homeric poems is that of men who have left the barbarous isolation and exclusiveness of clan life far behind them; men who, if they have lost much of the clansmen's equality, are gaining wider sympathies and

* *E.g.* the ship *Argo* is called "interesting to all" (πασιμέλουσα), *Od.*, xii. 70, an epithet implying a familiar story. For further examples, see K. O. Müller, *Hist. of Gk. Lit.* (Donaldson's translation), vol. i. p. 54.

artistic refinement under the guidance of chiefs and kings. Social life as depicted in the Homeric poems bears striking resemblances to that of the medieval seigneurs, allowing for great differences wrought among the latter by ideas of a world-religion and a world-empire. If the medieval priest was the mediator between the serfs and God, the Homeric priests are honoured by the commonalty (dêmus) as gods.* If the medieval singers wander from seigneur to seigneur, or enjoy their permanent patronage, the Homeric bard enjoys like patronage or security in his wanderings.† But in all this we have personal power and personal poetry. We have left far behind us the communal life and song of the clan; and we must not suppose, because we have thus left these out of sight, that the banquets of the princes are the true homes of early song, and that the *aoidos* or the troubadour are the earliest of song-makers. The truth is that the sentiment of the lines—

> "Lordship of the many is no good thing,
>   One lord let there be, one king to whom Zeus,
> Son of crafty-counselled Kronos, giveth
>   Sceptre and *themistes* ‡ for his rule" §—

is almost equally removed from the spirit of the clan and that of the city republic; and the makers of such lines are the poets neither of the commune nor the commonwealth. Let us, then, try to discover the character of the songs which we believe to be older than those of either the cities or the kings.

Critics of Greek literature have long distinguished the lyric poetry of the Dorians, intended to be executed by choruses and accompanied by choral dances as well as instrumental music, from the Æolian lyric, meant for

---

* *Od.*, xiv. 205.   † *Ibid.*, xvii. 383 *sqq.*
‡ Inspired decisions. Cf. Maine, *Ancient Law*, ch. i.
§ *Iliad*, ii. 204–206.

recitation by a single person who accompanied himself with some stringed instrument, such as the lyre, and with suitable gestures. The former, public and often religious in its character, preferred subjects of general interest, while the thoughts and feelings of the individual were the appropriate themes of the latter. It is true that no hard-and-fast line can be drawn between these Doric and Æolian lyrics; we know, for example, that Lesbian poems were sometimes composed for choral recitation, such as the *humenaios* of Sappho imitated by Catullus. Still, the general difference between these choral and personal lyrics is clear; and no less clear is the difference of social conditions which such lyrics respectively reflect. Like the communal institutions of the Dorian states, their choral poetry keeps before our eyes those groups of kinsmen, with common property and feasts, which lie in the prehistoric background of Greek history. The contrast of personal and impersonal poetry is indeed found in literatures which have passed far beyond the clan age. Thus, the epic poetry of medieval France has been divided into the popular and the individual narrative, the former sung or chanted to a monotonous tune, the latter artistically recited.* But the contrast of the choral and personal lyric carries us back much farther than feudalism, and brings out some of the earliest characteristics of song and consequently of literature. Some pictures of communal festivals will enable us to realise how much older are these choral songs than any courtly makings of the troubadours.

We are among the Dacotahs of North America. We are present at the sacred feast of one of their clans, "The Giant's Clan," as it is called. High festival is now being

* Hueffer's *Troubadours*, p. 11.

held in honour of Ha-o-kah, "The Giant." We enter the wigwam within which the ceremony is taking place. Round a fire, over which are boiling kettles full of meat, there are Indians dancing and singing. They wear no clothing but a conical cap of birch, so streaked with paint as to represent lightning, and some strips of birch round their loins. As they sing and dance they thrust their bare hands into the boiling pots, pull out pieces of meat and eat them scalding hot. For does not the god, Ha-o-kah, in whose honour they dance and sing, shield them from all pains?* Here, and in many like cases, it is clear that the words of the choral song are altogether of secondary importance—the magic symbolism of dance and gesture is nearly everything. We watch an infant drama, a savage mystery-play, in which dance and music and gesticulation are as yet confusedly blended. Perhaps in the next tribe we meet we may find another of these infant dramas going on. Here the supply of buffalo-meat has fallen short. The prairie is deserted by the herds. Somehow a new supply must be secured; and the magic dance which the braves are now performing is designed to lure back the herds to the old hunting-grounds. The Indians, dressed in buffalo skins, are dancing the Buffalo-Dance; and, as each tired warrior drops out, acting as he does so the death of the buffalo, another brave takes his place; and so the dance goes on, perhaps for weeks, until the object of the magic rite is secured and a herd discovered on the prairies. Here, again, the symbolism is everything; as yet we are far from having reached the stage at which the words of the choral song are separated from the music and the dancing, much less written down.

* Dr. Schoolcraft's *History, Condition, and Prospects of the Indian Tribes in the United States*, pt. iii. p. 487.

Let us pass from the hunting-grounds of the Red Indian to the *Mir*, or village community, of Russia. It is a fine spring day, and the girls* of the *Mir* have determined to hold their "circle" or *Khorovod*, their village festival of blended dance and song. In holiday dress they are now streaming towards the open space where the *Khorovods* are held—the *choros*, or "dancing ground," of the commune, as a Greek of the Homeric age would have called it. "When the appointed spot is reached," says Mr. Ralston, in his *Songs of the Russian People*, "they form a circle, take hands and begin moving this way and that, or round and round. If the village is a large one, two *Khorovods* are formed, one at each end of the street; and the two bands move towards each other, singing a song which changes, when they blend together, into the Byzantium-remembering chorus, 'To Tsargorod will I go, will I go; With my lance the wall will I pierce, will I pierce.'" Little dramas, too, we might see these *Khorovods* performing, if we had time. But we must pass on to another picture of communal song-dances; only let us note in passing how the singing and dancing are of greater import than the words or the authorship of the song. The village, like the tribal, community has far less to do with written poetry and personal authorship than with the dramatic dance.

But now we are in Sparta, spectators of the *Gymnopædia*, or festival of "naked youths." Large choruses of men and boys are taking part in the festival; and, as in medieval towns the burghers assisted at the mystery-plays, the general body of the Spartan citizens joins in the song and dance, and has not yet become mere onlookers at a professional performance.† The boys in

* Cf. the *Parthenia*, or "Maidens' Choruses," of the Greeks.
† Cf. Müller's *Dorians*, bk. iv. ch. 6.

their dances are imitating the movements of wrestling and the *panoration*; and soon they will begin the wild gestures of the Bacchanalian worship. It is a choral carnival in which an outburst of communal feelings has for the moment drowned the little voices of self-interest. These choral dances and songs contrast remarkably with the personal and artistic lyrics of an Alcæus or Sappho; and perhaps this is one reason why the intensely personal art of later Greece cared so little to preserve them. However this may be, our communal song-makers of the Greek city, as of the Russian village community and the Indian tribe, are a group in which individual song-making and the celebration of individual feelings are still in the background.

§ 29. Dr. Hans Flach, in his *History of the Greek Lyric*,* has written with all a German scholar's usual erudition on the folk-songs of the Greeks, their development of flute-playing, the Oriental influences on their lyric, and other topics deeply interesting to the special student of Greek literature. We cannot, however, regard Dr. Flach's book as an adequate study of the choral or the personal lyric from the standpoint of social life in early Greece. We believe that K. O. Müller's method of studying the beginnings of Greek song in close company with social life has been too much neglected by recent subjective criticism. Nay, farther, we believe the study of early Greek poetry as dependent on social development in Greece to be only a step towards a larger comparative study, which shall forget classic exclusiveness to learn from Norse or Arab as well as from Thrace and Pieria. The truth is that when we soberly survey the materials out of which Dr. Flach and others would build up a history of lyric poetry in Greece, we find them

* Tübingen, 1883.

singularly inadequate. We find ourselves hazarding theories of Greek lyrical progress without real knowledge of early Greek music and dances—two-thirds at least of the old choral poetry. Moreover, when it is remembered to how small an extent the evolutions of dancing, especially when of a dramatic character, can be expressed in words, and how improbable it is that the Greeks, in days when even writing was unknown, should have possessed any system of musical notation, it is hard to believe that accurate information on these subjects can have reached us through such channels as the works of a Plutarch or an Athenæus. We shall be contented, therefore, to listen here to some echoes from old Greek choral song, observing how faint they are compared with the many voices of the personal lyric, and to support our belief that the choral was the oldest form of the Greek lyric, by comparison with other fragments of ancient song and by the communal organisation of early social life.

Who does not remember the picture of the vintage-festival on the Shield of Achilles? The beautiful vineyard, wrought in gold, is heavy with grapes, the black bunches hanging overhead, and ladders wrought in silver are standing all through the vineyard. Round about are the trench and hedge, and a single path leads to and fro for the grape-bearers at the vintage. Maidens and youths are gleefully bearing the luscious fruit in wattled baskets; in their midst is a youth, playing delightfully on a clear-sounded harp and "singing with sweet voice the lovely Linus Hymn," while others, with measured beat of foot and with reels (σκαίροντες), are following with the cry of *ai Line*. The scholiast on this passage has preserved for us a specimen of this Linus Hymn which critics have variously emended. Adopting the emendation of Bergk,* we may thus express the meaning and metre of the song in English :—

> " O Linus, honoured of all gods,
> For unto thee have they given,
> First among men, to sing ditties
> Sung with the clear-sounding voices;
> Phœbus in jealousy slays thee,
> Muses in sorrow lament thee."

It has been observed that a pair of these lines with slight alteration can form an hexameter; and, accordingly, the origin of the hexameter, with its strong cæsura, has been found by some writers in the junction of two such lines. However this may be, both the form and spirit of the Linus Hymn are thoroughly primitive; and whether we believe, with Müller, that it laments the tender beauty of the spring burned by the summer heat of Phœbus, or see in it the dirge of some human hero like the yearly lament of the Hebrew maidens over Jephthah's daughter, we cannot but feel in it the communal air of the choral lyric in which, as in the *Ialemus* song, or the Tegean *Scephrus*, or the Phrygian *Lityerses*, or the Syrian laments for Adonis, " not the misfortunes of a single individual but a universal and perpetually recurring cause of grief was expressed." †

Again, this communal spirit meets us in traditionary choral songs of ancient Greece, consisting, like the Indian choral songs described by Dr. Schoolcraft, of a few words in which the principal thoughts were rather touched than worked out. Thus, as Plutarch tells us in his *Life of Lycurgus* (ch. xxi.), there were in certain Spartan festivals responsive choruses of old men, young men, and boys. The chorus of old men began and sang—

" Valiant young men once were we; "

---

* *Fragg. Lyr.*, 1297.
† K. O. Müller, *Hist. Gk. Lit.* (Donaldson's tr.), vol. i. p. 25.

the chorus of young men reply—

"We are still so; if it please you, look upon us and rejoice;"

and the chorus of boys rejoin—

"Yes, but we are yet to be stronger far than all of you." *

So the women of Elis, Plutarch tells us,† used to sing the ancient hymn—

> "Hero Dionysus, come
> To a holy ocean-shrine,
> With the Graces to a shrine,
> Rushing on with hoof of ox;
> Holy ox!
> Holy ox!"

But here we must be careful to draw a distinction between merely popular songs and the old communal poetry. Just as Simonides and Pindar represent that lyric which in the growing unity of Greek tribes and cities found an opportunity to rise above local idioms and local sympathies, just as in the Homeric epics we find a feeling of Greek unity in spite of local kings and tribal distinctions, so in the old choral songs we should expect strongly local feelings and a much weaker sense of common Greek kinship than is to be found either in the personal lyric or in the epic poetry. We cannot, therefore, hope for light on the character of the early Greek choral lyric from such fragments of popular songs as the address of the wandering minstrel to the potters (*Kerameis*), or the *Eiresiône* of children going from house to house, levying what they can, in autumn during Apollo's feast, preserved in the pseudo-Herodotean life of Homer. These are no more indications of clan poetry than the English street-ballad, or the Indian songs which

---
* Ἀμὲς ποκ' ἦμες ἄλκιμοι νεανίαι.
Ἀμὲς δέ γ' ἐιμές· αἰ δὲ λῇς, αὐγάσδεο.
Ἀμὲς δέ γ' ἐσσόμεσθα πολλῷ κάρρονες.

† *Quæs. Græc.*, 36.

civil servants in India have heard from the lips of wandering singers, and sometimes taken down in writing as specimens of primitive song-making. Such fragments, perhaps all extant fragments of Greek song, belong to days when the local life of the Greek tribes and cities had lost much of its early separateness; indeed, the development of Greek language as well as sympathy must have been largely fatal to the preservation of old local song. Even the specimens of early song just given cannot, therefore, be accepted as really carrying us back to the local *origines* of Greek poetry. Still we may gain from them some conception of such poetry. In the same way, there are ancient descriptions of these choral lyrics which may be accepted as truthful, and graphic pictures of early, though not the earliest, Greek song-makers. Two of these we shall now present as belonging respectively to the autonomous city, and to the sacred festival of leaguered clans meeting at the seat of their league-god's worship. Students of the Amphiktionic League need not be reminded of the prominent part played by such tribal federations in early Greek life, a part which at one time promised to be as prominent in the social life of Greece as the *Berîth* or Sacred League ("The Covenant") in that of the Hebrews, or the Sacred Months in the early history of the Arab tribes.

§ 30. One of these descriptions brings before us the *humenaios*, or choral song of marriage, in the life of the old Greek city. The marriage festival is going on, and under the flashing lights of torches the bride is being conducted through the streets. "Then a loud *humenaios* arises; dancing youths were whirling round ($ἐδίνεον$), while among them flutes and harps resounded; and the women, standing at their thresholds, one and all admired and wondered." * A like picture of the *humenaios* song

* *Iliad*, xviii. 490–496.

and dance is given in the Shield of Hercules, attributed to Hesiod. "Some bear the bride to the husband on the well-formed chariot; while a loud *humenaios* arises. Burning torches borne by boys cast from afar their lights; forward move the damsels beaming with beauty. Both are followed by joyful choruses. One chorus, of youths, sing to the clear sound of the pipe with tender mouths, and make the echoes to resound; the other, of damsels, dance to the notes of the harp."* In this choral song of marriage in the early Greek city, the publicity of the festival and the communal sympathy of the citizens remind us that as yet the city *dêmus* is not far removed from the settled clan or village commune, and that the feelings of common kinship and *connubium* have not yet been altogether lost by the clans and tribes of the city. The *epitaphios* of Adonis is scarcely so far removed from the *thrênos*, or dirge of the clan, as is the marriage song-dance of the commune from the artificial marriage-songs of modern poetry, such as, for example, the *Prothalamion* of Spenser.

In the hymn to the Delian Apollo we have a glimpse of a Greek tribal league-festival, which reminds us of the Hebrew tribes going up to the place which Yahveh chose, or the Arab at the Fair of 'Okâdh. No doubt this hymn as it has reached us, written in hexameter verse of thoroughly epic tone, is no true specimen of the old and sacred "chorlyrik" of Greece. But it may be accepted as an echo of those sacred chants which are known to have prevailed in the early worship of Greek communities, and a truly ancient picture of choral singers. The allusion, at the end of the lines here translated, to dramatic imitations of different languages or dialects shows that the religious hymn of the Greeks, like some

* Hesiod, *Scut.*, 274-280. Cf. K. O. Müller, *Hist. Gk. Lit.*, vol. i. p. 29.

of the Vedic hymns, or like the medieval service of the Mass, contained the germs of a drama.

> "But in Delos, Phœbus, thou art happiest;
> There Ionians long-robed gather for thee
> With their children and their lovely ladies;
> So with boxing and with dance and singing
> When the games are set they gladly praise thee.
> He who met Ionians thus assembled
> Well might think them gods, to old age strangers,
> Looking on the men and well-girt women,
> Ships of speed, and many forms of wealth,
> And, beside, that wonder ne'er to perish,
> Girls of Delos, handmaids of Apollo,
> Handmaids of Apollo, the Far-Darter,
> Who, when first they hymn Apollo's praises,
> Next remember Artemis and Lêto,
> Artemis rejoicing in the arrow;
> Then a hymn of ancient men and women
> Sing they, and delight the tribes assembled;
> For they know to mimic tongues of all men
> And the rattle of the castanets,
> So that each would think his own speech uttered;
> Such the skilful song they fit together." *

§ 31. The war-song, the marriage-hymn, the dirge, chants to the ancestral gods, songs of the spring and autumn festivals—these and such as these would nearly exhaust the varieties of the clan's choral poetry. Many of these we perhaps hear at a distance in the more refined music of individual song-makers—the war-song, for example, in the *embatéria* or anapæstic marches of Tyrtæus, the dirge in such fragments of the *thrénos* as those of Pindar. In any work aiming at an exhaustive treatment of early choral song, the close communion of music and early poetry would require a special study of vocal and instrumental music in their beginnings. Such treatment in the present work, however, is clearly impossible; and the student can only be referred to the works of specialists, such as that of Dr. Flach previously mentioned. The beginnings of music and metres appear

* Hymn to Delian Apollo, ll. 146-164.

to have been almost as closely connected in Hebrew, Indian, and Chinese literatures as in the early lyrics of Greece, and the development of music and religious ritual seem, at least up to a certain point, to have been closely united in all these literatures. Without entering on any technical discussions of Greek or Hebrew, much less Indian or Chinese, music, we can discover abundant evidences showing that clans or guilds of bard-musicians, for the most part sacred, were the chief makers of early poetry; and without some such organisation it is difficult to imagine how the old song-dances could have been developed.

Among the early composers of Greek hymns stand out prominently the Eumolpids of Eleusis in Attica. To this clan the chief sacerdotal functions in connection with the worship of Demeter are known to have descended as an hereditary privilege. The very name of the clan— "Beautiful Singers" *—points to their original office of sacred choristers; and, if the social development of the Greeks had resembled that of the Indian Aryans or the Hebrews, these hereditary musician-priests might have grown into Bráhmanic or Levitic castes. In the Lycomids of Attica we have another clan of sacred singers; and at Athens the playing of the *Kithara* at processions belonged to another clan, the Eunids. But these clans of musicians were by no means confined to Attica. Like the Hebrew clans of musician-poets, to which we shall presently refer, the flute-players of Sparta continued their art and their rights in families. To a family of musicians Terpander, the Lesbian, the reputed founder of Greek music, belonged. Simonides of Keos, who exercised the functions of chorus-

* Cf. Swinburne's *Erechtheus*, ll. 52, 53—
   "Eumolpus; nothing sweet in ears of thine
   The music of his making," etc.

teacher at the town of Karthæa, belonged to another such family. Other members of this family were Bacchylides and Simonides the younger, the writer on genealogies. Finally, Pindar himself seems to have belonged to a family in which music was a kind of hereditary art.* Early epic poetry, also, was apparently arranged and perfected for recital, perhaps in some cases actually composed, by similar clans or castes of bards. Such, for example, were the Homêridæ of Chios, who, even if they were not a clan ($\gamma \acute{\epsilon} \nu o \varsigma$) of really common descent, were organised on the clan model like the Hebrew "sons of the prophets." Even the dramatic poets, as we shall see hereafter, did not altogether lose the hereditary culture of the poetic art.

Turning to the united cultivation of music and song among the Hebrews, we find the clearest evidences of its communal nature. Before the organisation of Yahveh's central worship we find local bodies, apparently organised on the clan model, engaged in this culture under the guidance of a leader, much as each town in early Greece appears to have had its *chorodidaskalos*, or teacher of the chorus. In one place† we have a picture of "a band of *Nâbîs*"—a word by no means satisfactorily translated by the Greek word "prophet"—"descending from the high place, and before them lyre, and timbrel, and flute, and harp, while they dance and sing together as *Nâbîs*" (*mithnabbëim*). There is another bard-clan at Naioth— "an assembly of *Nâbîs* singing and dancing, with Samuel standing as leader over them."‡ Such also are the "sons of" (an ordinary Hebrew and Arab expression for clan) "the *Nâbîs*" at Jericho, and the "sons of the *Nâbîs*"

* K. O. Müller, *Hist. Gk. Lit.*, pp. 34, 199, 263, 275, 289, vol. i.; and cf. authorities cited.
† 1 Sam. x. 5. ‡ 1 Sam. xix. 20.

who sit before Elisha at Gilgal.* After the establishment of central government, however, among the Hebrew tribes, the service of the temple was directly modelled on the hereditary system of the clan or caste; and "sons" of Asaph, Heman, Jeduthun, became not only the performers but apparently the arrangers and composers of sacred hymns.

How far communal hymn-making extended in the early literatures of India and China it is now possible only to conjecture. Each of the *Súktas* (metrical prayers or hymns) of the Rig-Veda is attributed to a *Rishi*, or holy and inspired author. But the hymns of the Rik— evidently the oldest of the Vedas from the manner in which its hymns enter into the composition of the three later Vedas, Yajur, Sáma, Atharva—contain no directions for their use, the occasions on which they were to be employed, or the ceremonies at which they were to be recited; these were pointed out by later writers, in the *Sútras*, or precepts relating to the ritual; and even the deities in whose honour the hymns were composed are for the most part known to us through independent authorities, especially an *Anukramaniká*, or index accompanying each Veda. We cannot, therefore, attach much value to the reputed authorship of these ancient hymns. Yet it is worth observing that the *Súktas* of the Rik are arranged on two methods, one of which would seem to bring before us directly the communal authorship of the hymns. The arrangement by *Khandas* (portions), *Ashtakas* (eighths), *Adhyákas* (lectures), does not seem to depend on any fixed principle; but in the arrangement by *Mandalas*, "circles," six out of the ten "circles" comprise hymns by the same person or by *members of the same family*. Thus the hymns of the third *Mandala* are ascribed to Viswámitra

* 2 Kings ii. 5; iv. 38.

I

and his sons or kinsmen; of the fifth, to Atri and his sons; of the seventh, to Vasishtha and his descendants. The ceremonies (offerings of clarified butter and the fermented juice of the Soma plant) of which these ancient hymns formed the verbal portion, seem to have taken place in the dwelling of the worshipper in a chamber set apart for the purpose; and the absence of allusion to temples or other public places of worship in the hymns apparently implies their family or clan character. We may, therefore, agree with Professor Wilson that the hymns of the Rik "were probably composed in many instances by the heads of families, or of schools following a similar form of worship, and adoring in preference particular deities."* And if it is probable that different Indian families "had their own heroes, perhaps their own deities, and kept up the memory of them by their own poetic traditions,"† if parts of the Veda are represented as actually belonging to such illustrious families, is it not still more probable that in China, the ancient seat of ancestor worship, the old hymns to the dead (some of which have come down to us in the Shih King) were regarded as the common property of the family or clan?

§ 32. In the Roman song of the Arval Brothers we have a specimen of the sacred guild-chant more closely allied to the solemn psalm of the Hebrew musician-castes, or the earnest appeals to Indra and other deities in the Vedic hymns, than to the artistic spirit of the Delian Hymn. In Rome, as among the Hebrews and the Indian Aryans, clan life long retained an intense vitality; and when it is remembered how the archaic family-system of the Romans, itself descended from the clan, formed the

* Preface to translation of *First Ashtaka*, or Book of Rig-Veda, p. xvii.
† Max Müller, *Hist. Anc. Sans. Lit.*, p. 55.

basis of Roman law, it need not surprise us that this song of a religious brotherhood is to be reckoned among the oldest of Rome's literary monuments. This primitive hymn was discovered at Rome in 1778, on a tablet containing the acts of the sacred college. Varro tells us that these Arval Brothers—"Brothers of the Fields"—were a rustic priesthood whose duty it was "to perform public rites that the fields (arva) may bear fruits." * At the *Ambarvalia*, or Lustration of the Fields, the Arval Brothers apparently performed for the Roman people as a community what each house-father did for his own farm. Cato † and Tibullus ‡ have described these Ambarvalian ceremonies, which seem to have been thoroughly in keeping with the agricultural spirit of certain Hebrew festivals. As in the *Carmen Sæculare* of Horace, in spite of Sapphic measure having displaced the old Saturnian, and sundry other signs of Greek influence, we may fancy an elegant improvement of the old communal hymns of Rome, so in the elegiac poem of Tibullus on the *Ambarvalia* we may find, if not an imitation of the Arvalian prayer, at least a description of the festival.

> "Whosoe'er is by, be silent:
> Fruits and fields we purify
> As the rite, from hoary ages
> Handed duly, doth ordain.
> Bacchus, come with tender vine-branch
> Hanging from thy horns, and Ceres
> Bind thy temples with the corn-ears.
> Rest the earth this holy dawning,
> Rest the ploughman from his toiling,
> Let his heavy work be ended
> While the ploughshare idle hangs.
> Loose the yoke-chains: now by full stalls
> Oxen with wreathed heads shall stand.
> For the god be all things sacred;
> Nor let any set her hand
> Woollen-weaving to the task-work. . . .

---

* Varro, *L. L.*, v. 85.   † *R. R.*, 141.   ‡ *El.* II. 1.

> Look you, how to shining altars
> Goes the consecrated lamb,
> While a white-robed crowd attendeth,
> All their locks with olive bound."

The next few lines seem to contain the prayer, which in its simplicity has at least all the appearance of being imitated, so far as elegiac metre and classical Latin would allow, from the old hymns.

> "Gods ancestral, we are purging
> Fields and country-folk together;
> Drive ye mischief from our confines;
> Let no crop with shoots deceptive
> Mock the harvest, nor the slow lamb
> Fly the bounding wolves in fear."

The prayer is over, and the worshippers, confident in their due performance of the rites, may now enjoy their domestic amusements.

> " Blithely, then, for full fields trustful,
> Let the countryman pile up
> On the blazing hearth the big logs,
> While a crowd of household slaves,
> Goodly marks of thriving farmers,
> Dance and build of twigs toy-houses." *

The rest of the poem is modern enough in thought and sentiment, at one moment smacking of the Horatian wine-jar, at another recalling Lucretian theories of social progress.

The legendary origin of the *Ambarvalia* was that Acca Laurentia, foster-mother of Romulus, had twelve sons, with whom once every year she sacrificed for the fields. On the death of one of these sons, Romulus took his place, it was said, and with his eleven foster-brothers constituted the first college of the *Fratres Arvales*. At the yearly festival, which took place in May, the members of the college wore, as a sign of their priestly rank, crowns

---

* Tibullus, *El.* II. i.; for last line translated, cf. Hor., *Sat.* II. iii. 247, aedificare casas.

of ears of corn bound with white ribbons. The following translation of the ancient hymn is taken from Wordsworth's *Fragments and Specimens of Early Latin.**

"Help us, O Lares, help us, Lares, help us!
    And thou, O Marmar, suffer not
    Fell plague and ruin's rot
    Our folk to devastate.
Be satiate, O fierce Mars, be satiate!
    Leap o'er the threshold! Halt! now beat the ground.
Be satiate, O fierce Mars, be satiate!
    Leap o'er the threshold! Halt! now beat the ground.
Be satiate, O fierce Mars, be satiate!
    Leap o'er the threshold! Halt! now beat the ground.
Call to your aid the heroes all, call in alternate strain;
    Call, call the heroes all.
Call to your aid the heroes all, call in alternate strain.
Help us, O Marmar, help us, Marmar, help us!
Bound high in solemn measure, bound and bound again;
    Bound high and bound again!"

§ 33. This primitive hymn clearly combined the sacred dance (suggestively marked by such a name as the *Carmen Saliare*) with the responsive chant; and the prominence of the former suggests how readily the processional or stationary hymn might grow into a little drama symbolising the supposed actions of the deity worshipped. Professor Réville, in his interesting study of Mexican and Peruvian religions as illustrating the general growth of religious ideas throughout the world,† rightly assigns a very prominent place to the sacred dance. Referring to the Peruvian hymns to the sun which were chanted at great festivals, every strophe ending with the cry "Hailly," or "Triumph," he remarks that "the grand form of religious demonstration among the Peruvians was the dance. They were very assiduous in this form of devotion; and indeed we know what a large place the earliest of the arts occupied in the primitive religions generally. The dance was the first and the

* *Vide* pp. 386 *sqq.*   † Hibbert Lectures for 1884.

chief means adopted by prehistoric humanity of entering into active union with the god adored. The first idea was to imitate the measured movements of the god, or, at any rate, what were supposed to be such. Afterwards, this fundamental motive was more or less forgotten; but the rite remained in force, like so many other religious forms which tradition and habit sustained even when the spirit was gone. In Peru this tradition was still full of life. The name of the principal Peruvian festivals, *Raymi*, signifies a 'dance.' The performances were so animated that the dancers seemed to the Europeans to be out of their senses. It is noteworthy that the Incas themselves took no part in these violent dances, but had an 'Incas' dance' of their own, which was grave and measured." * When it is remembered that the choral hymn is not merely, as M. Burnouf tells us,† "the first literary form that poetic thought assumed among the Aryan race," but even contains apparently the germs of lyric and dramatic poetry alike in the West and East, this accompaniment of choral song by symbolic dancing, which is found in many parts of the world, and has left its marks on dramas so widely removed in their social conditions as those of Athens and Japan, must be regarded as a very significant fact in the growth of literature.

As the Russian *Khorovods* performed by girls may enable us to realise the Greek *parthenia*, or the hymeneal chorus with its responses of youths and maidens,‡ so the symbolical song-dances of American Indian tribes, while supplying interesting parallels to such dances as the

* Hibb. Lect. 1884, p. 224. † *Essai sur le Véda*, p. 31.
‡ Cf. Catullus, lxii.—a poem in which the burden, "Hymen O Hymenæe, Hymen ades O Hymenæe," like the αἰάζω τὸν Ἄδωνιν of Bion, or the ἄρχετε Σικελικαί of Moschus, seem like distant echoes of ancient hymeneal or threnic choruses.

Pyrrhic of the Greeks, may enable us to catch the spirit of the sacred dance in spite of the trivial associations of modern dancing. In the American Indian war-dance, the tribal leader, with his war-club in his hands smeared with vermilion to symbolise blood, raises the war-song, accompanied by drum, and rattle, and the voices of a few choristers. The song, brief and full of repetition, is repeated slowly and with measured cadence, to which the most exact time is kept, the singer every few minutes stepping out of his circular path to shout the war-cry. Clearly the words he sings are far from occupying the most prominent place in the æsthetic appreciation of the Indian; for him the graceful dance, the graphic symbolisation of battle and victory by vehement gestures, the familiar music of drum and rattle and the voices of the choristers carry a significance scarcely imaginable by bookish minds. Still, a specimen of the words may be here quoted from Dr. Schoolcraft's work on the Indian tribes as an aid in realising the nature of these song-dances.

> "Hear my voice, ye warlike birds!
> I prepare a feast for you to batten on;
> I see you cross the enemy's lines;
> Like you I shall go.
> I wish the swiftness of your wings;
> I wish the vengeance of your claws;
> I muster my friends;
> I follow your flight.
> Ho! ye young men that are warriors,
> Look with wrath on the battle-field!" *

In the same work Dr. Schoolcraft gives us a picture of the famous *Arrow-Dance*, as described by an eye-witness, Surgeon Ten Broeck, who served in the United States army in New Mexico, 1851–2. Part of this description may be here quoted as a very vivid illustration of the

* *Hist. Ind. Tribes in U.S.*, pt. ii. p. 60.

symbolic dance. "After dancing and singing fifteen or twenty minutes, the sound of another *tombe* (Indian drum) is heard, and another brave, with a *malinchi* (girl specially attired) and his friends, shouting and whooping, enter on the north side (a similar party having previously assumed a position on the south side of the *plaza*), and, ranging themselves opposite to the first party, commence the same kind of performance. The *tombe* of the first party then ceases; and one of the men, going out, leads the brave in front of his friends, who are drawn up in two ranks. Here he is placed on one knee, his bow and arrow still in his hand, while the *malinchi* commences the *Fleeka* or *Arrow-Dance*. At first she dances along the line in front of him, and by her gestures shows that she is describing the 'war-path.' Slowly she pursues, but suddenly her step quickens—she has come in sight of the enemy. The brave follows her with his eye, and the motion of his head intimates that she is right. She dances faster and faster—suddenly she seizes an arrow from him, and now by frantic gestures it is shown that the fight has commenced in earnest. She points with the arrow—shows how it wings its course—how the scalp was taken and Laguna victorious. As she concludes the dance, and returns the arrow to the brave, firearms are discharged, and the whole party wend their way to the *Estufa*, to make room for another warrior and his friends; and thus the dance was maintained, warrior succeeding warrior, until dusk." If any one doubts the world-wide influence of such symbolical dancing on the development of early lyric and dramatic poetry, let him reflect upon the prominence of symbolic action in a sphere in which it was far less to have been expected—early law.[*]

Side by side with these American examples of symbolic

[*] Cf. Maine's *Ancient Law*, ch. x.

dancing may be placed some Chinese illustrations of like symbolism. Just as the Sanskrit term for "drama" (*nataka*) properly applies to "dancing," so the earliest kind of dramatic spectacle among the Chinese seems to have been pantomimic dances closely connected with religion. "The majority of these dances," says M. Bazin,* " were symbolic, and represented the business of tillage, the pleasures of harvest, the fatigues of war, or the comforts of peace. The dancers bore shields, battle-axes, and banners, according to the various religious ceremonies. . . . In his notes on the *Chou-King*, Gaubil speaks of a Chinese treatise on the dance; the author has there given the following description of an ancient pantomime. 'The dancers sallied out on the northern side. Scarcely had they taken a few steps when, suddenly changing the order in which they had come, they symbolised by attitudes, gestures, evolutions, a battle array. In the third direction the dancers kept advancing southwards; in the fourth, they formed a kind of line; in the fifth, they represented the two ministers, *Tcheou-kong* and *Tchao-kong*, who aided *Wou-wang* with their advice; in the sixth, they kept motionless like the mountains. This dance was a history of the conquest of China by *Wou-wang*, who, entering the empire, defeated King *Cheou*, penetrated farther and farther, fixed the limits of his states, and governed them by the wise counsels of his two ministers.'" These old Chinese pantomimes, like the rude farces of early Rome, became after a time, in spite of their religious origin, so obscene that they required to be checked by law. But the early union of dance and song in China seems to have left its marks on Chinese criticism. In the *Great Preface* to the collection of ancient Chinese odes known as the Shih

* *Théâtre Chinois*, pp. ix., x.

King, poetry, song, and dance are pictured as a kind of graduated scale of emotional expression. The passage, as translated by Dr. Legge, is as follows: "Poetry is the product of earnest thought. Thought cherished in the mind becomes earnest; exhibited in words it becomes poetry. The feelings move inwardly, and are embodied in words. When words are insufficient for them, recourse is had to sighs and exclamations. When sighs and exclamations are insufficient for them, recourse is had to the prolonged utterance of song. When these prolonged utterances of song are insufficient for them, unconsciously the hands begin to move and the feet to dance."

§ 34. Like the Indian and Chinese, the Greek symbolised the actions of battle in his dances. The dancers in the Pyrrhic dance even bore the same name as the practised and armed combatant (*prulis*);* and we learn from a passage in Plato's *Laws*† that this Pyrrhic dance imitated all the attitudes of defence—avoiding the thrust, retreating, springing up, crouching down—and the opposite movements of attack with arrows and lances. We have now scanty means of estimating the perfection to which artistic dancing was brought in the progress of the Greek choral lyric save the complicated strophes and antistrophes of Pindar and the dramatic chorus. But the union of symbolic dance with choral song at the beginnings of Greek literature may be easily illustrated.

In the choral dance which Vulcan represents on the shield of Achilles we have clear indications of dramatic action accompanying the choral song, as it sometimes does in the dance-songs of the Russian *Mirs*. "At one time the youths and maidens dance round nimbly with measured steps, as when a potter tries his wheel whether

---

* Cf. Müller, *Dorians*, bk. iv. ch. 6. † vii. p. 815.

it will run; at another they dance in rows opposite one another. . . . Among them sang and played upon his harp a bard divine, and two tumblers whirled among them as the song directed."

δοιὼ δὲ κυβιστητῆρε κατ' αὐτοὺς
Μολπῆς ἐξάρχοντος ἐδίνευον κατὰ μέσσους.*

So, in the hymn to the Delian Apollo, Delian maidens in the service of Apollo sing a hymn which pleases the assembled multitude, and consists partly in a dramatic imitation of different languages or dialects, and partly in the production of certain sounds by instruments apparently resembling the Spanish castanets.† Again, Ulysses, looking at the Phæacian youths who form the chorus of the song of Demodokus, admires not the sweetness of their voices but (as Gray might have expressed it) the glance of their many-twinkling feet. "So spake the godlike Alkinous, and a herald uprose to bear a hollow lyre from the royal house. Then judges of the folk, nine chosen men in all, who were wont to order all things well in the contests, stood up; they levelled the dancing-place (χορὸν) and made a fair wide ring. So, bearing a loud-sounding lyre for Demodokus, the herald drew near; and Demodokus gat him into the midst, and round him stood boys in their first bloom, skilled in the dance, and they struck the good floor with their feet; and Ulysses gazed at the twinkling feet (μαρμαρυγὰς θηεῖτο ποδῶν) and marvelled in spirit." ‡ Indeed, the very words *molpé* and *melpesthai*, applied as they were by the Greeks to singing, dancing, and even any graceful gesticulation (as in a game at ball §), significantly mark

* *Il.*, xviii. 590-606.
† ll. 161-164, translated above; cf. K. O. Müller, *Hist. Gk. Lit.*, pp. 32, 33.
‡ *Od.*, viii. 256-265.   § Cf. *Od.*, vi. 101.

the close union of song, instrumental music, dance and mimetic action in early Greece.

As the dancer speaking the epilogue at the end of Shakspere's *Henry IV., Part II.*, or the allegorical herald Rumour "painted full of tongues" at the beginning of the same play, or the Vice "with his dagger of lath" in *Twelfth Night*, or the Shaksperian clowns with their tag-ends of popular songs, carry us back to the rude beginnings of the Elizabethan drama, so in these choral dance-songs we may see survivals from the rude efforts of literary art in early Greece. How far these combinations of dance, and song, and symbolic gesture were infant dramas our scanty means of information do not now enable us to decide. But we are by no means left to picture their nature from choral songs of early Greeks alone. Among the Hebrews, for example, we find a similar connection between music, dance, violent gesticulation, and choral song. Early Hebrew, like early Greek, song, discloses itself in the form of the choral lyric. Indeed, the dance-song seems to have occupied a more prominent place in Hebrew than in Greek literature, just as the clan and tribe retained a stronger hold on Hebrew than on Greek life.

From the days of tribal and local worship to those in which the centralised religion of Yahveh had cast its shadow over old local associations and traditions, the dance-song is the choral hymn of Israel. Thus, in the early days of tribal federalism, at the feast of Yahveh held from year to year in Shiloh, the maidens of the town come out to "dance in the dances;"* and, long after the worship of Yahveh has been centralised and organised, his worshippers are exhorted in one of the choral lyrics collected in the books of psalms "to praise

* Judg. xxi. 21

the name of Yahveh in the dance."* So important was song in national tradition and worship, that not only do we find the Hebrew law-chronicle appealing to folk-songs as among the earliest sources of the history of the tribes,† but the teaching of song (possibly a leading duty of the early *Nâbîs*) is directly ordained by the priestly law-book.‡ Old polytheistic worship, against which Yahvism waged a long conflict, also possessed the choral song-dance as the essence of its ceremonial. Thus, we find the early Hebrews before the idol of the calf singing and dancing songs of such a rude description that it was possible for them to be mistaken for shouts of war.§ The violent character of the sacred dance among the Hebrews reminds us of the Peruvian *Raymi*; and a still more interesting parallel is observable in the degradation which such dancing seems to have undergone among the Hebrews as among the Peruvians. The *Nâbîs* combined dance and song; for example, Miriam "the prophetess," *Nebiah*, takes a timbrel in her hand while the women "go out after her with timbrels and with dances." ‖ "To play the *Nâbî*" apparently meant to sing, dance, and violently gesticulate, so violently indeed that the verb *nâbâ* is used of madness and excited raving. In a well-known passage of Hebrew story this violence of gesticulation is very prominently brought out. Saul has sent messengers to seize David at Naioth, a centre of *Nâbî* culture, and the king's messengers, thrice sent, have thrice been infected by the spirit of the place and joined in the sacred festival. "Then Shâûl himself went to the high place and came to the large well that is by the

* Ps. cxlix. † For example, the song of the well, Numb. xx. 17.
‡ Deut. xxxi. 19. § Exod. xxxii. 17-19.
‖ Exod. xv. 20. The word *yâtzâ*, "go out," is the same as that applied to the maidens of Shiloh "going out" of their town to dance in the dances (Judg. xxi.), and seems to betray the social conditions under which the author writes, viz. those of settled city life.

hill and asked, 'Where are Shemûêl and Dâvîd?' Men said, 'Yonder in Nâyôth at the high place.' So he went thither to the high place at Nâyôth; and even on him came the spirit of God, and, as he walked on, he acted the *Nâbî* till he reached the high place at Nâyôth. Then he stripped off his garments himself, and himself acted the *Nâbî*, and fell down naked before Shemûêl all that day and all that night. Wherefore they say, 'Is Shâûl also among the *Nâbîs*?'" (1 Sam. xix. 22 *sqq*.). But such violent dancing was not altogether decorous for a king. David "whirls about" (*mekarkêr*, "whirling in a circle," a word with which the Homeric expression ἐδίνευον, applied to the two "tumblers," should be compared) "with all his might before Yahveh," but in the eyes of Michal he has "uncovered himself as one of the vain fellows shamelessly uncovers himself;"* and, though the incident is made to reflect honour on the king's devotion to Yahveh, we may be sure that the orgiastic dance-song was softened down into stately processions in the civilised and centralised worship of Yahveh. Perhaps the latest survival of the violent gesticulation with which the *Nâbîs*' name and worship had been associated among the early "sons of Israel" is to be seen in the symbolical action of later *Nâbîs*, as when Ezekiel takes a tile and portrays upon it the beleaguered city of Jerusalem. But these men were rather lyrical preachers than leaders of communal song; and if the gesticulations of the *Nâbîs* ever contained the germs of a drama, the progress of social life among the Hebrews was clearly fatal to any such form of literary expression. The strength of clan life among the Hebrews (as that of family life among the early Romans) prevented the distinctness of personal character and the

* 1 Sam. vi. 14, 20.

EARLY CHORAL SONG. 127

degree of individual independence without which the drama has little or no place.

§ 35. Thus, looking on choral songs of war or peace as the primary sources from which literature has everywhere been developed, we may accept the vulgar canon that all literature begins in song; but it is song widely differing in nature and in impersonal authorship from any to which modern art is accustomed; it is a hymn strangely unlike the choral services of our civilised religions both in form and spirit. In this primitive song the words, the dance, the music (such as it is), and gesticulations contribute to make a unity nameless in the languages of peoples far removed from the beginnings of social life. These curious combinations of mimicry and music, dancing and words, vary in their purposes. Sometimes they are magic incantations, sometimes they are war-songs, sometimes they are songs of marriage, sometimes they are dirges of death. In some the gestures predominate, in others the rude music, in others the refrain of a few simple words. But the main points to be borne in mind are that these elements are confused together, and that the mere preservation of the words alone cannot enable us to imagine the true nature of primitive song. Hence the impossibility of applying our highly-developed modern ideas of prose or verse to such performances. For not only have dance and gesticulation among us ceased to convey any sacred meaning, not only have we long distinguished these from the mimetic action of the regular drama, but we have also separated words from any accompaniment of music or dance, poetry from recitation as well as from these accompaniments, and prose from metrical forms which, far from being joined to dance and melody, or sustaining the memory in an age when writing was unknown, simply appeal to the reader's sense of harmony through the medium of printed letters. Accustomed to artistic ideas based upon distinctions impossible in early social life, it is not strange that we neither possess the words, nor in many cases the imaginative powers, needful to carry us out of our own literary conditions into the primitive homes of literary development.

In the progress of this literary differentiation we may observe some striking changes, not of course capable of chronological data—for they have everywhere occurred insensibly in the course of social development—but none the less real because they lie outside the range of such measurements. The gradual severance of acting, dancing, and musical accompaniment from the words of the song marks a whole series of such changes partially illustrated by the rhapsodists of early Greek, and the Râwy or reciter of early Arab, literature. Another and greater change than any of these is introduced by the invention of writing, parting still farther the music and gesticulation (which once supplied excellent props to the memory) from the bare words, and turning the attention of the makers of literature to the study of metres as distinct from music and recitation. Finally, the rise of prose composition as a distinct species of literature, at first apparently constructed largely on the older metrical models (as, for example, in the rythmical prose of the Qur'ân), but afterwards passing by degrees into a plain reflection of public or private conversation, and finding its proper sphere in the speech or philosophic discussion, brings us far on the road to that severance of science from literature which characterises the most civilised communities. It is clear that the status of early song-makers must have undergone prodigious changes during this evolution of literary forms. It is clear that the communal culture of early literature, which among the Irish Celts, for example, seems to have left its traces in "Literary Fosterage,"* breaks up with the decomposition of clans into their component families, and the farther development of personal freedom from such family restraints as those of the Roman *patria potestas*. But, before we turn to this individualising process or to the evolution of literary forms, we shall illustrate another side of clan literature, viz. that on which the clansman's personality, so far as communal sentiments permit, is most distinctly visible.

* Sir Henry Maine (*Early History of Institutions*, pp. 242 *sqq.*) has cited evidences of Literary Fosterage in India resembling the Celtic. Signs of communal literary culture, however, are to be found in any literature with which the author of the present work is at all acquainted.

CHAPTER III.

PERSONAL CLAN POETRY.

§ 36. IF we mean by "personal" poetry such laments for the individual's growing age and regrets for his fleeting youth as appear to have been common in the songs of the Greek lyrical poets who represented an age of aristocratic individualism, if we mean the poetical expression of that individualising spirit which dwells with a kind of sad pleasure upon personal recollections of youth and the contrast of the ideal future of self with its real past, and which fondly dallies with reminiscences of times, and places, and persons, and things never again to be seen in the golden dream-light of vanished childhood—then we must admit that the poetry of the clan cannot be called "personal." The life-view of the clan, like that of the lyric Greek, is indeed confined to earth, but its strong feelings of unity with kindred leave no place for such personal regrets, and look forward to the prolonged existence of the group not as a mere substitute for individual immortality (for of that ambition the clan knows little), but as the only kind of life worthy of enthusiastic contemplation. Poets of clan life, or deeply imbued with the spirit of clan life, know not the Greek melancholy of individual decay nor the modern melancholy of individual hopes unsatisfied—the latter far more frequently the result of limitless personal ambitions than of any such spiritual cause as Mr. Browning seems inclined to assign it. Like Ezekiel picturing the ideal future of Israel under the figure of national clanship, the true clan poet socialises everything he touches. He knows nothing of personal introspection. His theme is not self, but the group of kinsmen to which he belongs; if he sing of any hero, the whole body of clansmen share the eulogy; in short, his poetical pictures are rather of men in groups than of individuals. We must not, therefore, expect "personal" poetry in the modern sense from the clan.

But neither must we suppose that the clan age knows no personal poetry of its own, or that such poetry is less real than ours because it is conceived from a totally different standpoint. Sentiments and emotions are not, indeed, conceived as the peculiar property of the individual; they are projected outwards like visible threads uniting the clansmen in a common objective existence. But they possess on this very account a peculiar vividness which the poetry of individual reflection fails to reach. There is an intensity in clan affections, in clan hatreds, which, compared with the passions of individualised life, stands out like the figures in relief on the Arc de Triomphe contrasted with the flat surface of a painting;

"Sibb acfre ne maeg
Wiht onwendan þám þe wel þenceð." *

It is only by remembering this *objectiveness* of early personality and the social conditions it denotes that we shall solve an apparent paradox in the development of civilisation and literature. The barbarians, says M. Guizot, introduced into the modern world the sentiment

* "Naught can alter ties of kinship
In the man who thinks aright."
(*Beowulf*, 2600-1.)

of personal independence and the devotion of man to man. The progress of society, says Sir Henry Maine, has been from communal restraint to personal freedom. Both of these apparently conflicting statements are true. The personal independence of which M. Guizot speaks is the communal equality of fellow-clansmen, an independence which each possesses not because he is a man but because he is a *clansman*, an independence which, far from implying any "offhangingness" from the group, simply results from the union of the individual with his group. On the other hand, the personal independence in which Sir Henry Maine sees the latest outcome of a slow and fitful evolution is one which (to apply an expression of Savigny) draws a circle round each individual as distinct from his group and the government of his group, an independence which sets him apart from every tie of kinship in an isolation which primitive socialism would have contemplated and treated as a terrible calamity—the isolation of the clanless and the lordless man.

§ 37. Over and above the choral song-dances of the clan, over and above communal hymns of all descriptions, we shall therefore be prepared to find some sort of personal poetry in clan life. Moreover, it need not surprise us if such poetry should give the clearest insight into clan sentiments, for it is evidently in the relation of the clansman to his group that such sentiments are most distinctly expressed. Self-sacrificing devotion to the cause of the clan, uncompromising vengeance for the blood of slaughtered kinsfolk, justice in the distribution of the common property, faithfulness in the discharge of funeral obsequies—these and such as these are the ideal characteristics of the clansman; and clearly they may be best illustrated where conditions of climate and soil have allowed the largest personal freedom compatible with a vigorous clan life. Such conditions may be found among the Arabs of the burning deserts. The Arab, on his horse or camel, shifting from spot to spot, cannot feel or express the impersonality of clan feelings with the intensity peculiar to settled village communities. In the early poetry of the Arab clans we shall accordingly find some of the best specimens of that personal expression of the clansman's feelings which we seek to illustrate.

Marzûki, in the preface of his Commentary on the *Mufaddalian Poems* (so called from their collector, Al Mufaddal, who made the anthology about the year 160 of the Hejîra), tells us that a great deal of early Arab poetry owed its origin to tribal wars. "I have been told," says the Arab authority,* "that Ali ben Mahdi, the Kisrawite, reported that in Attâïf there were both poetry and reciters, but not in abundance. For poetry increased only during the wars between the tribes, such as happened among the Ausites and Kasragites, and in the engagements and expeditions which were continually going on. Among the Kuraishites poetry was rare, for there were no inveterate animosities among them." The passage reminds us of our Border Ballads; but the presence of genuine clan sentiments, such as those of Blood-revenge, in the early Arab poems carries us far nearer the beginnings of literature than Chevy Chace. Some examples of this Arab poetry we shall now offer from the *Hamâseh,* or "*Valour,*" an anthology so called because the first chapter contains verses on valour and manly behaviour. Collected about the year 220 of the Hejîra by Abu Tammâm, this anthology contains many short pieces of verse and fragments selected from complete odes. The collection is distributed into ten chapters, the first of which takes up

* The words are translated from a Berlin manuscript by Professor Kosegarten, in the introduction to his edition of the Huzailian Poems.

nearly half the work. The Arabic text, accompanied by a commentary of Tabrizi, Latin translation and notes, was published by Freytag at Bonn in 1851.

Perhaps the best specimen of the poetry of Blood-revenge to be found in any literature is a poem of this *Hamáseh* assigned to Ta'abbata Sherrâ, but attributed on better grounds to his sister's son, and believed to refer to the vengeance taken by the nephew on his uncle's slayers. Mr. C. J. Lyall, who has attempted to translate the poem into a metre resembling the Arab in the *Journal of the Asiatic Society of Bengal* for 1877, would find its author in Khalaf el-Ahmar, a famous imitator of old Arab poetry. But when we remember that early Arab poems were regarded as partially the property of the poet's clan, we cannot treat the authorship of these poems as a profitable inquiry. So far as Mr. Lyall's effort to express the Arab metres in English is concerned, we can only regard it as a brilliant failure. Even if the English language permitted exactly the same metres as the Arabic—which was not to be expected and is not the case—the repetition of the same rime throughout an entire poem, a repetition which Mr. Lyall has not attempted except in a few very short poems translated in the same journal for 1881, would be fatal to such well-intended efforts. No moderniser of the *Chansons de Geste* could try to reproduce in modern French the medieval monorimes with any hope of success; and in English the attempt to transplant the Arab monorimes in any poem longer than a few lines must only result in a comic repetition of sounds so far as the attempt is even practicable. Since, therefore, the very structure of the English language prevents imitation of the most striking characteristic of early Arab poetry in point of form, why should we with Mr. Lyall seek to retain the Arab measures *wâfir, tawîl,* and the rest?

These measures are scanned by feet, as in the Greek and Latin systems, and from the length of the Arab lines are often much more opposed to the English than hexameter, elegiac, or alcæic. In fact, the attempt to exactly reproduce Arab forms of poetry in English is based on a mistaken view of poetical form as something which has no necessary connection with the structure of languages. We shall, therefore, offer the following poem in a metre not unfamiliar to English ears, yet not very widely removed from the Arabic measure if the reader bears in mind that two lines of the English will generally correspond to one in the Arabic. Goethe, in his *West-Oestlicher Divan*, translated the poem into German from the Latin of Schultens, and though the effort to reproduce the Arab metre would have been much easier in German than in English, he has made no attempt of the kind.

"Dead in rocky cleft below Sal'
Lies a man whose blood drips vengeance.
He has left the burden to me,
And I lightly lift and bear it—
Heritage of bloodshed for me,
Fearless son of his own sister—
One whose grip none loses lightly,
One whose downcast eyes are dripping
Poison like the hooded asp.
Ah! the fearful tale has reached us,
Saddest tale that ever sped!
One whose friend none dared belittle
Tyrant Fate has severed from us;
Sunshine he in wintry season;
When the dog-star burned, a shadow;
Lean he was, but not from lacking,
Open-handed, open-hearted;
Where he journeyed, where he halted,
Wariness and he were banded;
When he gave, a rushing rain-flood;
When he sprang, a mighty lion;
Black his hair among his kindred
Flowed, and trailed his robe of peace;*
But in war a thin-flanked wolf-whelp;

---

* In peace the Arabs allowed their *izâr*, or waistwrapper, to trail on the ground; in war it was girt tightly about their loins—a practice of the desert reminding us of the Roman "girding up his gown."

> So he savoured gall and honey,
>   One or other all men tasted;
> Fear he rode without companion
> Save his deep-notched blade of Yemen.
> Many warriors when the night fell
>   Journeyed on until the dawning,
> Halted keen of eye and sword-blade,
>   Sword-blades flashing like the lightning;
> They were tasting sips of slumber,
>   They were nodding—thou appearest
>   And they scatter at thy face!
> Vengeance we have wreaked upon them,
>   None escaped us but a few;
> And if Hudheyl broke his sword-blade
>   Many notches Hudheyl won!
> Oft on rugged rocks he made them
>   Kneel where hoofs are worn with running,
> Oft at dawn he fell upon them,
>   Slaughtered, plundered, and despoiled.
> Valiant, never tired by evil,
>   One whose sword drinks deep the first draught,
> Deep again the blood of foemen,
>   Hudheyl has been burned by me.
> Wine no longer is forbidden,
>   Hard the toil that made it lawful!
> Reach me, Sawâd son of 'Amru,
>   Reach the cup—my strength is wearied
>   With the winning of revenge.
> Drink to Hudheyl we have given
>   From the dregs of Death's own goblet—
>   Shame, dishonour, and disgrace.
> Over Hudheyl laugh hyenas,
>   Grin the wolves beside their corpses,
> And the vultures, treading on them,
>   Flap their wings, too gorged to fly."

The poem will summon up recollections of the *Coronach* over Duncan in the *Lady of the Lake,* and the deed of vengeance in *Cadyow Castle*. But the pale cheek, glaring eyeballs, and bloody hands of Bothwellhaugh, as he springs from his horse and dashes his carbine to the ground, are melodramatic compared with the consuming passion of revenge in the terrible Arab fresh from that cleft of rocks below Sal' and the sight of his slaughtered kinsman, and glancing from his downcast eyes the poisoned glance of the hooded asp. We have here no "spectre gliding by," as in the Scotch tale, to watch the winning of revenge. The heart and hand of the Arab are remembered, his blood is to be avenged, but his spirit haunts not the rocks any more than that of his dead camel. The heritage of blood is a material burden which must be taken up and borne; it is no ghost-voice crying from the grave. All this is in keeping with the clan spirit which turns away from the shadow-world of kinsmen, where punishment or reward are yet unknown, to the sphere of the dead man's achievements and the very real work of revenge. For the murdered Arab is only the central figure of a group; around and behind him move his avenging kin, and even the virtues he possesses are rather those of a kinsman than of an individual in our modern conceptions of character.

In Burckhardt's *Notes on the Bedouins and Wahabys* * occurs a passage which, as fully describing this communal nature of Arab Blood-revenge, deserves to be here quoted; it will show how widely the personal vengeance of a Bothwellhaugh is socially separated from the feelings of clan duty. "It is a received law among the Arabs that whoever sheds the blood of a man owes blood on that account to the family of the slain person; the law is sanctioned by the Qur'ân, which says, 'Whoever shall be unjustly slain, we have given to his heir the power of demanding satisfaction.' The Arabs, however, do not strictly observe the command of their holy volume; they claim the blood not only from the actual homicide but from all his relations, and it is these claims which constitute the right of *Thâr*, or Blood-revenge. . . . This rests within the *Khomse*, or fifth generation, those only having a right to avenge whose fourth lineal ascendant is at the same time the fourth lineal ascendant of the person slain; and, on the other hand, only those male kindred

* Vol. i, p. 149.

of the homicide are liable to pay with their own blood for the blood shed whose fourth lineal ascendant is at the same time the fourth lineal ascendant of the homicide.* . . . The right of *Thâr* is never lost; it descends on both sides to the latest generations. It depends upon the next relation of the slain person to accept the price of blood. If he will not agree to the offered price of blood, the homicide and all his relations who are comprised within the *Khomse* take refuge with some tribe where the arm of vengeance cannot reach them. . . . A sacred custom allows the fugitives three days and four hours, during which no pursuit after them is made. These exiles are styled *djelâwy*, and some of them are found in almost every camp. The *djelâwys* remain in exile till their friends have effected a reconciliation, and prevailed on the nearest relations of the slain to accept the price of blood. Families of *djelâwys* are known to have been fugitives from one tribe to another (according as these became friendly or hostile to their original tribe) for more than fifty years."

§ 38. It is not difficult to collect examples of Blood-revenge inspiring the early poetry of the Arabs. Thus another poem of the *Hamâseh* begins—

> "Surely shall I wash the blood-stain
> With my sword away,
> Ay, whatever fate of Allâh
> Come across my way!" †

In another poem of the same anthology an ideal warrior is described as

> "A man who girdeth night on;
> Seldom cometh sleep for him; his greatest care
> Is vengeance and to break the ranks right on."‡

---

* Cf. Exod. xx. 5, "Visiting the iniquity of the fathers upon the children, *upon the third and upon the fourth generation* of them that hate me" ('al shillêshîm ve-'al ribbê'îm). † *Ham.*, p. 355.

‡ *Ibid.*, p. 405. "To gird on night" is an Arab phrase for "daring the dangers of the night."

Again, another poem on Blood-revenge in the same collection ends with the words—

"Vengeance have I taken fully
 For my father and forefather,
Nor in aught betrayed the household
 Which my shoulders must sustain." *

This prominence of communal sentiment should prevent us from picturing the chiefs of an Arab clan as corresponding to the knights of medieval Europe. The Arab's sense of honour has been compared with the feelings of medieval chivalry; Antar has been called the Bayard of Pagan Arabia; and the Arabs of the days of Ignorance (that is, before the Prophet's birth) have been described as the forerunners of our Western chivalry. In all this there is but a grain of truth. No doubt the Arabs in Spain and during the Crusades often supplied models of chivalrous deportment to European knights. But, in the first place, the old clan feelings of the Arabs underwent great changes during the Mohammedan conquests, and under the military organisation such conquests required. Feelings of honour resembling those of the German *gefolge* towards their military chief were developed and tended more and more to take the place of clan ties. Moreover, without some such loosening of these ties, without some such expansion of Arab sentiments as these conquering hosts brought about, it is hard to see how the common creed of Islâm could have subdued the tribal antipathies with which it had a long and troublesome contest. But these poems of Blood-revenge display feelings of duty and honour altogether older than the chivalry of Christian knight or Moslem soldier, just in this, that clan kinship—not military service, or nationality, or universal religion—is still the bond of social union. In fact, it was military combination for purposes

* *Ham.*, pp. 487-497.

of conquest which almost everywhere broke down the old communal organisations, created distinctions of rank and property before which the clansmen often have sunk into serfs, and ultimately displaced sentiments of kinship by mere ties of local contiguity and self-interest.

The communal character of Arab honour is therefore to be carefully distinguished from any bonds of military service; and the poetry of Blood-revenge illustrates the distinction more accurately perhaps than any other. To another and final example of such poetry we accordingly turn—the Mo'allaqah of Zuheyr. This poem has been excellently translated by Mr. C. J. Lyall,* and wherever the exact words are offered we shall avail ourselves of Mr. Lyall's translation in the following sketch of its contents:—The pasture-lands which the tribesmen leave at the end of spring are deserted, and over the camping ground of Umm Aufa's tents—those "black lines that speak no word in the stony plains"—roam "the large-eyed kine, and the deer pass to and fro." Umm Aufa was the poet's wife, whom one day in an angry mood he had divorced; since then he had repented and prayed her to return, but she would not. Here where her tents had stood he stands and gazes—twenty years have passed since last he saw the spot—hard was it to find again "the black stones in order ranged in the place where the pot was set, and the trench,† like a cistern's root, with its sides unbroken still."

Then the poet turns to the praises of the makers of peace for the clans of 'Abs and Dubyân, and swears, "by the Holy House which worshippers circle round," the Ka'beh, that the work of peacemaking is good. "Busily wrought they for peace when the kin had been rent in

---

* *Journal of the Asiatic Society of Bengal*, 1878.
† Dug round the tent to receive the rain.

twain, and its friendship sunk in blood. Ye healed 'Abs' and Dubyân's breach when the twain were well-nigh spent, and between them the deadly perfume of Menshim * was working hate. Ye said, 'If we set our hands to Peace, base it broad and firm by the giving of gifts and fair words of friendship, all will be well.' . . . The wounds of the kindred were healed with hundreds of camels good; he paid them forth, troop by troop, who had no part in the crime. Kin paid them forth to kin as a debt due from friend to friend, and they spilt not between them as much as a cupper's cupful of blood."

Then the tribes are exhorted to keep faithfully their pact of peace. "Ho! carry my message true to the tribesmen together leagued and Dubyân—Have ye sworn all that ye took upon you to swear? War is not aught but what ye know well and have tasted oft; not of her are the tales ye tell a doubtful or idle thing. . . . She will grind you as grist of the mill that falls on the skin beneath; year by year shall her womb conceive, and the fruit thereof shall be twins." After this reference to the deadly nature of tribal feud the poet tells the deed of Hoseyn, son of Damdam, how he slew his foe while the kins were making peace. "Yea, verily good is the kin and unmeet the deed of wrong Hoseyn, son of Damdam, wrought against them, a murder foul! He hid deep within his heart his bloody intent, nor told to any his purpose till the moment to do was come. . . . So he slew; no alarm he raised where the tents stood peacefully, though there in their midst the Vulture-mother † had entered in to dwell with a lion fierce, a bulwark for

---

* Said to refer to an Arab custom of plunging hands into a bowl of perfume when swearing to fight to the death. Hence, "to bray the perfume of Menshim" (said to have been a seller of perfume in Mekkeh) became a proverbial expression for deadly strife.
† Death.

men in fight, a lion with angry mane upbristled, sharp tooth and claw, fearless; when one wrongs him, he sets him to Vengeance straight, unfaltering; when no wrong lights on him, 'tis he that wrongs."

So the wars break out afresh and more blood is spilled, and the Gheydh clan, though themselves without blame, pay from their herds. "They pastured their camels athirst, until, when the time was ripe, they drove them to pools all cloven with weapons and plashed with blood. . . . But *their* lances—by thy life—were guilty of none that fell; Nehik's son died not by them; nor had they in Naufal's death part or share, nor by their hands did Wahab lie slain, nor by them fell el-Mukhazzem's son. Yet for each of these that died did they pay the price of blood—good camels unblemished that climb in a row by the upland road to where dwells a kin of great heart, whose word is enough to shield whom they shelter when peril comes in a night of fierce strife and storm; yea, noble are they! The seeker of Vengeance gains not from them the blood of his foe." The poem terminates with reflections on life and conduct, in the manner of the Hebrew *máshál*, or proverbial maxim; the poet has seen the Dooms "trample men, as a blind beast;" and the fellowship of the clan is the only safeguard.

"Who gathers not friends by help in many a case of need
　　is torn by the blind beast's teeth or trodden beneath its foot. . . .
And he who is lord of wealth, and niggardly with his hand
　　alone is left by his kin; naught have they for him but blame. . . .
Who seeks far away from his kin for housing takes foe for friend."

Blood-revenge in various forms of early song is easily discovered by any wanderer in the uplands of early literature. Even long after he has descended to homes of poetry in which a note of clan sentiment is rarely heard, he may be startled by the old sound among the streets of cities like an echo from the life of the wild woods, the desert, the haunts of the barbarous communes. Such are the words which suddenly voice the spirit of Blood-revenge in the speech of Ajax *—

"Ay, for a murdered brother or son have we taken the *wehrgeld;*
So in his commune stayeth the murderer, much having paid down;
So the avenger's passion is soothed by the gift of the *wehrgeld.*"

And among the Christian associations of *Beowulf* the same feelings of old clanship break out in a curious mixture of the spiritual and material;

"Spake the son of Ecgtheow,
'Clearly was our dread encounter,
Higelac, a time of strife,
On the plain where Grendel harried
Sige-Scyldings sick of life.
All their griefs have I avengèd
So that Grendel's kindred may
Ne'er on earth, however long-lived,
Boast about that twilight-fray.'" †

§ 39. Closely allied in spirit to these poems of Blood-revenge are the death-songs of clansmen; here, again, there is scope for the expression of such personal feelings as do not conflict with clan duties. Among the many examples of such poems we shall select two, which, as coming from the most distant parts of the world, and belonging to widely different conditions of climate and race, may be aptly compared—the death-song of the Arab 'Abd Yaghûth,‡ and that of the famous Ragnar Lodbrok thrown by Ella into a dungeon full of vipers.

The song of Lodbrok partly sketches the hero's past victories, and partly describes the sentiments with which he meets his death; it is only with the latter part that we are at present concerned. The chant of death is put dramatically enough into the dying hero's mouth, and would no doubt have been wonderfully effective as delivered by the Scald. Some of the concluding stanzas

* *Iliad*, ix. 632 *sqq.*   † *Beowulf*, 2005 *sqq.*   ‡ *Aghâni*, xv. 75.

may be here quoted as illustrating the spirit of the poem.

> "Ay, we have struck with the sword!
> Each of us follows his fate;
> None can escape the Nornes.*
> But never had I believed
> That Ella should take my life
> When, to sate the falcons of blood,
> We launched our ships on the waves,
> And far in the Scottish gulfs
> Gave to the wolves their prey.
>
> "Ay, we have struck with the sword!
> Ever I joy as I think
> How tables are ready for feasting
> In the hall of Balder's father; †
> Soon shall we drink of the beer
> From the branching, bending horns.
> In Fiölner's ‡ splendid palace
> No hero groans for death;
> Nor ever with cries of anguish
> Shall I reach the hall of Vidrer.‡
>
> "Ay, we have struck with the sword!
> The latest moment comes;
> The raging serpents tear me;
> In my heart the viper coils.
> Soon shall the dart of Vidrer ‡
> In Ella's heart be buried.
> My sons shall rage for their father's death,
> Warriors brave they shall never rest."

Ah! all Asloga's § sons would fight to the death if they only knew their father's tortures. Has he not fought battles, fifty and one, "by the messenger-arrow announced"? "But the Ases come to call me—my death is not for weeping. Yea, would I die! The Dises, Odin's messengers, invite me to the Heroes' Hall. Gladly I go to drink on a throne by the Ases' side;

> 'The hours of my life are finished—
> I die with a smile on my lips!'"

The sensual pleasures of Lodbrok's rude paradise are

---

* The Parcæ of the North.   † Balder was the second son of Odin.
‡ Names of Odin.   § Wife of Ragnar.

perhaps the most striking thought in these lines. Like the future blessedness of the Egyptian,* Lodbrok's paradise is merely the best of his earthly good things, which in the cold regions of the North are scant and coarse enough. But though there is no thought of future life as a moral sanction, though personality has not yet passed beyond a sense of animal pains and pleasures, Lodbrok's song sets the person of the chief in the front and thrusts the kinsmen well into the background; and we could readily imagine the Heroes' Hall developed into the privileged paradise of the chiefs, while the body of the kinsmen, like the common herd in Mexico, remained in some dreary realm of Mictlan. Whether it was that clanship lost much of its communal spirit during the expeditions of the sea-robbers, devotion to the chief taking the place of kinship ties, or that Northern conditions of soil and climate never permitted the same closeness of clan co-operation and sentiments as the sunny lands of the South, Lodbrok's song is pitched in a more personal key than most early Arab poems. Ideas of fate and revenge, common enough in Arab poetry, are thus personalised. Moreover, in the Arab death-song the idea of future

* "The blessed is represented as enjoying an existence similar to that which he had led upon earth. He has the use of all his limbs, he eats and drinks and satisfies every one of his physical wants exactly as in his former life. His bread is made of the corn of Pe, a famous town of Egypt, and the beer he drinks is made from the red corn of the Nile. The flesh of cattle and fowl is given to him, and refreshing waters are poured out to him under the boughs of sycamores which shade him from the heat. The cool breezes of the north wind breathe upon him.... Fields also are allotted to him in the lands of Aarru and Hotep, and he cultivates them" (Hibbert Lectures for 1879, p. 180). If, as M. le Page Renouf here adds, "it is characteristic of an industrious and agricultural population that part of the bliss of a future state should consist in such operations as ploughing and hoeing, sowing and reaping, rowing on the canals and collecting the harvests," the Hebrew *Sheól*, or gathering-place of the clans, and the Scandinavian Warriors' Hall, or paradise of the chiefs, are no less interesting reflections of social conditions in ideas of a future life.

happiness is conspicuously absent. 'Abd Yaghûth knows nothing of a heroes' paradise; his face is turned not to the shadow-world of the clan which he is about to enter, but to the comrades who drank with him in Nejrân "who shall never see him more;" even now he would gladly purchase life from the Blood-avengers with all his wealth; but, alas, it is no use, he must "hear no more the voice of the herdsmen who shout for their camels in the distant grazing-grounds."

'Abd Yaghûth has been taken captive, and 'Ismeh son of Ubehr of Teym has carried him to his home, where the captive is about to be slain in revenge for the death of en-No'mân son of Jessâs, the leader of Temîm. Then said he, "O ye sons of Teym, let me die as befits one noble." "And how wouldst thou die?" asked 'Ismeh. "Give me wine to drink and let me sing my death-song." "So be it," said 'Ismeh, and plied him with wine and cut one of his veins. Then, as his life ebbed, and 'Ismeh's two sons standing by began to upbraid him, this was the death-song of 'Abd Yaghûth : " Upbraid me not, ye twain! Shame is it enough for me to be as I am: no gain in upbraiding to you or me. Know ye not that in reproach there is little that profits men? It was not my wont to blame my brother when I was free. O rider, if thou lightest on those men who drank with me in Nejrân aforetime, say, 'Ye shall never see him more!'—Abû Kerib and those twin el-Eyhem, the twain of them, and Qeys of el-Yemen who dwells in the uplands of Hadramaut. May God requite with shame my people for el-Kulâb—those of them of pure race, and the others born of slaves! Had it been my will there had borne me far away from their horse a swift mare, behind whom the black steeds flag in a slackening throng: but it was my will to shield the men of your fathers' house, and the

spears all missed the man who stood as his fellows' shield.
The matron of 'Abd-Shems laughed as she saw me led
in bonds, as though she had seen before no captive of
el-Yemen; but one knows—Muleykeh my wife—that
time was when I stood forth a lion in fight, whether men
bore against me or I led on. I said to them when they
bound my tongue with a leathern thong—' O kinsmen of
Teym, I pray you, leave me my tongue yet free! O kinsmen of Teym, ye hold me fast: treat me gently then; the
brother ye lost was not the equal in place of me. And,
if ye must slay me, let me die at least as a lord; and if
ye will let me go, take in ransom all my wealth.' | Is
it truth, ye servants of God—I shall hear no more the
voice | of herdsmen who shout for their camels in the
distant grazing-grounds? | Yea, many a beast did I
slay and many a camel urge | to her swiftest, and journey
steadfast where no man dared to go; | and ofttimes I slew
for my fellows my camel at the feast | and ofttimes I rent
my robe in twain for two singing girls, | and ofttimes
withstood a host like locusts that swept on me | with
my hand alone when all the lances on me were turned. |
Now am I as though I never had mounted a noble steed, |
or called to my horsemen—' Charge! give our footmen
breathing space!' | or bought the full skin of wine for
much gold, or shouted loud | to my comrades stout—
' Heap high the blaze of our beacon fire!'" *

§ 40. But, beside the songs which have come down to
us reeking of bloodshed, we have early Arab poems in
which the personal character of the clansman is less
violently expressed. Thus in the Mo'allaqah of Lebid
the poet draws a picture of the clansman's generosity
which reminds us of Antar, but is again to be distin-

---

* In order to convey some idea of the Arab metre (*tawil*, second form)
Mr. Lyall's version is here retained, his lines being also marked in the
latter part of the poem.

guished from medieval chivalry by its communal rather than personal spirit; it is, in fact, the generosity of a group rather than that of an individual, of a brotherhood of kinsmen alike noble and not of an isolated knight. The lines occur after a graphic description of the camel (to which we may elsewhere refer), and have been rendered as follows by Mr. Lyall in the *Journal of the Asiatic Society of Bengal* for 1877. "There sought refuge by my tent-ropes, every wretched one clad in scanty rags and wasted like the camel by his master's grave. And they fill brimful with meat, when the winds are blowing shrill, great bowls of broth in which their fatherless ones come to drink. Verily we of 'Âmir, when the tribes are met together, there wants not of us a chief to lead in the doing of a noble deed, or a divider to portion out to the tribe its due, or a prince to give less or more as he deems right and good in his headship; or a generous man who helps men with his bounty freehanded, a gainer of all good gifts and one who takes them by force. For he comes of a stock to whom their fathers laid down the way—and every people has its own way and its leader therein."

It is interesting to contrast this picture of the open-handed Bedouin with another Semitic poem, in which, however, the desert is in the background and city life in the front. Ibn Khaldoun tells us that "writing in towns reaches a degree of beauty greater or less in proportion to the progress men have made in civilisation; so we see that the nomads for the most part can neither read nor write." This difference between the culture of the towns—purchased by division of labour and new distinctions of property and rank—and the rude freedom of the desert was deeply experienced by the Hebrews; their ideal life was clearly that of the pastoral tribe, the Hebrew state of nature so vividly symbolised by the preference of Abel the shepherd over Cain the tiller of the soil, and indirectly expressed in the curse of labour; but agricultural villages with their periodic allotments of land, and towns or larger villages with their elders (*zeqênîm*), are the foremost figures in the practical life of Israel. So, when we turn to the Book of Job, the most Arab of Hebrew poems, we find that we have passed from the associations of the desert to those of the city, and that feelings of communal generosity have been largely lost in the transition to that settled life in which the higgling of the market (to use Adam Smith's phrase) must soon come to be based on individual self-interest. "When I leave the gate of the citadel (*qereth*) in the open space I set my seat; greybeards rose and stood; princes stayed their words and placed their hands upon their mouths; the voices of the nobles ceased and their tongues clave to the roofs of their mouths." Here in the settled community, with its social grades dependent largely on the possession of wealth, its trading spirit and competitions in miniature, the bettering of the outcasts is not an act of Bedouin generosity, but the rise of upstarts whose early poverty may be cast in their teeth as a disgrace. " Now they of fewer days laugh against me, whose fathers I disdained to set with the dogs of my flock.—Ay, what use to me was the strength of their hands? Age lay dead upon them. Lean for want and hunger they were gnawing in the desert, yesternight in waste and ruin; they were cutters of orachs by the bushes, with the roots of juniper for food. They are driven from among us (shouts are raised against them as against the thief) to settle in the horrid beds of torrents, caverns in the earth, and crags. They bray like hungry asses in the bushes, under nettles are they clanned*

---

* *Yesuppâchu*; this use of *sâphach* should be compared with *shâphach*, from which *mishpâchah*, the familiar Hebrew expression for "clan," is derived.

together. Sons of folly, sons without a name too, they are too afflicted to live. But now am I become their song of satire, ay, to them have I become a byword." *

Thus in the city old ties of kinship and the generous feelings of the desert were to be spoiled by that huckstering spirit of the market to which the Bedouin has ever shown the contempt of Cyrus. Action from self-interest, the very gospel of townsmen, was of all things most distasteful to clan character, for the true clansman is always ready to sacrifice self for communal interests, even where he believes the conduct of his kinsmen to be ill advised. An excellent example of such self-sacrifice is to be found in a poem of the *Hamâseh* attributed to Dureyd, son of es-Simmeh.† The poet has warned both Ârid and the men who went Ârid's way; he has said, "Think, even now two thousand are on your track;" yet his warning goes unheeded. "But when they would hearken not, I followed their road, though I knew well they were fools and that I walked not in Wisdom's way—For am I not one of Ghaziyyeh? And if they err, I err with my house; and if Ghaziyyeh go right, so I. I read them my rede one day beneath where the sandhills fail; the morrow at noon they saw my counsel as I had seen." For a shout arises, a voice, "The horsemen have slain a warrior!" "Is it Abdallah?" cries the poet, and springs to the warrior's side. "The spears had riddled his body through, as a weaver on outstretched web plies deftly the sharp-toothed comb;" and his champion, whose counsel was yesterday set aside, now stands "as a camel with fear in her heart, and thinks is her youngling slain."

This readiness to share foreseen disaster with the

* Job xxx. 1-10.
† *Ham.*, pp. 377-380. For Mr. Lyall's translation in full, see *Jour. As. Soc. of Bengal*, 1881.

clan, even where personal forethought might have averted it, is an expression of communal sympathy curiously contrasting with the personal lyric for which our modern literatures have made such wide room. The Arab knows the folly of his clansmen, but he will die by their collective folly rather than live by his individual wisdom; and so the poem goes on, "I fought as a man who gives his life for his brother's life, who knows that his time is short, that Death's doom above him hangs. But, know ye if Abdallah be gone and his place a void; no weakling unsure of hand, no holder-back was he!"

But it would be a mistake to suppose that early Arab poetry contains no indications of personal quarrels with the clan, that the clansman's self-sacrificing devotion was never weakened by any sense of injustice experienced at the hands of his kindred. Lest the reader should carry away any such mistaken impression, we shall here offer one more specimen from the *Hamáseh* which will illustrate the conflict of personal with communal action; and it is worth noticing how the subject of the dispute is the defence of personal property by the clansman's kindred.

Certain men of the Benû Sheybân had fallen upon the herds of Qureyt, son of Uneyf, of the Bel-'Ambar, and carried off thirty of his camels. So he asked for help of his kin the Bel-'Ambar, but they helped him not. Then he betook himself to the men of Mâzin; and a company of these went forth with him and drove away a hundred camels of the herds of Sheybân, and gave them to him and guarded him until he came to his tribe. Upon this incident the following poem, which is the first of the *Hamáseh*, was composed.

"Had I been a son of Mâzin,
　Never had my herds been ta'en
By the sons of Dhuhl of Sheybân,
　Sons of children of the dust.

> Straightway to my help had risen
> Kinsmen of a heavy hand,
> Smiters good when help is needed
> And the feeble bend to blows;
> Men, when evil bares before them
> Gaping jaws of hindmost teeth,
> Gay to rush upon and meet him,
> Joined in bands or e'en alone.
> When a brother in his trouble
> Tells the story of his wrong,
> They are not the men to question
> And to ask for proofs of truth.
> But my people, though their numbers
> Be not small, are good for naught
> 'Gainst whatever evil cometh
> Howsoever light it be;
> They are men who with forgiveness
> Meet the wrong their foes have done,
> Men who meet the deeds of evil
> Kind of heart and full of love!
> Just as though the Lord created
> Them among the sons of men,
> Them alone, to fear before Him
> And beside them no man else.
> Would I had instead for clansmen
> Kinsmen who, when forth they ride,
> Swiftly strike their blows and hardly,
> Or on horse or camel borne!"

§ 41. This peculiar objectiveness of personality in clan life will enable us to see in their true light certain characteristics of early poetry which have been constantly misinterpreted by the sentiments or philosophy of modern life. "Poetry," says Victor Hugo in his famous preface to *Cromwell*,* has three ages, each of which corresponds to an epoch of society—the ode, the epic, the drama. Primitive ages are lyrical, ancient times are epical, modern are dramatic. The ode sings of eternity, the epic celebrates history, the drama paints life. The character of the first is *naïveté*, of the second simplicity, of the third truth. The rhapsodists mark the transition from lyric to epic poets just as the romancers mark that from epic to dramatic. With the second

* p. 18.

epoch historians appear; chroniclers and critics with the third. The personages of the ode are colossal—Adam, Cain, Noah; those of the epics are giants—Achilles, Atreus, Orestes; those of the drama are men—Hamlet, Macbeth, Othello. The life of the ode is ideal, that of the epic grandiose, that of the drama real. In fine, this triple poetry springs from three grand sources—the Bible, Homer, Shakspere. Such are the diverse aspects of thought at different eras of man and society. Here are its three faces—youth, manhood, old age. Examine a single literature by itself or all literatures *en masse*, and you will always reach the same fact—the lyric poets before the epic, the epic before the dramatic." Nor is this all. The supposed law of literary progress extends beyond the domain of social and individual humanity, and the same triple aspect of progress may be observed in the magnificent phenomena of physical nature. "It might be consistent to add that everything in Nature and in life assumes these three phrases of progress—the lyric, the epic, the dramatic—since everything has its birth, its action, and its death. If it were not absurd to intermingle relations fancied by the imagination with strict deductions of reason, a poet might say that sunrise, for example, is a hymn, noonday a brilliant epic, sunset a sombre drama in which day and night, life and death, struggle for the mastery."

All this is something more than that abuse of words—"lyric," "epic," "dramatic"—below which there lurks so often an abuse of reasoning; it is something more than an imaginative will-o'-the-wisp mistaken for the steady light of science; it is nothing less than an inversion of the true order in which the personality of man has been developed. Just as Rousseau's ideal state of nature dissolves into a dream as soon as we recognise the fact that communal groups of kinsmen, not free individuals, are the starting-points of social progress, so the poetic fancies of Victor Hugo disappear into dreamland at the touch of historical facts which prove the "colossal" individualism of his "primitive" ages to be a myth. Hugo, in fact, seems to waver between two theories alike unhistorical. Partially he seems to retain the Platonic fancy that personal character is not essentially different in different stages of social evolution, that the range of social life within which the individual acts and thinks does not profoundly affect his character, and that consequently "lyric" means the same bundle of facts and ideas for the clan, the city, the nation, the world-empire. Partially, on the other hand, he seems inclined to adopt the old religious and poetic theory of human degradation from a race of gods and heroes, as if individual character (and physique, no doubt) at first "colossal" had gradually sunk into the more moderate dimensions of a giant—the Titans reduced to Nimrods, let us suppose—and finally narrowed down into the average stature and age of men as we find them. But the main source of Victor Hugo's brilliant errors is the same as that of Rousseau's fallacies—the assumption of individual freedom, objective and subjective, under social conditions which by their communal narrowness of thought and sympathy and action, their communal restraints on personal independence by innumerable chains of custom, prevented any but the weakest and most material sense of personality. Hugo's theory of "lyric," "epic," "dramatic" progression is, from one standpoint, not unlike Carlyle's Hero-worship; and neither Hugo nor Carlyle seems to have discovered the profound differences which separate the merely objective and animal personality of primitive groups from the subjective depths of highly developed individualism. As for Hugo's fancy that the critical terms "epic," "dramatic," "lyric," may be viewed apart from the conditions under which they arose as marks of literary distinctions universally discoverable, it would be easy to show that the meanings of these words changed in the social history of Greece itself, the country of their origin, and that, far from being marks of universal ideas common to every literature, their meanings have continually altered in the mouths of the European peoples and critics who have used them. But it rather concerns our present purpose to observe the unhistorical criticism which overlooks the profoundly significant facts that neither the individualism of the "lyric" author nor that of the human character he celebrates, in truth few of the personal feelings of the modern "lyric," are possible in the really primitive conditions of social life which Victor Hugo and many in his company are accustomed to label "lyrical." The "lyric" of modern life sees all things, expresses all things, in the thoughts and feelings of a personal being connected, indeed, with far wider circles of kinship than it entered into the heart of primitive man to conceive, but only connected by vague ties of infinite and incomprehensible destiny. The so-called "lyric" of early life sees all things, expresses all things in the thoughts and feelings of little groups narrowly exclusive in their ties of common obligation, but feeling the reality of such ties with a force which now can scarcely be conceived. How, then, it may be asked, have such misrepresentations of the spirit of early literature become so common in our European criticism?

We have previously alluded to certain causes of such misrepresentation. In our modern European life individual character has so long occupied the foreground, so strongly have individualised passion and sentiment become associated with literary art and criticism either distinctively our own or inherited from Athens and Rome, that only very recently and under the influence of a new uprising of corporate life have we cared to remember that personality in primitive is very different from personality in civilized communities. Moreover, we have been long content to regard the beginnings of literature as socially ascending little farther than the feudal castle, and for the most part dependent upon the rise of monarchical courts or of polished city commonwealths such as those of Greece and Italy. To penetrate beyond such forms of social life, to reach conceptions of personality quite different from those which the lord's castle, the city, or the court have produced, to even explain survivals from the earlier types of social and individual life in these later organisations, has been up to the present the tentative work of a few scholars who have scarcely affected popular views of literature at all. Moreover, it is exceedingly difficult even for scholars possessing a thoroughly historical turn of mind to grasp facts so subtle in their nature as the historical changes of human personality. One illustration will suffice to show the difficulty with which even profoundly historical minds have reached the conception of types of personality dependent on the changing forms of social organisation.

Montesquieu, in his *Essay on Taste*, left unfinished at his death, saw clearly enough the importance of the senses as sources of our ideas of the beautiful neglected by Platonic idealists. Deriding such idealism as converting internal perceptions into real and positive qualities, he observed how different our emotions and feelings would have been had we possessed one organ of sense more or less, or if, possessing the same number of senses, our sight or hearing had been greatly different in their powers. Other species of poetry and eloquence would have arisen; the plans of architects would have introduced fewer ornaments and more uniformity had our sight been more feeble and confused; and had our sense of hearing been constituted like that of many other animals, most of our musical instruments would have required a different construction or modulation. "Hence, the perfection of the arts consisting in their presenting to us their respective objects in such a manner as will render them as agreeable and striking as possible, a different constitution of *our nature* from the present would necessarily require a change in the present state of the arts adapted to the change which that new constitution would occasion in the means of enjoyment." Had Montesquieu paused to ask what he intended by "*our nature*," he might have found that the "nature" of which he spoke was a certain average humanity, a certain type of character which by no means results from the mere possession of the human senses. He would have found that this type is largely the outcome of peculiar social conditions; indeed, he himself admits—without making much use of the admission—that, beside the senses and intellect, "those impressions and prejudices which are the result of certain institutions, customs, and habits" have moulded our ideas of taste. Nay, more, he would have discovered that even the senses themselves, sight and hearing for example, possessed a far higher degree of average acuteness, though an inferior degree of æsthetic discrimination, among American Indian clansmen of the prairies than in the average Frenchman or Englishman of his day. Finally, if he had compared together the music of France and China, or the languages of these countries as indices to average discrimination of sounds, he would also have discovered that the type of humanity he had in view was only one among many diverse types, and that his statical view of human sensations and their effects on the arts would require to be supplemented by dynamical views of human development, and the effects of different social systems on music, sculpture, architecture, painting, literature.

If one of the very founders of historical science experienced such difficulty in rising above the associations of personality to which he had been himself accustomed, we need not be surprised that few have yet grasped the historical fact that types of personality have come into being and disappeared with different stages of social evolution. But neither should we allow the imperfect philosophy of a Montesquieu or the poetic fancies of a Victor Hugo to stand between us and the light.

§ 42. Had space permitted, we might here pause to trace the rise of those social conditions which permitted an epic poetry of personal prowess and kingly descent. We might show that such conditions are to be found in the decadence of communal life before the growth of personal property and personal rank. It is when the head men of the clan have assumed the privileges of hereditary chiefs, and come to stand alone in the golden sunset of a divine ancestry once common to the entire group, when the mass of clansmen have sunk into simple freemen or even serfs, and the chief's men stand apart from the common folk as their lord's *comitatus*, that both the choral and the personal poetry of the clan give way to the songs of the chief's hall. Perhaps one of the earliest shapes of heroic poetry was the genealogical poem, familiar to students of Celtic literature, blending the communal personality of the clan with the individual heroism of the chief, and drawing no clear distinction between his exploits and those of the kinsmen in general. Old songs of eponymous clan-ancestors would meet such beginnings of epic poetry half-way, and the glory of the clan's ideal parentage would be easily transferred to the personal ancestry of the chief. It has even been proposed to find the roots of epic poetry in hymns of ancestor-worship similar to those of the Shih King. It has been suggested that the oldest epic poems were little else than hymns extolling the deeds of the dead at the celebration of ancestral sacrifices; and wherever ancestral worship has possessed such influence as in China, we may be sure that there was little scope for an epic of any description save through sentiments of such worship. But without laying undue stress on the fact that the Chinese, so far as their literature is at present known to European scholars, possess nothing which can be said to resemble an epic poem, and even admitting that ancestral worship of great families may have contributed something to epic poetry, we must remember that heroic poetry derives its main inspiration from individualised life. Wherever physical and social conditions have allowed the clan or family to maintain their strength, we need not expect such poetry. Hence its absence in early Rome as in China; and if it be replied that India, with its caste-system and village communes, offers us specimens of the epic, we may reply that the *Rámáyana* and *Mahábhárata* are rather stories of the gods than celebrations of human heroism, and that their very tissue is the handiwork of a priestly caste.

But space we have not to enter the lists of epic criticism in which so many belted knights of the pen have fought and fallen. We prefer to leave our Homeric battle of the books in the hands of specialists, merely observing that up to the present the wordy war has savoured rather too much of the modern study and blotting-pad, and rather too little of early social life in Greece. If our laborious German scholars would only devote a little spare time to the comparison of the social conditions under which the poetry of heroism has flourished in different countries and ages, we might know more about the beginnings of the epic than we are likely to learn from any number of textual emendations and verbal skirmishings.

It would have been part of our treatment of the epic to have traced or attempted to trace the changes through which the makers of literature passed in the social transition from communal to personal life; for the rise of personal authorship is one of the main literary effects of the decadence of clan life. So long as dance and music and mimicry form as integral parts of the literary performance as the words said or sung, property in song is almost inconceivable; and, long after priestly castes had commenced to create a kind of religious literature of hymns and legal ordinances belonging to the sacerdotal oligarchy, the conception of personal property in literature seems to have remained practically unknown. To examples of communal authorship and apparent survivals from it we have previously referred; and, if space permitted, we might have treated the universal prevalence of verse in early literature as closely connected with this communal song-making, or might have watched the gradual rise of prose as accompanying the development of personal freedom, and aided by that invention before which assonance and rime and metre ceased to perform the practical function of supporting the memory, and became ornaments of art—writing. But neither the changes in the status of early song-makers * nor the progress of literary forms from verse to prose can here receive more than a passing notice. We prefer to devote the space at our command to a brief outline of the aspect which physical nature assumes under the eyes of clansmen.

* Such changes in status were due to a great variety of causes. Thus, the introduction of writing reduced the value which recitation, with or without musical accompaniment, had possessed in days when this invention was either unknown or little used. (Cf. Renan, on the *Kasida*, *Hist. des langues Sémitiques*, p. 359, edit. 1878.) Another influence powerfully affecting the status of early song-makers is the growth of central government. By a statute of the thirty-ninth year of Elizabeth, for example, "minstrels wandering abroad" are included among "rogues, vagabonds, and sturdy beggars"; so low had the early song-maker of England sunk in the Elizabethan centralisation of force and culture. (Cf. Percy, Essay on Ancient English Minstrels, prefixed to his *Reliques*, vol. i.)

CHAPTER IV.

THE CLAN AND NATURE.

§ 43. ALTHOUGH Alexander von Humboldt [*] and others after him have observed the influences of a great political union, such as that effected by the Roman empire or that of Great Britain and her colonies, on human views of the physical world, no one, so far as the present writer is aware, has undertaken to trace the different aspects which Nature assumes for man under the varying and expanding forms of social organisation he has experienced. The studies of Montesquieu, to whom we owe so much as one great founder of truly historical inquiry in Europe, tended to treat social life too exclusively as the resultant of physical forces—climate, the nature of the soil, extent and character of sea-board, and the like. But though the physical conformation of the country they inhabit powerfully affects the commercial and political, the philosophical and artistic life of men, we must not forget that the structure of their social system, however dependent upon physical causes, supplies the aspects of Nature with certain lines peculiarly its own. Humboldt

---

[*] Perhaps the best introduction for students beginning the interesting study of literature in its relations with Nature would be the section on *Poetic Descriptions of Nature* in Humboldt's *Cosmos*, and the works of M. Victor de Laprade *Le Sentiment de la Nature avant le Christianisme* and *Le Sentiment de la Nature chez les Modernes*.

with great felicity compares the poetic descriptions of
Nature left us by Indians and Persians, Hebrews and
Arabs, Greeks and Romans, and the literatures of modern
Europe. But his point of view, though not quite so
passive as that of Montesquieu, though not directly
intimating the creation of human ideas by physical
forces, is that of the physical, not of the human, world.
It is one thing to watch the effects of Indian or Italian
scenery as they disclose themselves in Sanskrit or Italian
poetry; it is another to observe the different aspects
under which the same physical environment presents
itself to social groups differently organised. The latter
is the study to which at present we propose to direct
attention—the sentiment of Nature as dependent on
social organisation, that of the clan in particular.

We must at the outset carefully distinguish the two
faces which early social conditions present—that of the
clan and that of the chief's hall, the communal poetry
of the Hebrew or the Arab, and the heroic songs of
Homeric *aoidoi* or of Saxon *Scôps*. Nature presents herself in different garb to the village community and the
household of the chief. To the former she is thé maker
of the harvest, the bounteous giver or the offended with-
holder of the corn and wine and oil; the whole community
lives in constant companionship with her, and (as the
Hebrew when he spoke of sunrise as the sun's "going
forth," like man to his labour, and sunset as the sun's
"coming in," like man to his rest) transfer to her the
associations of their agricultural life. To the household
and retainers of the chief she is less interesting than the
ancestor from whom the chief derives his divine lineage,
or the deeds of martial prowess in which he and his
immediate following take pride. The epic rhapsodist
may, indeed, clothe his heroes in the dress of Nature's

godship, but the personality of his chief shines through. Hence, wherever the clan community falls under the domination of chiefs (as, in the absence of a strong priestly centralism, it has at least for a time almost always fallen), the powers of Nature are thrust into the background by divinities, or demi-gods, or heroes whose connection with the physical world is obscured by aristocratic associations; wherever communal life has for any length of time held its own against the chiefs, the poetry of Nature, comparatively unhumanised, has been kept alive.

In Homeric Greece and Saxon England the development of social unity found its main channel in the individual enterprise of military chiefs; and the *Scôp* of the mead-hall or Demodokus in the palace of Alkinous are the song-makers whom such a turn of social circumstances brings to the front. In early Israel or Arabia before the Prophet the progress of social unity moves along another channel—that fusion of leaguered clans which in the Amphiktionic League looks out upon us like a survival from unsuccessful prehistoric efforts after Hellenic unity. In the poetry of Israel and Arabia, accordingly, Nature plays a more prominent part than in that of Homeric Greece or Saxon England. The point of view from which Nature is conceived is also different in these cases—she is the grand unity of the Hebrew and Arab, before which all social differences "are as dust that rises up and is lightly laid again;" she is the grand diversity of the Greek and Saxon, looking out from every place with a new face and a changed name, and a sympathy for none but her local friends. The same principle meets us in the poetry of India. Here Nature, too, predominates, not merely because the splendour of Indian scenery is passively reflected in the

Indian hymns, epics, dramas, but because human life in India has been such as to make the social predominate over the individual factors, the Indian village community having always been the most stable institution of Indian life. Indian, like Hebrew, literature is full of the social sentiment of Nature, but knows little of the individualised Nature of Theocritus or Wordsworth.

"Now sleeps the deep, now sleep the wandering winds,
But in my heart the anguish sleepeth not," *

sings the Greek idyllist; but the song of his own heart outsings through the stillness of Nature.

"Yon cloud with that long purple cleft
Brings fresh into my mind
A day like this which I have left
Full thirty years behind,"

sings the English poet of Nature; but the cloud bears no rainbow of social hope, it is a private sign of personal recollections.

§ 44. In order to reach the point of view from which the clan regards Nature we must remember the one grand characteristic of clan thought which has been previously explained at some length. This is the want of *personality* in any sense resembling the modern. Just as the responsibility of a child for the deeds of generations buried long before it was born does not appear irrational to men who have no clear notion of personal intention, of personal as distinct from communal life, so in dealing with the phenomena of Nature—wind and cloud, rain and thunder, sun, moon, stars—the names given by such primitive minds and expressing for the most part ideas of human action are not really *individual*

---

* Idyll ii. 38—

ἠνίδε σιγᾷ μὲν πόντος, σιγῶντι δ' ἀῆται·
ἁ δ' ἐμὰ οὐ σιγᾷ στέρνων ἔντοσθεν ἀνία κ.τ.λ.

names. The Hebrew and Teuton heard without surprise that the eponymous ancestor of the human race was "Man" (*âdâm, mannus*), because the difference between a general idea and an individual name was not yet conceived with any distinctness, because, in fact, the sense of personality was not sufficiently developed to admit of such distinctness. In the same way the phenomena of Nature are expressed in the terms of human existence, as it was then conceived, without either the desire or the ability to *personify* Nature in our modern sense. The early confusion of human and physical existence is, in fact, only an extension of that confusion of personal with social existence which so strikingly characterises the clan age. Both proceed from a condition of thought in which personal and collective, subjective and objective, abstract and concrete forms of being are confused; and the source of this confusion is to be largely discovered in the communal organisation of early social life.

Viewed in this light we may regard the work of myth-making as the peculiar function of the clan age; and the relations of the clan to myth are alike visible in the social and the physical aspects of myth-making. "Myth" (a word which had no fixed value among the Greeks, fables of invention, like the Choice of Hercules, and divine traditions of prehistoric origin being lumped together under the vague term *mûthos*) would seem to be now tacitly used by those who profess any accuracy of language to mean creations of imagination unconsciously working upon external nature; and philological scholars in England and Germany have sometimes displayed a tendency to narrow the term still farther, and make myths little more than a disease of language. But the makers of myth are really the narrow limits within which man's primitive action and thought are bound up; just

THE CLAN AND NATURE. 167

as the destroyers of myth are man's widening or deepening experiences of space or time, of social and individual life. The myth, which may consist in a rude effort to explain some element of physical nature or some form of animal life,* or some social custom or some rude sense of personality, does not become visible as myth until wider circles of comparison and contrast have superannuated the beliefs and corrected the experiences upon which it once reposed. The social aspect of clan myth-making may thus be easily conceived. Such myth-making constantly accompanies the fusion of clan groups, traditions of eponymous ancestry being interwoven as larger groups—clan-federations or nations—are developed. It is indeed mainly this social fusion that makes the beginning of every national history fade into masses of myth, blending their social and physical origins in darkness which science has hitherto done little to lighten.

The clan age, then, is the great maker of social as well as physical myths ; and, to return to the latter, it views physical Nature neither as a person in our modern sense of the word, nor as an impersonal entity; neither as invested with individuality as we conceive it, nor yet as divested of personality and conceived in the abstract. Ages later than those of the clan reach the individual view of Nature; and ages later still reach the abstract view of Nature.

But here our brief review of nature's aspects as modified by clan life must cease. The illustrations we had intended to offer must be reserved for another opportunity; and we shall willingly leave the corroboration or denial of our views to students who can spare the time and trouble to criticise them in the light of early poetry.

* Cf. the "Beast-epic," as studied by Jacob Grimm or Dr. Bleek ; or *Zoological Mythology*, by Professor Gubernatis.

There are many other aspects of clan literature to which we should have gladly given even passing attention. We might have discussed, for example, the treatment of animals in early poetry, such as that of the camel, in the Mo'allaqah of Lebid, taking refuge "in the hollow trunk of a tree with lofty branches standing apart on the skirts of the sandhills," while overhead is a starless night of rain; or that of the wild asses, in the same poem, raising as they gallop along "a train of dust with shadows flitting like the smoke of a blazing fire." But these and many other aspects of early poetry we must leave untouched. We have merely thrown out a few hints which have cost no little study, however small their value; and we shall be content if the path of our inquiries is honestly pursued, and not at all offended if real study discovers a good deal to be corrected even in this little glimpse of a vast subject.

BOOK III.
THE CITY COMMONWEALTH.

CHAPTER I.

THE CITY COMMONWEALTH GROUP.

§ 45. It has been said with truth that the "brief blossom-time" of the Periclean age has so far dazzled modern critics that they have come to identify the short-lived spirit of that age with the spirit of the Greek race in general. The error cannot, however, with fairness be laid at the door of the modern critic alone. The Athenian spirit in its full life and vigour could not brook the thought of a time when it was not, threw a kind of glamour over the past history of Hellas, and universalised its own ideas at the expense alike of contemporary states of Greek society less developed than its own, and of the early life of chief and clan. Thus, to select a literary example, the dramatic spectacles and forensic pleading of Athens underlie the general canons of Aristotle's poetic and rhetorical criticism, and supply the living particulars which his philosophy expands into ideal forms. Athens herself is, in fact, the type of a city commonwealth, her literature the ideal of ·such a city's literature. The custom of speaking of "Greek" literature or the Greek "nation"—the latter an abuse of language to be peculiarly condemned—obscures the real nature of that social and political development which has given us the masterpieces of Athenian thought and art. Inheriting the poetic treasures of the tyrannies and the Homeric kingships, songs of lyrists dependent on the tyrant's palace or the chieftain's hall, Athenian literature strikes its roots deep into the local life of prehistoric Hellas. The flowers and fruits of Athenian imagination and reason spring from a soil to which every part of Greece in its different degree of culture contributed somewhat; and under these external influences the mind of Athens may be observed progressing in the two directions so profoundly affecting literary growth — the evolution of individual character and the expansion of social life. Athens, gathering up into herself all the past and contemporary Greek life of lower evolution, develops within herself an individualism deeper than the Greeks had ever known before, and a width of social sympathy impossible in days of early Greek isolation. In the synoikism of the Attic demes described by Thucydides* we have Athens springing out of isolated village communities; in the days of Macedonian supremacy we have her old political hegemony exchanged for that intellectual centralism of Western civilisation which, from the time of Isokrates to the present, she has never lost. From the isolation and exclusiveness of clan life to world-empire of intellect—such is the brief epitome of Athenian progress; and it is this twofold relation to a narrowly isolated past and a world-wide future that makes Athens the type of the city commonwealth in social and individual development.

To illustrate this typical character we have only to contrast Athens with Rome and the Italian republics. Rome, like Athens, finds the roots of her social life deep down in the clan age. That age, in fact, left upon Roman character marks far more lasting than can be observed in

* Bk. ii. ch. 15 (vol. i. p. 203, Arnold's edition, 1868).

Athenian. From the time of the XII. Tables down to the utmost relaxation of the *Patria Potestas* the spirit of Roman life was more or less that of the clan narrowed for the most part into the dimensions of the *familia*. But it is just this conservatism that prevents Rome from competing with Athens as the proper type of the city commonwealth in literary development. The reconciliation of the clanned with the unclanned Romans is reached too late to allow a Roman literature, common property of plebeian and patrician, to spring up. The struggles of Plebs and Patres—essentially one of the clanless against the clansmen for equal rights of marriage, landed property, and political capacity—prevent the rise of Roman unity until the city commonwealth has become the metropolis of a municipal empire of force which must borrow its intellectual refinement from abroad. Not so with Athens. Here the commonwealth is neither parted asunder into *gentiles* and those who can boast no *gens* (plebs gentem non habet), nor widened, while thus internally divided, into the metropolis of a municipal empire. Nor like Florence, split into factions almost as permanently hostile as those of Rome, is Athens oppressed by membership of any world-empire; the freedom of her thought knows not the restrictions of a world-religion, and that of her art is unoppressed by models whose imitation cannot but disappoint and whose existence often damps the ardour of young genius. The burning of the Alexandrian Library by the Khalif Omar, it has been said, may not have inflicted so severe a loss on civilisation as some have supposed, " inasmuch as the inheritance of so vast a collection of writings from antiquity would, by engrossing all the leisure and attention of the moderns, have diminished their zeal and their opportunities for original productions." It would be interesting to estimate how far the genius of the Italian republics was diverted from literature to painting and sculpture by the presence of literary models which it must have seemed alike hopeless to surpass by creation and to equal by imitation.

§ 46. Athens, then, is the type of the city commonwealth as an organism internally united, free to pursue its own development, unshackled by inheritances from the past, uncurbed by relations with any larger social union, political or religious. But it may be questioned whether the city commonwealth is a phase of social life found with sufficient frequency to admit of its being taken as a stage of social evolution. It may be said that Athens, Rome, Florence, not only represent, as we have admitted, very different types of the city commonwealth, but that these are isolated cases possessing no widely found characteristics which would justify us in setting them apart as specimens of a defined social organism.

When we look at the East in general and the civilisation of India in particular, we must candidly admit that there are large districts of the world's surface in which city life has exerted no influence compared with the municipal systems of Greece and Rome and the nations which have risen among their ruins. If Rome passed at a single stride from a city commonwealth to a world-empire without waiting to grow into a nation, the social evolution of the East seems to have passed from the village community to world-empire without experiencing the stage of isolated city commonwealths. But the vast influence of municipal life and thought on Western progress abundantly demonstrates the claim of the city commonwealth to be regarded as a leading stage in social development. Objectors, accordingly, will probably shift their ground to the difficulty of defining the nature of the city commonwealth. But a little examination will show that this difficulty is exaggerated, and that the objection founded upon it is one on which all attempts at definition in social science would suffer shipwreck. No doubt, if we were simply to put forward "the city" as a social classification, we should expose ourselves to the very serious objection that so vague a term confuses clan-cities like the Hebrew, in which the inhabitants are regarded as "sons" and "daughters" of the place—a curious combination of kinship and local contiguity as social ties—with municipal life, like that of Athens and Rome, in which kinship of communal nature is gradually forgotten, and with royally or imperially chartered towns, like those of England, France, Spain, Germany, in which kinship ties are altogether lost and the connection between local and central government alone regarded. The term "city commonwealth" has been used to prevent any such ambiguity. It is intended to call attention to the fact that the "city" which occupies so conspicuous a place in social history is neither a village commune nor a chartered town, but a self-dependent unit, rising indeed out of clans and villages, and expanding, it may be, into an empire, but clearly distinguishable alike from communal and imperial systems. But the objection is really based on a mistaken view of social science which would destroy all its definitions. According to this view, our social classes must possess a clear-cut regularity of outline such as the insensible gradation of forms of social life renders impossible. We have previously referred to this irrational requirement, and can only repeat that the fallacy proceeds from the assumption that a class can ever possess the defined unity of individual being.

So far as the social classification under discussion is concerned, it may be added that the range of the city commonwealth, like that of the clan itself, has been concealed by the fact that rarely have physical and social conditions so combined as to allow the development of language and literature bearing distinct marks of a community so limited in extent. None the less clear is it that in passing from the localism of tribes and clans to the centralism of national life the city commonwealth is an intermediate stage which cannot be ignored, because some social groups have made it but a temporary halting-place, while others, from a variety of causes, have accepted it as their social ideal.

CHAPTER II.

CLAN SURVIVALS IN THE CITY COMMONWEALTH.

§ 47. WITH what kind of literary stock did the Athenians start upon their career of literary production? Without some such stock-taking we cannot know much about their real losses and gains, for losses as well as gains the spirit of this ideal city commonwealth certainly experienced.

To such stock-taking the true literary artist—and he is the deepest sympathiser with Athenian feelings—is no doubt altogether opposed; and to mark the difference between scientific and artistic handling of Athenian history we have purposely used an expression which suggests an inartistic but truthful treatment. "Art," says Goethe, "is called art simply because it is not nature;" and wherever the artistic view of social and personal character prevails we may be prepared for a good deal of feigned history, a good many ideas claiming universal sway on account of their approaching the artist's standard of the beautiful. Theognis made the Muses and the Graces chant as the burden of their song—

"'That shall never be our care
Which is neither good nor fair;'"

and it has been well said that the lines express the essence of that Greek feeling for the beautiful which in Athens reaches its culminating point. But such a feeling, whether expressed in words or music, in colours or in marble, in the sensuous ideas of a poet or in the naked generalities of a philosopher, contains a latent hostility to the spirit of historical truth. He who loves the beautiful with heart and soul is not likely to watch its development from rude beginnings with pleasure, or even to admit that its nature is so perishable as to have had a beginning at all. To pry into its secret growth were almost as painful to the true artist as to look upon its decay and death.

It is a noble sentiment, worthy of greater and better beings than men, thus to reserve enthusiastic worship for that which looks immortal. But it is also a sentiment full of sad delusions, ever adorning with wreaths of eternal spring that which at a touch crumbles into dust, building everlasting ice-palaces which a few rays of even human reason melt away. In truth, the artist lives and must live, if he will act at all, a life of limitation fancied to be limitless. If he should know and feel his limits, if he should eat of the fatal tree of science and his eyes be opened, the ideas he expresses are likely to be revealed ephemeral in their essence, and his hands are apt to lose their cunning in a craft which has lost its divinity. For, however paradoxical it may appear, the true glimmerings of human divinity are visible, not in the creation of the artist, but in the reflection of the critic. The former is limited by the particular conditions of space and time, individual and social character, in and through which he works. The latter through a thousand of these shadows may catch an infinitely distant glimpse of the light which the artist imagines in the little day of the group for which he works. The artist deals with τὰ πρὸς δόξαν, with appearances, simply because he is an *artist*, controlled by average language and thought, not a scientific discoverer delving at will for new ideas, and labelling them when found with strange word-marks. The critic also deals with τὰ πρὸς δόξαν, but their range is for him far wider, and he possesses a certain scientific freedom of treatment in idea and language. The artist of Japan or China must work with the materials his social conditions offer; the artist of Athens possessed a far finer quarry, but his materials were also socially limited; the true critic, the "*discerner*," compares and contrasts the most divergent types of social and individual character at will, and, if the development he observes is fatal to any universal æsthetic standard and deprives him of the enthusiasm such a standard might supply, he is at least superior to the artist alike in the range and quality of his knowledge.

The critic cannot, therefore, allow the art-conception of literature to stand for a moment between him and the object of his study, whether the champions of that conception are found among the Athenians themselves or their modern disciples.* And so, to return to our prosaic question, we ask again, With what kind of literary stock did the Athenians start upon their career of literary production?

* "The students of antiquity," says Mr. J. A. Symonds (*Greek Poets*, Second Series, p. 303), "attached less value than we do to literature of secondary importance. It was the object of their criticism, especially in the schools of Alexandria, to establish canons of perfection in style. . . . Marlowe, according to their laws of taste, would have been obscured by Shakspere; while the multitude of lesser playwrights, whom we honour as explaining and relieving by their comradeship the grandeur of *the dramatist* (ὁ τραγῳδοποιὸς they might have styled Shakspere, as their Pindar was ὁ λυρικός), would have sunk into oblivion, leaving him alone in splendid isolation. Much might be said for this way of dealing with literature. By concentrating attention on undeniable excellence, a taste for noble things in art was fostered, while the danger that we run of substituting the historical for the æsthetic method was avoided." Mr. Symonds, however, forgets that in their unhistorical criticism the Greeks committed the far more serious error of substituting the æsthetic method for the historical—an error which, decked in the beauty of Greek art, has done more to check the growth of historical science in modern Europe than can be easily estimated.

§ 48. In the first place, the Athenians, as Ionians, possessed a dialect which, carried by their kinsmen to the Ionic cities of Asia Minor, became the earliest vehicle of prose in the literary history of Greece—the Ἑπτάμυχος of Pherecydes of Scyros was the first attempt at a prose treatise in Greek. In common with other Ionians, also, they possessed certain religious festivals—the Thargelia and Pyanepsia of Apollo, the Anthesteria and Lenæa of Dionysus, the Apaturia, Eleusinia, and others. The federations of early Ionians may indeed be compared with Arab and Hebrew tribe-leagues marking their federal union by sacred festivals; and the eponymous ancestor of such leagues was long as highly respected in Athens as in Israel or Arabia. The *Ion* of Euripides, it has been remarked, was designed to extol the pure blood of Athenians, and to show that the Ionic stock from which they claimed descent was not, as represented in ordinary legends, that derived from the Hellenic stranger Xuthus, but had originated from Apollo himself; and though the ordinary legends probably went much nearer the truth (just as Ezekiel in his denunciations of Israel reminds his countrymen of their hybrid origin, "Thy father was an Amorite and thy mother a Hittite"), the eponym *Ion* and the purpose for which the story is dramatised seem to mark the influence of clan ideas in Athens, even in an age when her old religion and clan morality were being rapidly undermined by individualised thought. But the Athenians had something more than the mere instrument of literature in common with their Ionic kinsfolk of the East; from them they learned the A B C of philosophy, history, poetry. Among the Eastern Ionians chronicling had commenced at Miletus, the birthplace of the earliest philosophers of Greece—Thales, Anaximander, Anaximenes. An Ionic poet of the East, Callinus of Ephesus, has left the earliest extant specimen of the elegy. Archilochus, the creator of iambic poetry, and the next iambic poet, Simonides of Amorgos, were both East-Ionian satirists. But though the political and literary growth of Athens came later than that of her wealthy kinsfolk, though East-Ionian soil and climate were greatly superior to those of Attica, the progress of literature was to depend, as it ever depends, upon social freedom no less than wealth; and, while Asiatic conquerors subdued the Ionians of Asia, and warlike races preferred to turn to the fertile plains of Argos, Thebes, and Thessaly, the shallow and rocky soil of Attica allowed a peaceful though manly development of social life to the Attic village communities.

How far the old village life of Attica had given way to that of the city commonwealth, how far that marked opposition of men of the country to men of the town which so powerfully affected later Athenian life had disclosed itself in Solon's time, we shall not attempt to estimate. Suffice it to say that at this time the literature of Athens may be said to begin with the elegies and gnomic poetry of the great reformer himself. As a pioneer of Athenian literature, Solon seems to resemble an Oriental prophet rather than a literary artist. The strange delivery of the Elegy of Salamis, composed about 604 B.C., reminds us of the symbolical action with which the Hebrew *nâbî* sometimes accompanied his impassioned speech.* Nor is

* "Suddenly appearing in the costume of a herald, with the proper cap (πιλίον) on his head, and having previously spread a report that he was mad, he sprang in the place of the popular assembly upon the stone where the heralds were wont to stand, and sang in an impassioned tone an elegy which began with these words: "I myself come as a herald from the lovely island of Salamis, using song, the ornament of words, and not simple speech, to the people" (K. O. Müller, *Lit. of An. Greece*, ch. x. § 11). Müller might have added that the practice of poetic recitation was used by Xenophanes and Parmenides to disseminate their philosophic views. While writing is known to the very few (in East and West alike at first probably to the priests alone) and no reading public exists, the speech in verse or rhythmical prose, whether of Arab *kâwy*, Hebrew *Nâbî*, or Athenian reformer, is an effective appeal to an unlettered audience.

this the only respect in which Solon's poetry typifies the infancy of Athenian literature. Another elegy (quoted by Demosthenes in his speech on the Embassy) describes the misery of the poor in terms which might have been applied to the debt-oppressed plebs of Rome, and seems to imply a conflict of clanned and clanless, men of property and the proletariate, which at one time augured as badly for Athenian as for Roman literature. But Athenian factions were to be fused into tolerable unity by internal tyranny and external war—two disciplining influences which also come out in Solon's poetry, the former in an elegy which foretells the coming tyranny, the latter in the martial spirit of many of his verses, which have been contrasted in this respect with the effeminate tone of Mimnermus, one of his East-Ionian contemporaries. In Solon, then, we see Athenian literature beginning in the rough but manly expression of a social spirit, a spirit in which collective interests leave as yet but little room for that personal and artistic poetry which the individualism of the East-Ionians had created.

But in Solon's age the Athenian people needed to be fused into social unity; and it was the work of the Peisistratids to effect this fusion against themselves. Mr. Mahaffy, in his *Social Life in Greece*, has called attention to the work of the tyrants in diffusing artistic taste through Greece; and in Athens their fondness of art was sufficiently proved by their building the temple of the Olympian Zeus. But their patronage of poetry and music more directly interests the student of Greek literature. The character of the poetry thus patronised should not escape notice. It was not the drama in its rude beginnings, which, especially in comedy, required a popular inspiration; it was the lyric of Anacreon, Simonides, Lasus, so much better suited to the atmosphere of a court. And, whatever truth is to be found in the Peisistratidean redaction of the Greek epics, it is equally significant that the Peisistratids "were unquestionably the first to introduce the recital of the entire *Iliad* and *Odyssey* at the Panathenæa." The heroic songs of the Homeric bards were more in keeping with the tyrant's court than the dramatic spectacle. But the Athenian people had not yet expressed itself in any literary voice, and when that voice should make itself heard it was to be something very different from the personal lyric of the tyrants or the epic of the ancient kings.

Thus, in reply to our question, with what kind of literary stock did the Athenians start on their career of literary production, we have found that, so far as literary *form* is concerned, the epic, lyric, and iambic forms of poetry were known to them chiefly through their East-Ionic kinsfolk, and that prose in a somewhat poetic dress may be reckoned among the formal elements which their literary capital owed to the same source. East-Ionic prose, prior to the destruction of Miletus at the beginning of the fifth century B.C., was being developed in narrative and philosophical forms which have been contrasted by Mure with the rhetorical prose of Athens in her literary age. The *Makâmât* of Al Harîri, however, proves that rhetorical prose may be developed where Ekklêsia and law-courts such as those of Athens are unknown. Still, in Miletus we have a municipal centre of Greek intellect widely differing from Athens in its social and physical conditions—a metropolis which, if undestroyed, would in all probability have produced a literature differing widely from that of Athens alike in form and spirit.

But a more important question than that of poetical

or prose *forms* now awaits us; it is this : What stock of *ideas* did the Athenians at the beginnings of their literary production as a people possess? It is here that survivals from the clan age and the village community come thickly upon us.

§ 49. In the first place, the Athenians inherited from the days of their village communities the idea of inherited guilt, which, strange to say, never seems to have received among them the angry repudiation we find in the Hebrew Ezekiel. Nay, what is still more remarkable, the idea comes upon us in Athenian literature with almost fresher vitality than in the Homeric poems. In the most striking Homeric reference to the *Wehrgeld*, a passage from the *Iliad* already quoted, the old communal liability has been cut down into the banishment of the individual criminal from his δῆμος, or village community, until the *Wehrgeld* is accepted by the kindred of the murdered man; unlike the system of the Arab Thâr, no one can now suffer in the murderer's stead, but he is personally exiled for a time to avoid any pollution attaching to his group. This personal liability in the Homeric age ought to be contrasted with the dramatic prominence of inherited guilt at Athens probably three centuries later; for the contrast shows that, whatever social and intellectual progress had taken place in other parts of Greece and under different political or physical conditions, the clan spirit of the old Athenian dêmes retained sufficient strength even in the days of Sophocles to make itself felt in spectacles the pivot ethical conception of which is communal responsibility. While individualism elsewhere in Greece had been developed under the rule of kings or tyrants, the Athenian townsmen had retained enough of the primitive communal spirit to make it the life of their drama. Moreover, in this late survival of communal morality we may discover at least a partial explanation of one strange fact in Athenian literary development—the sudden burst and rapid decay of Attic genius.

After the rule of the tyrants and the successful resistance to Persian invasion had given to Athens social unity and the hegemony of states greatly her superiors in civilised refinement, the communal morality of old Athenian life was suddenly exposed to an influx of new ideas unknown to the early poverty and isolation of Attica. Hence a conflict set in between old Athenian sentiments and the individualism which had long before been developed in other parts of Greece, especially among the East-Ionians; and the material progress of Athens in wealth, which followed the Persian war and showed itself so notably during the administration of Pericles, allowed greater personal independence and far more leisure for debate than the early Athenians had possessed. It is in this conflict between things old and new that we find the chief source of Athenian genius; and if we are asked why that sunburst of creative power was so ephemeral, and why it was so soon obscured by clouds of verbal trifling and pedantic logomachy, we shall reply that the rapid destruction of old communal morality, when once the full force of Greek individualism had been let in on it, put an end to that duel of egoistic with altruistic thinking in which throughout the world's history the brightest sparks of genius have been struck out, and by completely individualising Athenian intellect and imagination made one-sided the later culture of Attic genius. As Müller observes, the traditional maxims of Athenian morality were, at the beginning of the Peloponnesian war, subjected to a scrutinising examination by a foreign race of teachers, chiefly from the colonies of the East and West; and we can easily understand how the exposure of clan ethics to this widened circle of comparison and contrast was certain to awake Athenian consciousness to defects in their old beliefs. The Socratic questioning is an outcome of this conflicting consciousness; the Platonic universalism is a dogmatic answer to the difficulties it raised; and the customary offering thrown into the sea for the sins of the Athenian people does not more graphically bring before us the early Athenian morality of vicarious punishment than Socratic speculations on the relation of law to morality,* or the contrast of customary with subjective morality,† bring before us the days of subtle debaters, when the simple ethic of her clan age was as impossible for Athens as it would be for an adult to force himself back into the ideas of his infancy. It was not to be expected that primitive doctrines of vicarious punishment and inherited sin could long retain their hold upon people accustomed to debate recondite problems of personal intention in their courts of law or legislative assembly. It was not to be expected that simple belief in the ancient morality could be retained while ties of kinship were steadily giving way to action from self-interest, and sophists were aiding the cleverness of Athenians bent on comparing the institutions and ideas of the various Greek states or analysing their own subjective thought. It made little difference whether the sophist was a Protagoras, ready to demonstrate the impossibility of truth from the conflict of Greek ideas alike claiming divinity, or a subtle Socrates prepared to raise moral problems which he could not, or at least did not, solve. In either case old ideas were being undermined; and the struggles of men like Aristophanes to ridicule the new notions out

---

* *Xenophon Memorabilia*, bk. i. ch. ii. § 42, *sqq.*
† *Ib.* Cf. bk. i. ch. iii., and bk. ii. ch. ii. § 13.

of sight were but efforts, tragically comic, to restore life to the ancient morality by choking attempts to answer problems which had been forced upon Athenian attention by altered social conditions and not merely suggested by hair-splitting sophists.

§ 50. But besides conceptions of inherited guilt and vicarious punishment, positive signs of the early communal life, the clan age left on Athenian thought a negative mark which deserves to be noticed in connection with the decay of Athenian morals. This is the absence of any profound belief in a future state of personal reward or punishment. Considerable progress toward the conception of such a state had been made in the interval between the Odyssean age and that of Pindar. In the Nekuia, or eleventh book of the *Odyssey*, the gathering-place of the clans * is as yet by no means divided into abodes of happiness and suffering. We are indeed introduced to the sight of suffering in Hades; but the persons singled out for punishment are not men, but demi-gods. Ulysses sees Tituos, son of far-famed Earth, outstretched many a rood, while two vultures on each side tear his liver for the wrong he had done to Latona. He sees Tantalus, expressly called a δαίμων,† thirsting while the water touches his chin, and putting forth his hands to touch the fruits which a wind "scatters to the shadowing clouds." Sisyphus, too, he sees, rolling with both hands the enormous stone that always falls back to the plain. But mere *human* personality is not yet distinguished in Hades by punishment or reward. The dead are but

* Cf.
περὶ δ' ἄλλαι ἀγηγέραθ', ὅσσοι ἅμ' αὐτῷ
Οἴκῳ ἐν Αἰγίσθοιο θάνον καὶ πότμον ἐπέσπον.
(*Od.*, xi. 388.)

In Ezekiel's famous picture of the fallen nations (ch. xxxii.) Hades admits not only clan but national distinctions.
† *Od.*, xi. 587.

empty images of mortal men;* to be king of their myriad clans is worse than to be a serf on earth; and if Hercules is better off it is not because he is in Elysian fields, but because only his image (εἴδωλον) dwells in the cheerless Shadow-land, "while he himself with the immortal gods enjoys the feast and lovely-ankled Youth." The gathering-place of the clans, with its pale reflection of the life then known, has not yet been separated into the torture-place of the Evil and the paradise of the Good, though Minos, holding his golden sceptre, sits like any earth-king giving his inspired commands to the dead (θεμιστεύων νέκυσσιν), "while those around seek decisions (δίκας) of the king."

So far the Greek conception of a future state was not greatly in advance of the Hebrew Sheôl. But the break-up of clan ties and the progress of individualism were to bring out the need of such sanctions for personal morality as the future state can create. In truth, the Heaven and Hell conceptions were to develop in parallel lines with the development of social life. In the poems of Pindar the punishments and rewards of a future state are no longer confined to dæmons and demi-gods; plain human personality is to suffer for the evil it has wrought, or to enjoy a paradise of holiness which is neither the abode of the gods nor confined to translated heroes like Hercules. In a famous passage of Pindar's second Olympian ode we have an evidence of this ethical progress worth quoting in full.† "But if one possesses wealth aright he knows the future lot, that reckless souls of men who died on earth pay straightway their *wehrgelds* (ποινάς),‡ for one

---

* πῶς ἔτλης Ἀϊδόσδε κατελθέμεν, ἔνθατε νεκροὶ
ἀφραδέες ναίουσι, βροτῶν εἴδωλα καμόντων;
(*Ib.*, 475.)

† εὖ δέ μιν ἔχων τις οἶδεν τὸ μέλλον, κ.τ.λ.

‡ Cf. the Homeric use of ποινή. The transference of the *Wehrgeld* to

there is who by a hateful fate pronouncing sentences awards the penalties for deeds committed in the realm of Zeus; but the good, enjoying sunlight ever equally by night and day, receive a life more free from griefs than ours, not harassing earth with strength of hand nor ocean wave for scanty sustenance. But all who joyed in keeping of their oaths, among the honoured of the Gods rejoice in tearless life; the others bear affliction too dreadful to be looked upon. They who have thrice endured on either side the grave to keep their souls unsullied by injustice, pursue the road of Zeus to Kronos' tower; there the ocean breezes blow round the islands of the blest, and the golden flowers are glowing, some on land from glistening trees, some the water nourishes; there with chaplets made of these the blest twine their hands and heads by the just decrees of Rhadamanthus, whom Father Kronos, spouse of Rhea, throned above all gods, keeps as assessor ever ready by him." Fragments of the Pindaric Threnoi contain similar ideas, for example one * which Professor Conington has translated thus—

> "But the souls of the profane,
>   Far from heaven removed below,
> Flit on earth in murderous pain
>   'Neath the unyielding yoke of woe;
> While pious spirits tenanting the sky
> Chant praises to the mighty one on high."

But Athenian life was not destined to *popularise* such ideas. In the *Frogs* of Aristophanes we have, though of course in caricature, a picture of Hades little in advance of the Odyssean. Bacchus, with a lion's skin thrown over his saffron-coloured robe and armed with a club, imitates Hercules, and, as Hercules had gone to fetch

Hades recalls the presence of Blood-revenge in the spirit-world of the Grendel. See passage from *Beowulf* translated above.

* ψυχαὶ δ' ἀσεβέων ὑπουράνιοι
γαίᾳ πωτῶνται ἐν ἄλγεσι φονίοις, κ.τ.λ.

the dog Cerberus, descends to bring back Euripides from the infernal world. On his way, Bacchus inquires of Hercules "what entertainers he had met when he went to fetch Cerberus, what harbours, bakers' shops, lodging-houses, springs, roads, cities, hostesses"—earthly associations well kept up when Proserpine's servant tells the pseudo-Hercules that "the goddess, when she heard of his arrival, began baking loaves, boiled some pots of soup of bruised peas, broiled a whole ox, and baked cheese-cakes and rolls." But two innkeepers of Hades think they recognise in the pseudo-Hercules "the villain who came into our inn one day and devoured sixteen loaves, twenty pieces of boiled meat at half an obol apiece, and vast quantities of garlic and dried fish." For these depredations the innkeepers determine to take vengeance; and Bacchus, in fear of the coming evil, gets his slave Xanthias to assume the lion's skin and club of Hercules. Æacus, attended by three myrmidons, now enters; but the slave-hero holds his own, tells Æacus to go to the mischief, and as a proof of innocence offers Bacchus, now supposed to be his slave, to be tortured for evidence in true Athenian fashion. Xanthias and Æacus, farther on in the play, congratulate each other on the delight they take in prying into their masters' secrets, and then "blabbing them out of doors;" and Æacus tells his fellow-servant of the quarrel between Æschylus and Euripides, with whose famous contest the rest of the play is taken up. "There is a law established here," says Æacus, "that out of the professions, as many as are important and ingenious, he who is the best of his own fellow-artists should receive a public maintenance in the Prytaneum and a seat next to Pluto's." Æschylus had held the "tragic seat," as being "the best in his art;" but Euripides, when he came down, "began to show off to footpads, and cutpurses, and parricides, and housebreakers—a sort of men there is a vast quantity of in Hades—and they, hearing his objections and twistings and turnings, went stark mad and thought him the cleverest. So Euripides was elated, and laid claim to the throne on which Æschylus was sitting."

It has been remarked that in this thoroughly Athenian Hades, with its Prytaneum and Athenian law giving public maintenance to such as excelled their fellow-artists, "the under-world is an exact copy of the upper;" but the remark by no means exhausts the significance of the *Frogs* as an index to average Athenian notions of the future state. The treatment of the under-world as a mere reflection of Athenian life shows what little way the Athenians had made towards utilising the future state as the most solemn sanction for personal morality. Hercules, indeed, at the opening of the play, makes a passing allusion to those who "have wronged their guests, beaten their parents, sworn false oaths, or transcribed a passage of the dramatist Morsimus," as "lying in the mud" by way of punishment; but the jocular allusion to Morsimus is not calculated to make us think of the Athenian conception of future retribution as at all a serious matter. We must regard such theories as those of Plato in his *Phædo* as expressing the deep reflection of a very few who, like the philosopher, felt the need of sanctions for personal morality. But outside esoteric circles, such as the initiated in the Eleusinian mysteries, there was little opportunity for earnest belief in the moral sanctions of a future state; and one great obstacle to the popularity of such belief is to be found in Athenian slavery. The prominence of the slave in the *Frogs*, among all sorts and conditions of Athenian men and women in Hades, is a sharp reminder of this obstacle. How could the master

of slaves picture himself in Hades either with or without
his slaves? If they accompanied him into Hades, all the
social distinctions of Athenian life would logically follow,
and the exact reflection of Athens in Hades would be too
grotesque even for the most pious and least sceptical of
minds. If, on the other hand, there were no slaves in
Hades, how could the freemen of Athens realise without
inward ridicule a privilege which any of them might lose
with his civil status? But, over and above this hostility
of slavery to a future state, Athenian ideas of future
reward and retribution had to meet another cause of
weakness. In the political life and poetical sentiments
of Athens clan facts and feelings were long retained; and
as long as men believed in the inheritance of guilt in
groups—as during the height of Athenian power and
dramatic genius the Athenians undoubtedly did on the
average believe—there was little moral need for the personal rewards or punishments of the under-world. The
very strength of this survival from the clan age concealed
the want of sanctions for personal morality till it was too
late for Athenian intelligence to do more than debate, as
some among us are now debating, scientific bases for
morality.

§ 51. While survivals from the clan spirit supply the
ethics of Athenian tragedy, while the conflict between
such survivals and growing individualism produces the
masterpieces of Athenian philosophy, the clan spirit in
Rome brings about very different effects in Roman character and, through character, in Roman literature.
Where Solon and Peisistratus had commenced the conservative patricians of Rome were determined to remain,
and for a long time did remain. Clan life, retained and
in some respects hardened in the Roman *familia*, left
little scope for either literary or philosophic progress

where childen *sub potestate,* women in *perpetuâ tutelâ,* wives *sub manu viri,* showed how personal independence and character were still in communal leading-strings. While Roman life was socially ruled by the *familia* and politically ruled by patrician *gentes,* there was little opportunity for any literature save that of sacred hymns and religious law-books such as the priestly castes of the East have so frequently produced; indeed, if the clanless element at Rome had not been sufficiently strong to modify this social and political system, there is little reason to think that Rome, physically or intellectually, would have risen above the level of these Eastern priest-oligarchies. But, though the conflict between plebeian and patrician could not strike out Athenian intelligence, it saved the "urbs æterna" from such a fate; it struck out that vigorous political life of law-court and assembly in which Roman prose and jurisprudence were developed by a permanent progress remarkably unlike the sudden outburst and decay of Athenian genius.

When the personal relations of Roman citizens under the despotic system of the *familia* are clearly realised Rome's need of external aid in the development of her literature is manifest. Mommsen has said with truth that the culminating point of Roman development was reached without a literature; and two causes are sufficient to explain this fact—the rigid family system which among full citizens proscribed individualised action and thought, and the deadly enmity between these full citizens and the clanless proletariate, so far as it prevented an enthusiastic political union which might have made itself felt in popular song. If the conflict of plebeian with patrician was needed to break down gentilic exclusiveness, it at the same time retarded and perhaps altogether prevented the rise of a *popular* Roman literature. Not until the Persian war had fused Athenians into a political unity they might otherwise never have attained did the fruits of Attic genius show themselves; and, had internal clan distinctions survived the age of Solon and Peisistratus in anything like their patrician vitality at Rome, Athenian verse and prose would probably never have attained any remarkable degree of beauty and symmetry. The reason for the absence of literature in early Rome has been sought in "the original characteristics of the Latin race;" but, like the answer of Molière's famous doctor, or M. Renan's explanation of Hebrew and Arab monotheism by "Semitic instinct," this explanation simply repeats the problem in another form. The true explanation must be found in causes affecting the general character of men and women at Rome; and any student of Roman law and early social life need not be at a loss for such causes. The conscious contrasts of patrician, plebeian, alien, and servile status, and the strong conservatism of clan character, are the primary causes of that unimaginative life which made the Roman law-court the fountain-head of European jurisprudence, but compelled the mistress of force to look for literary guidance to the mistress of intellect. Without any store of common sympathies which plebeian and patrician might feel alike, Rome had no social ideals such as literature desires; and if she had heroes of her own, they only served to summon up recollections of kingly or aristocratic despotism.

The production of Roman literature, about the middle of the third century B.C., opened with a stock of materials and ideas meagre in the extreme. No kinsmen of Rome had created a vehicle of verse like the hexameter, iambic, or elegiac of Greece; the rude Saturnian seems to have been the only metre known. Nor had any Miletus of the West laid the foundations of Roman prose; chronicles, of the barest kind conceivable, and laws, apparently without note or comment, seem as yet to have been the only types of Latin prose. Dionysius,* indeed, speaks of πάτριοι ὕμνοι as still sung in his own time by Romans; and Cicero twice refers to a passage in Cato's *Origines* which speaks of old Roman songs sung at banquets to the accompaniment of a *tibia* in praise of great men. But, in spite of Niebuhr's and Macaulay's inferences from these authorities, it cannot be seriously maintained that Rome ever possessed a popular ballad-poetry. For, in the first place, Rome possessed no background of myth which such early poetry might have used as its wonderland. This absence of myth has been attributed to the nature of Rome's early religion; and it must be admitted that such transparent names as Saturnus (Sowing), Fides, Terminus, were not likely to aid the creation of poetic mythology. But deeper reasons for the absence of heroic mythology in early Rome are discoverable in her ancient social life. Whatever germs of epic poetry may have existed in the private hymns or songs of patricians, they had no opportunity to ripen into a genuine epic among the constant conflicts of clansmen, who had "Fathers" to celebrate, with the clanless plebs. The traditional stories of Roman gentes were too closely interwoven with political associations to be quietly gathered into the beautiful poetic forms of the Greek myths, which might never have reached their æsthetic perfection had they been so closely bound with things of daily life. Niebuhr's conception of a Roman ballad-poetry overlooks the fact that the true home of the ballad, out of which the epos may grow, is not the life of a city, nor that of clans seeking to keep up their exclusiveness in the presence of city life, but the halls

* Cf. Macaulay, preface to *Lays of Ancient Rome*, pp. 13 and 15, notes.

of chiefs where individual character is surrounded by a divine halo which the democratic intercourse of the city cannot tolerate.

§ 52. The semi-dramatic Fescennine Dialogues, the Saturæ, Mimes, and Fabulæ Atellanæ (the last, according to Livy, exclusively in the hands of freeborn citizens and not polluted by professional actors), show that even at the beginnings of Roman literature city life, in spite of *gentile* aristocracy, was roughly producing its characteristic literary product—the drama. But here, too, the patrician clan spirit opposed the progress of the Camenæ and left a clear way for the Muses of Greece. It would have been untrue to Roman social life to have exhibited as Roman the relations of father and son, husband and wife, as Plautus and Terence borrowing from Greek models exhibit them always on a thoroughly Greek stage. The scene of the *Amphitruo* is at Thebes, of the *Asinaria* probably at Athens, of the *Aulularia* at Athens; of the *Bacchides, Casina, Epidicus, Mercator, Mostellaria, Persa, Pseudolus, Stichus, Trinumus, Truculentus,* at Athens; that of the *Captivi* in Ætolia, of the *Cistellaria* at Sicyon, of the *Curculio* at Epidaurus, of the *Menæchmi* at Epidamnus, of the *Miles Gloriosus* at Ephesus, of the *Pœnulus* at Calydon, of the *Rudens* in Africa near Cyrenæ; so that not one of the twenty extant plays attributed to Plautus has its action in Italy, much less in Rome. The Greek places, names, characters, of the Plautine and Terentian dramas are to be accounted for not merely by the desire of avoiding offence and by their close imitation of Greek models, but also by the comparative absence of such characters and personal relations at Rome as would suit the dramatist. Neither the Roman son, whose *peculium* reminds us rather of a slave's status than that of a free man, nor the Roman father, with the solemn despotism of *patria potestas*, nor above all the Roman matron, wife, or daughter, in their perpetual tutelage, possessed that kind of freedom which was required by the drama of individualised life. The Roman drama, tragedy and comedy alike, had to wear Athenian livery in order to get out of associations which met dramatic freedom at every turn with the cold *status* of patrician life.

Thus the clan spirit in Athens and Rome affected the beginnings of Athenian and Roman literatures very differently. Not strong enough in Athens to keep the city divided into hostile camps, yet strong enough to remain the inner life of traditional morality, it sets Athenian genius on fire by its conflict with individualised ideas pouring in from all parts of Greece, and required by the rapidly altering conditions of Athenian social life. Too strong in Rome to allow even physical, much less intellectual, freedom, it stops the progress of Roman unity and literature alike, and forces the founders of the Roman drama to seek in Greece the social and personal characteristics their art requires.

CHAPTER III.

POETRY OF THE CITY COMMONWEALTH.

§ 53. THE peculiar poetic production of the city is the dramatic spectacle, whether in the rude shape of such plays as those of Hans Sachs or in the exquisite symmetry of Sophocles' *Antigone*. We do not, of course, mean to maintain either that all cities, if left to their own literary evolution, will of necessity produce a drama, or that no social conditions save those of city life have produced this form of literature. The Indian, Chinese, and Japanese dramas show the weakness of any such general assertions; and wherever an audience can be gathered together, to a passion-play like the Persian or a court-play like the Japanese, we may be sure that religion or royalty will supply the place of the city audience to a certain extent. But the religious or courtly spectacle cannot be regarded as a perfect substitute for the city drama. It is in the organisation of city life that the greatest variety of human character within the smallest space is produced; and this variety of human types allows dramatic analysis of character its fullest scope. Accordingly, the most admirable specimens of dramatic art have been the work of cities, from the Athens of Pericles to the London of Elizabeth and the Paris of Louis Quatorze. We are, however, at present concerned, not with the drama of national capitals, but only with that of the city as a self-developed community—the city commonwealth. In the drama of the city commonwealth we may not meet certain interesting features of the Chinese and Indian theatres—the prominence of physical nature, for example. In the same drama we may not find such a variety of character as in that of a national capital like Elizabethan London. But in the narrow range of the city commonwealth we shall perhaps be able to trace the effects of social evolution on the form and spirit of the dramatic spectacle with greater clearness than in the complicated life of modern nations, or the comparatively motionless society of India and China.

Still it must not be supposed that the dramas of the East are altogether unlike that of Athens. The singing-character of the Chinese theatre, for example, reminds us in some respects of the Athenian chorus, only that (like Shakspere's use of the chorus) an individual actor here takes the place of the Athenian group. Indeed, the lyrical drama of Japan presents so many likenesses to the Athenian that we shall here quote Mr. Basil Hall Chamberlain's description of the origin and form of this Eastern theatre.

"Towards the end of the fourteenth century," says Mr. Chamberlain,* " in the hands of the Buddhist priesthood, who during that troublous period had become almost the sole repositories of taste and learning, arose the lyric drama, at first but an adaptation of the old religious dances, the choric songs accompanying which were expanded and improved. The next step was the introduction of individual personages which led to the adoption of a dramatic unity in the plot, though the supreme importance still assigned to the chorus left to the performance its mainly lyric character till, at a some-

* *Japanese Classical Poetry*, p. 13.

what later period, the theatrical tendency became supreme and the romantic melodrama of the modern Japanese stage was evolved." Farther on Mr. Chamberlain describes the manner of representing this lyric drama. "The stage, which has remained unaltered in every respect from the beginning of the fifteenth century, when the early dramatists Seama and Otourmi acted at Kiyauto before the then Shiyauguñ (Shogun or Tycoon, as Europeans usually pronounce it) Yoshimasa, is a square wooden room, open upon all sides but one and supported on pillars, the side of the square being about eighteen English feet. It is surrounded by a quaint roof somewhat resembling those to be seen on the Japanese Buddhist temples, and is connected with the green-room by a gallery some nine feet wide. Upon this gallery part of the action occasionally takes place. Added on to the back of the square stage is a narrow space where sits the orchestra, consisting of one flute-player, two performers on instruments which in the absence of a more fitting name may be called tambourines, and one beater of the drum, while the chorus, whose number is not fixed, squat on the ground to the right of the spectator. In a line with the chorus, between it and the audience, sits the less important of the two actors during the greater portion of the piece. (Two was the number of the actors during the golden days of the art.) The back of the stage, the only side not open to the air, is painted with a pine tree, in accordance with ancient usage, while, equally in conformity with established rules, three small pine trees are planted in the court which divides the gallery from the space occupied by the less distinguished portion of the audience. The covered place for the audience, who all sit on the mats according to the immemorial custom of their countrymen, runs round three sides of the stage, the most honourable seats being those which directly face it. Masks are worn by such of the actors as take the parts of females or of supernatural beings; and the dresses are gorgeous in the extreme." Mr. Chamberlain then notices "the statuesque immobility of the actors and the peculiar intonation of the recitative. When once the ear has become used to its loudness it is by no means unpleasing, while the measured cadences of the chorus are from the very first both soothing and impressive. The music unfortunately cannot claim like praise, and the dancing executed by the chief character towards the close of each piece is tedious and meaningless to the European spectator. The performance occupies a whole day. For, although each piece takes on an average but one hour to represent, five or six are given in succession, and the intervals between them are filled up by the acting of comic scenes. Down to the time of the late revolution much ceremony and punctilious etiquette hedged in on every side those who were admitted to the honour of viewing this dramatic performance at the Shiyauguñ's court. Now the doors are open to all alike, but it is still chiefly the old aristocracy who make up the audience; and even they, highly trained as they are in the ancient literature, usually bring with them a book of the play to enable them to follow with the eye the difficult text, which is rendered still harder of comprehension by the varying tones of the choric chant."

In this description of the formal elements of the Japanese drama we cannot but be struck by several resemblances to the Athenian stage. The prominence of the chorus, of dance and song and music, the gradual introduction of individual actors distinct from the chorus, the gradual subordination of the chorus to the actors in the development of the drama, the small number of the actors, the use of masks and splendid dresses, the "statuesque immobility of the actors," the "intonation of the recitative," the representation of several plays in succession, have all their parallels in the famous drama of Athens. The chorus, as is well known, with its combination of dance, and song, and melody, and mimetic action, makes the central figure of the Athenian drama, the figure round which the rude beginnings of that drama take their rise and whose disapperance heralds its decay. Some of the leading differences between the dramas of modern Europe and that of Athens may be attributed to the choral and lyric source of the latter contrasted with the early predominance of dialogue in the former; and it is to be remembered that this Athenian chorus carries us back to those choral songs in which we have previously found the beginnings of literature. When we trace the rise of the Attic drama from sacred mysteries in which priests and priestesses acted the story of Demeter and Cora, or from the betrothal of the second archon's wife to Dionysus at the Anthesteria, or from such festival rites as that in which a maiden "representing one of the nymphs in the train of Dionysus" is pursued by a priest "bearing a hatchet and personating a being hostile to the god,"* we must not forget that the choral song carries us back from the adult city community of Athens to the village festivals of early Attica. If the ethical ideas of the Athenian drama take their rise, as we have already seen, from the village community and clan, so also does the choral form. The chorus in the rapid progress of Athenian life and art is far more interesting than in the comparatively stationary civilisa-

* K. O. Müller, *Hist. Gk. Lit.* (Donaldson's translation, vol. i. p. 381).

tion of Japan; at Athens its rise and decay curiously illustrate early communal life and the evolution of individual action and thought; and the social development of the city commonwealth is thus reflected in the form as well as in the spirit of its drama.

§ 54. In Athens a group of persons—for such, of course, is the nature of the chorus—is the earliest centre of dramatic interest. The songs and dances of this group make the body of the dramatic spectacle; and though its leaders may now and then come forward separately (like the leaders of a Russian *Khorovod*), or its members may answer each other assembled round the altar of Dionysus, such responses and glimpses of individual action do not yet bring us to any regular dialogue, much less to any display of personal character. The chorus is the literary link between the sacred festivals of early Attic village communities and the semi-religious theatre of Athenian tragedy; but the æsthetic pleasures of character-drawing are only developed out of this group of worshippers by that profound change in the social character of Athenian men and women which allowed the tragic stage to become the vehicle of Euripidean casuistry, and converted the idealism of the old comedy into the everyday personages of Menander. Let us follow some of the formal and spiritual changes through which the Athenian drama passed in the course of this individualising process.

One of the first steps towards a drama of personal character seems to have been taken about 536 B.C., when Thespis is said to have added to the choral group one actor (he was called the ὑποκριτής, or "answerer," because he "answered" the songs of the chorus) whose dialogue with the chorus offered some scope for the display of individuality. This new departure of the old Athenian spectacles was carried still farther by Phrynichus (B.C. 512), who made this actor play female parts for the first time. Meanwhile the chorus itself was becoming more flexible; the old chorus of Satyrs, the appropriate accompaniment of the Bacchic festival, was being displaced by choruses suited to the particular subject of the play, and in the time of Chœrilus (524 B.C.) the Satyric drama seems to have been separated from regular tragedy. Thus, on the one hand, the old group of worshippers are being gradually transformed into a group personage with a general character conformable to the particular play, while, on the other hand, the individual actor is introducing dramatic personality distinct from groups or abstract personages. The Bacchic festal costume of the actors, their "stiff angular movements," their tragic masks, the monotonous kind of chant in which the dialogue is rather sung than spoken,* may remind us still of theatres so slightly developed as the Japanese, but the progress of dialogue and character is rapidly carrying us towards a dramatic region into which Japanese, Chinese, and even Indian dramatists, compared with the Athenian masters, have hardly ever penetrated. For the Athenian dramatists, becoming secular artists instead of religious teachers, are learning to depict personality with all its shades of thought and sentiment even through the hackneyed heroic personages of their sacred spectacle, and the vigorous growth of Athenian life is beginning to supply them, perhaps unconsciously, with new types of human nature.

But though the ἠθοποιία, or character-drawing of *individuals*, marks the master-hand of the Athenian

* K. O. Müller quotes from Lucian the phrase περιᾴδειν τὰ ἰαμβεῖα, "to *sing round* the iambics," which certainly gives us a very graphic idea of the tragic "mouthing" referred to by Demosthenes in his savage attack on Æschines.

dramatist, both the formal and spiritual elements of the Athenian stage long retained survivals from the choral group of earlier days. The whole structure of the Athenian theatre, as Müller says, "may be traced to the chorus whose station was the original centre of the whole performance." The orchestra grew out of the χόρος, or "dancing place" of Homeric times, to which we have previously alluded in connection with the choral song-dances of the clan. In the centre of the orchestra the altar of Dionysus, round which the dithyrambic chorus used to dance in a circle, gave way to a sort of raised platform, the *thymele*, as it was called, which, besides serving as a resting-place for the chorus, significantly marked the religious origin of the Athenian drama. The openness of the theatre to the sky and the remarkably long but shallow stage—two formal features of the Athenian theatre not to be overlooked—may likewise be attributed to the presence of the chorus. Again, whatever the mixed origin of the " unities " as expressed by French critics may have been, there can be little doubt that a certain fixity of time and place was in a manner necessitated by the chorus, which could not be easily shifted either in space or time. Finally, the Athenian conception of dramatic authorship, which subordinated the word-composition to the public production of the play, was partially due to the trouble and expense of teaching the choral songs and dances.

§ 55. But the formal prominence of the chorus in the early Athenian drama is scarcely more marked than the spiritual. It is here, indeed, that we find the clearest links between the chorus and the social conditions of early Attica. The dramatisation of human action in groups or abstract personages closely reflects the prominence of group life and unindividualised thought in early societies; hence it was only when individualised conduct and sentiment became the groundwork of average Athenian character that the subtleties of Euripides showed their hostility not only to the old prominence of the chorus, but also to those mythical personages of the sacred spectacle who were too abstract to suit an age of small personalities. Three striking features of the Æschylean drama are therefore to be explained by the early social life of Athens—the predominance of the chorus in the plays of Æschylus, his leaning to abstract or impersonal *dramatis personæ*, and his ethical machinery of inherited guilt. The chorus is the central point in the spiritual as well as in the formal elements of the old Attic drama; but the reason for this is not to be found in the chorus itself as the production of conscious dramatic art—for the rude drama of early Attica had as little to do with art as an Indian Buffalo-dance—but in the dême life of early Attica, in the small social groups which here, as everywhere else in the world, once subordinated all personal action and thought to their own collective being. It was one great work of city life at Athens to cut down this collective being into individual units, each with his separate personal character and destiny, and the progress of this work is reflected very closely in the progress of the Attic drama.

In the seven extant plays of Æschylus there are only about seventeen individual personages, the rest of the forty-five *dramatis personæ* being either groups, as the chorus itself, or general and abstract personages such as the herald and the messenger, Might and Force. In the *Suppliants* personal character has hardly any place at all; for neither Danaus nor the king of the Argives (who with the chorus and a herald make up all the *dramatis personæ*) can be called a study of character. In

Prometheus allegorical and divine personages interest themselves in that vast struggle between Man and Fate before which all the necessary littleness of personal humanity disappears. In the *Persæ* we can hardly count the ghost of Dareius as a personal character—it rather typifies the sunken sun of Persian conquest; and if Atossa and Xerxes are real human personages, they are also general types of Persian ostentation and pride; for the play, like some Chinese plays, rather points the moral of a great historical event than attempts to describe human character in individuals, and, as even Müller is forced to admit, "looks at first glance more like a lament over the misfortunes of the Persians than a tragic drama." Again, in the *Seven against Thebes*, Eteocles, Ismene, Antigone are no doubt human personages, but the "pivot upon which the whole piece turns"—Polynices' resolution to meet his brother in combat while recognising the fatal act as the effect of his father's curse—carries us back to the early life and morals of Attica as plainly as any abstract personage or the choral group itself. But it is needless to run through all the extant plays of Æschylus in our search for impersonal or, as modern critics would say, "undramatic" elements. No doubt even within his extant plays there are signs of a growing subordination of the chorus—that of the *Choëphoræ*, as Mr. Mahaffy observes,* is not only the confidant but the accomplice of the actors. But the fact that the chorus is the central character (if we may so apply a term long restricted to personal action by modern criticism) in the *Suppliants, Persæ*, and *Eumenides* would be alone sufficient to prove the prominence of the group on the stage of Æschylus.

In the drama of Sophocles the chorus is being sup-

* *Hist. Class. Gk. Lit.*, vol. i. p. 269.

planted by individual characterisation. Only one of Sophocles' extant plays derives its name from the chorus —the *Trachiniæ*; and here, in marked contrast with the *Suppliants* of Æschylus, the figures of Hercules and Deianira keep the chorus completely in the background. The dialogue, the true medium of character-drawing, was now being developed by the increased number of actors. If a third actor had been introduced in the *Agamemnon, Choëphoræ*, and *Eumenides* of Æschylus (his other extant tragedies are constructed for two actors), all the plays of Sophocles are adapted for three actors, excepting the *Œdipus at Colonus*, which could not be acted without the introduction of a fourth; and, with this increase of actors, dialogue was narrowing the domain of choral song. This reduction of the choral element in the Athenian drama is easily seen by comparing the proportion of the entire play assigned to the chorus in the tragedies of Sophocles with the proportion so assigned by Æschylus. In Sophocles' *Œdipus Rex* a little more than one fourth of the play is assigned to the chorus; in his *Antigone* a little less than one fourth; in his *Ajax* a little more than one fifth; in his *Œdipus at Colonus* a little less than one fifth; in his *Trachiniæ* one sixth; and in his *Electra* and *Philoctetes* about one seventh. Thus, using the extant plays of Sophocles as the basis of calculation and allowing for some uncertainty in the choral lines, we may say that on the average he assigned about one fifth of his play to the chorus. But, on examining the extant plays of Æschylus, we find that more than one half of the *Suppliants* is assigned to the chorus; that somewhat less than one half is so assigned in the *Agamemnon, Seven against Thebes, Persæ, Choëphoræ*, and *Eumenides;* and that in the *Prometheus** alone does the proportion sink so low

* The proportion of this play assigned to the chorus is plainly an

as that of one-fifth. Hence it appears that the chorus occupies about twice as large a space in the Æschylean as in the Sophoclean drama; and an increased prominence of individual character in the latter is profoundly in accordance with this change. Sophocles' Antigone, Electra, Ajax, Philoctetes, Œdipus, stand out more independently from the choral group than any Æschylean personage, and transfer dramatic interest from the choral ode to the individual dialogue. It is true that in the plays of Sophocles associations of early clan life still live side by side with the growing dominion of individualism; in the *Antigone*, for example, the conflict between family rites (such as the *familia* of Rome would have sternly maintained) and the commands of the State—a conflict sure to set in as clan custom gave way to State law—is the mainspring of the dramatic action; and inherited guilt is almost as powerfully depicted in the *Œdipus Rex* as in the Æschylean trilogy. But in the extant plays of Sophocles we have nothing resembling the abstract personages of the *Prometheus Bound*, nothing resembling the allegorical spirit of that famous tragedy; on the Sophoclean contrasted with the Æschylean stage character is being reduced from the dimensions of group life and colossal personifications to individuality like that of men and women, but still ideally great.

In the drama of Euripides this double process of individualising character and subordinating the chorus to the dialogue reaches its farthest tragic development, and most clearly reflects the altered conditions of social life at Athens. Aristophanes, in his *Frogs*, notes this

imperfect index to the impersonal action it contains. To judge this impersonal element fairly we should not only add to the chorus the lines attributed to Κράτος, but should decide how far Io, Okeanus, and even Prometheus himself are personages at all; for in this highly abstract play personality, as might be expected, is deficient.

P

prominence of dialogue at the expense of the choral songs. "Let some one bring me a lyre," says Æschylus in his contest with Euripides; "and yet what occasion for a lyre against him? Where is she that rattles with the castanets? Come hither, Muse of Euripides, to whose accompaniment these songs are adapted for singing." Not mediating between opposing parties (save to some extent in the *Medea*), as the chorus of Sophocles had fulfilled its dramatic function, much less dominating the entire drama as in Æschylus, the chorus of Euripides is often an inferior actor, the confidant of the protagonist, while its odes are frequently " arbitrarily inserted (*embolima*) as a lyrical and musical interlude between the acts without any reference to the subject of the play, much in the same way as these pauses are nowadays filled up with instrumental music *ad libitum*." Of the nineteen extant tragedies of Euripides, five indeed derive their names from the chorus—the *Hérakleidæ, Suppliants, Trojan Women, Bacchæ,* and *Phœnissæ ;* but we need only compare the proportion of each of these dramas assigned to the chorus with the proportion so assigned in the *Suppliants* of Æschylus to realise the complete subordination into which the central figure of the old drama has fallen. In the *Suppliants* of Æschylus, as we have already observed, considerably more than one-half of the entire play is assigned to the chorus ; in the *Hérakleidæ* of Euripides less than one-fifth of the play is so assigned ; in his *Suppliants* and *Trojan Women* about one-fifth is so assigned ; in his *Bacchæ* about one-fourth belongs to the chorus, and in his *Phœnissæ* little more than one-sixth.

This subordination of the chorus to the dialogue in Euripides is accompanied by the withdrawal of the ethical pivot of the old drama. None of the extant plays of Euripides makes the clan ethic its real centre of interest.

The religious horrors of inherited guilt are supplanted by subtle analyses of personal character, and the rhetoric of the contemporary law-court and assembly are now much more effective than the moral preaching of early tragedy. On the stage of Euripides everything of real interest is individual, nothing impersonal; the chorus has here survived into conditions of action and thought in which it is out of place, and the stereotyped practice of taking the *dramatis personæ* from the old mythical heroes of Hellas is now a lumbering impediment to a tragedian who had little in common with old Greek morality or heroism. The chorus of Æschylus, says Euripides, in the *Frogs*, "used to hurl four series of songs one after another without ceasing, while the few characters he used were silent." The "son of the market-place," the "gossip-gleaner," prays to his "own peculiar gods"— "O Air and thou well-hung tongue and sagacity and sharp-smelling nostrils, may I rightly refute whatever arguments I assail!"—but Æschylus claims to have fulfilled the true poetic function ("to make the people in the cities better") by composing a drama "full of martial spirit" (the *Seven against Thebes*)—"every man that saw it would long to be a warrior"—while Euripides had been teaching men "to practise loquacity and wordiness." Such had been the progress of the Athenian drama—from the moral and religious spectacle, with its central group of worshippers, to an æsthetic exhibition of personal character; and now the conservative comedian was revolting from the new drama of art to the old drama of moral teaching—an Athenian victory for the Chinese ideal of the theatre.

§ 56. But, in truth, Aristophanes' dramas reflect the individualism of contemporary Athens, the characteristics of the men and women who subjected the old traditional morality of Athens to the dissolvent of all creeds—individual reason—almost as clearly as any dramas of Euripides. The conservative comedian saw farther than the tragic sophist, but his penetrating sight was sharpened by the same conscious contrast of things old and new in which Euripides found the pleasures of purely negative thought. The secret of Aristophanes—by far the most astonishing figure in the whole crowd of Athenian poets and philosophers and orators, a man whose poetry, exquisite in spite of being perpetually draggled through the mire, is full of profound reflection in spite of its uproarious wit—the secret of this solemn jester, this conservative revolutionist, this religious atheist, this communistic defender of Attic aristocracy, is also the secret of Euripides. The time-spirit of individualism is in each; but the one accepts it as a blessing because he sees only the freedom of negative thinking, the other scorns and derides and hates it because his eagle glance foresees the destruction of old Athenian sympathies it must effect. But Aristophanes just as little as Euripides can live out of or above the new conditions of Athenian thought and action; he is a citizen not of his own Cuckoo-town, but of Athens with all its limitations of space and time.

It is, in fact, through the Aristophanic comedy that the Attic drama from Euripides onwards accompanies the development of social life at Athens. Tragedy had now run its course, and in the hands of men who disbelieved the myths and customary morals upon which it had been founded must have tended more and more to run into burlesque. In the lyrical tragedies of the æsthete Agathon; in the dramas in which Critias and Dionysius, tyrant of Syracuse, aired their speculations on political and social topics; in the plays of Chæremon, whose

Centaur seems to have been "a compound of epic, lyric, and dramatic poetry,"* and who is called by Aristotle "a *poet to be read,*" we may trace the gradual extinction of Attic tragedy. The glorious odes of the tragic chorus seem to have died away into descriptive and rhetorical writing intended rather for the scholar's eye than the public ear; and this stage-oratory belongs rather to the development of Attic prose than to that of Attic verse. The rapid decline of tragedy is, in fact, due to the decay of those moral characteristics of the Athenian audience which had primarily given to tragedy its vital force. Even dramatic studies of personal character gradually lost their interest when divorced from social sympathy and great moral problems; and soon little remained but a spectacular medley enlivened by descriptions of female beauty, or natural scenery, or by rhetorical declamation of a thoroughly metallic ring. The majestic spirit of tragedy departed at the touch of an individualism which could only laugh at its own littleness.

Both the processes we have already observed in the development of the tragic drama—the subordination of the chorus and the reduction of abstract and heroic to human and individual character—are repeated in the progress of Attic comedy; to this progress we shall accordingly now turn. The comedy like the tragedy of Athens had originated in the choral worship of Bacchus; but the development of the comic chorus seems to have been checked by the tyranny of Peisistratus. We know little or nothing of the earliest Attic comedians. Susarion, who probably flourished in Solon's time, before Thespis; and Chionides, who is reckoned by Aristotle the first of Attic comedians; even Cratinus, who died so late as 423 B.C., and Eupolis, who began to bring out

* K. O. Müller, *Hist. Gk. Lit.* (Donaldson's translation), vol. i. p. 509.

comedies as late as 429 B.C., are for us little more than names. We cannot, therefore, recover any such graduated change in the chorus and characters of comedy as the tragedies of Æschylus, Sophocles, and Euripides enable us to observe. Still, the eleven extant comedies of Aristophanes compared with fragments of later comedians and the Latin imitations of the "New Comedy" made by Plautus and Terence, enable us to watch a part of the development of comedy at Athens, a part which the better-known development of tragedy aids us in understanding. As in tragedy, the comic stage represented an open space in the background of which were public and private buildings; as in tragedy, the number of the comic actors is limited to three, and masks and gay costumes, such as would have been used in the old choral carnival of Bacchus, are worn. The chorus, indeed, is almost as prominent in the earlier dramas of Aristophanes as in Æschylus, and the *parabasis*, or address of the chorus to the audience in the middle of the comedy, whether it was the nucleus of the comic drama or an afterthought, at least marks the chorus as the central figure. Out of the eleven extant comedies of Aristophanes six [*] are named after the chorus; and though the *Thesmophoriazousæ* and *Ecclesiazousæ* do not necessarily take their names from their choruses of women, they also seem to look to the chorus as the centre of the piece. No extant play of Aristophanes, not even the *Plutus*, which approaches so closely to the later comedy in its want of political allusions, is without a chorus; but the new comedy of Menander and Philemon, which, by borrowing its characters and incidents from contemporary

---

[*] The *Acharnians*, the *Knights*, the *Clouds*, the *Wasps*, the *Birds*, the *Frogs*. Among non-extant dramas of Aristophanes called after the chorus we may name the *Babylonians* and the *Feasters* (*Dætaleis*).

Athenian life, completed the humanising process begun by Euripides in tragedy, gave up the choral form altogether; and even the Middle Comedy, which preceded the New, according to a remark of Platonius "had no *parabasis* because there was no chorus."

This disappearance of the chorus in comedy may, no doubt, have been hastened by the inability of the State or the wealthier citizens to meet the choral expenses in the days of Athenian decline; but that the impoverishment of Athens is in itself no sufficient explanation of the disappearance of the chorus, is clear from the fact that in the age when comedy and tragedy began and were developed in their choral forms Athens was a far poorer city than in the days of the Middle and New Comedy. The rise and fall of the choral form in comedy as well as in tragedy are to be explained by causes more deeply connected with average Athenian character than the presence or absence of wealth; and one notable feature of the old comedy serves as a guide-post to such causes. This feature is the constant use of allegorical and abstract personages throughout the Aristophanic comedy; and we shall now illustrate this usage at some length.

§ 57. In the earliest play of Aristophanes, the *Dætaleis*,[*] or *Feasters*, so called after its chorus, "the chorus were conceived as a company of revellers who had banqueted in a temple of Hercules (in whose worship eating and drinking bore a prominent part), and were engaged in witnessing a contest between the old frugal and modest system of education and the frivolous and talkative education of modern times, in the persons of two young men, *Temperate* (σώφρων) and *Profligate* (καταπύγων). Brother *Profligate* was represented, in a dialogue between him and his aged father, as a despiser

[*] Performed in B.C. 427, but no longer extant.

of Homer, as accurately acquainted with legal expressions (in order, of course, to employ them in pettifogging quibbles), and as a zealous partisan of the sophist Thrasymachus, and of Alcibiades, the leader of the frivolous youth of the day."* Passing from this earliest but non-extant comedy of Aristophanes to the extant *Plutus*, which came out nearly forty years later (388 B.C.), and was "the last piece which the aged poet brought forward himself," we are again met by allegory and allegorical personages—Plutus, the god of wealth, Just Man, Poverty. The intervening plays of Aristophanes are full of similar personages—Dêmus (People), the old citizen of Athens, in whom the Athenians are personified in the *Knights*; Just Argument (Logos) and Unjust Argument, in the *Clouds*, reminding us of such "characters" as Heresy and Understanding in Calderon's *Divine Philothea*; War and Tumult in the *Peace*, itself the name of another allegorical personage. Indeed, as any careful reader of Aristophanes must have observed, many of his apparently real personages dissolve into groups and general types the moment we examine them: such are Dicæopolis in the *Acharnians* and Trygæus in the *Peace*, representatives of the Athenian peace-party; Lysistrata, a female representative of the same party, in the *Lysistrata*; and Praxagora, the female exponent of women's rights in the *Ecclesiazousæ*. In these and other examples Aristophanic personages turn out, on closer inspection, not to be individuals at all, but only types of a certain class or group. In fact, to such a degree does this class character prevail in Aristophanes' plays, that even living persons do not seem to be introduced simply as *persons*, but as types of philosophic, poetical, or political thought. Thus the name of Socrates is used in the *Clouds* rather as

* K. O. Müller, *Hist. Gk. Lit.*, vol. ii. p. 21.

a class-name for the sophists in general than as the proper name of the famous ethical philosopher, with whom Aristophanes would seem to have been on very friendly terms; and though Euripides and Cleon are certainly hit at as persons, no one can read the passages in which they are introduced without observing that they are also general names, the former for the sophistic corrupters of what Aristophanes regarded as the best morals and æsthetic taste of Athens, the latter for the demagogues who at once flattered and enslaved the populace.

In the dearth of extant Athenian comedies it is, of course, impossible to feel certain that this use of abstract and allegorical personages is derived from the earliest practice of the comic stage. But when it is remembered that early Athenian tragedy discloses the same impersonal tendency alike in its characters and its ethical principles, when it is farther remembered that the group-nature of the chorus in comedy as in tragedy easily lends itself to impersonal and allegorical uses,* and when the weakness of personality is found to be one of the most striking points of likeness in all early communities, it may be regarded as highly probable that this characteristic of the old comedy is to be taken as a survival from the early social conditions of Attica through the earliest forms of the comic spectacle. Moreover, there is a special reason for this survival having become in time the peculiar property of the *comic* drama. In tragedy, so long as Athenian average character was rather social than individual, character-types were as free from the grotesque as Justice, Mercy, or any other abstract personages of the medieval morality-play. But just as the development

---

* The chorus of the *Clouds* and that of the *Wasps* will sufficiently illustrate such usage on the comic stage.

of individualism in England produced the thoroughly individualised drama of Marlowe, Shakspere, and their followers; just as its inferior development in Spain allowed the allegorical personages of Calderon's *autos sacramentales** to retain their intense interest for a Catholic audience; so its rapid development in Athens made mere types of character more and more grotesque, and less and less in keeping with serious thought. In this way, far more than through any sense of restriction, the habit of taking dramatic personages from the early Greek myths aided the fall of Attic tragedy; for though, as has been often observed, the tragedians were by no means tied down to any one view of a mythical character, their use of these types must have strongly militated against the seriousness of tragedy as soon as individualism of character came to be expected by the audience. Comedy, accordingly, after a time stepped into the shoes of tragedy, and applied to its own purposes the worn-out properties of the tragic stage. But the farther progress of Athenian individualism (much like the same progress in modern Europe) failed to find even a comic interest in typical and allegorical personages at all to be compared with the ridiculous little units of everyday life, and so the new comedians made their own kith and kin the puppets of their stage.†

* Thus in *Belshazzar's Feast* the *dramatis personæ* are the King Belshazzar, Daniel, Idolatry, Vanity, and a curious personage, called "The Thought," who in the first scene enters, dressed in a coat of many colours, as the fool. Among the *dramatis personæ* of the *Divine Philothea* are Sight, Hearing, Paganism, Judaism. See Denis Florence M'Carthy's translations of these *autos sacramentales*.

† Bearing in mind the historical development of the dramatic chorus at Athens as given above, we cannot but regard certain imitations of the classic form in modern times as singularly incongruous. The introduction of the Athenian chorus among the Hebrews in such plays as Racine's *Athalie* or Milton's *Samson Agonistes* is like writing Hebrew ideas for an English or French audience in Greek words. Yet the presence of the Athenian chorus and stock characters (the Κῆρυξ and Messenger, in *Samson*

§ 58. Thus the social development of Athens is reflected with peculiar accuracy in her dramatic—a development from the life of the group to that of the individual, from the ethics of the clan to personal responsibility, from a spectacle in which groups of men and women, or impersonal abstractions, or heroic types predominate to a drama of character in which persons borrowed from contemporary life humanise the stage. In Rome the development of individualism was a slower and more confused process; yet even here, in spite of Greek imitation and patrician culture, we may find in the progress of the drama some marks of social evolution. For in Rome, as in Athens, the rude forms of the early drama foreshadowed a *popular* literature; and, had her political and social factions amalgamated before her acquaintance with Greek civilisation, a truly Roman drama might have been produced. Plainly the old ritual of Rome, as in the hymn of the Fratres Arvales previously translated, contained, like some of the Vedic hymns, the germs of a dramatic spectacle. Responsive songs, too, like the Fescennine and the triumphal, would aid this dramatic tendency; and the absence of epic or lyric (personal) poetry would allow greater room for a drama of some kind. Professor Teuffel, indeed, tells us that "the Romans possessed a tendency to preserve and cherish the recollection of past events, and, as they perceived that metre facilitated both recollection and

Agonistes) among Hebrew associations never seems to strike critics as out of place, though if the Vidúshaka, or Buffoon of the Indian drama, had been transferred to Athens that incongruity would scarcely have been so great as this. But, in truth, the confusion of Hebrew and Greek with modern thought has done much, not only to close our eyes to such incongruities, but to stop the progress of that historical consciousness which cannot exist so long as such confusion is not felt. Of course such imitations of the Athenian drama as the *Atalanta in Calydon* or the *Erechtheus* are free from this charge of incongruity; for they represent the use of the Greek form within the legitimate range of the Greek spirit.

tradition, we find here a field favourable to the development of epic poetry."* But peoples who have never developed an epic (the Chinese, for example) have possessed in a high degree this "tendency to cherish the recollection of past events," and the value of metre as a support for the memory has been recognised all the world over. It would be as absurd to suppose that the fables of a Lokman should suffice to create a drama (as Voltaire seems to have supposed in his introductory letter to *L'Orphelin de la Chine*) as to think that the use of metre and a desire to chronicle the past suffice to create "a field favourable to the development of epic poetry." The form and spirit of poetry depend to a large extent upon social life; and, as already observed, Niebuhr's theory of an early ballad-poetry (with which the imaginary epic of early Rome has been closely connected) strangely overlooks this dependence. The life of the city commonwealth is not favourable to the growth of epic poetry; for the heroes of the epic are always exalted above the level of human character, always hostile to the democratic sentiments of the city. Moreover, the city life of Rome was peculiarly opposed to the individualised spirit of epic poetry; for the communal organisation of the *gentes* checked the rise of any literary forms in which personal character would predominate. We shall, therefore, believe that Roman poetry, if left to itself, would have assumed neither the epic nor the lyric, but the dramatic form.

The nature of the early Roman drama, so far as we can now recover it by the aid of a few scattered references, was exactly such as the social conditions of early Rome would lead us to anticipate. This drama (if we may so call it) was a comic spectacle in which personal character

* *Hist. Lat. Lit.* (Wagner's translation), vol. i. p. 27.

had little or no place. Thus the Atellane plays (so called from Atella, a small town in Campania) admirably suited the unindividualised life of early Rome, for their principal personages were not "characters" in the modern artistic sense, but fixed types. Such are Maccus, Pappus, Bucco, Dossenus, and the peculiarly Roman Mania, Lamia, Pytho, Manducus. Maccus, for example, is a stupid glutton wearing ass's ears; Pappus, a vain old man constantly cheated by his wife and son; Dossenus, a cunning sharper. These typical personages remind us of the Cain * or the " Vice with his dagger of lath" in our old morality plays, and like them belong to an age in which personality was weakly realised. It is to be remembered that the diction of the Atellane plays, like that of the Mimes, was plebeian —an index to the popular character of these rude dramatic spectacles.

But the plebeians were not destined to be the makers of Roman comedy, much less of Roman literature in general, nor were such types as Maccus and Pappus to be individualised by the internal evolution of Roman society. The increase of Roman wealth and consequent pressure of strangers to Rome from the era of the First Punic War reproduced, but within a relatively narrower circle, the effects of the great Persian War on Athenian mind; and among the earliest of these effects was the discovery of Rome's literary nakedness compared with the intellectual riches of Greece. How to convey some of this intellectual wealth to Rome and there give it currency became the literary problem of the day; and

* Shakspere's expression, "Cain-coloured beard" (*Merry Wives*, I. iv.), referring to the red hair worn by this stock personage of the morality-plays, reminds us of the custom on the Roman stage for old men to appear in white wigs (*e.g.* "Periplecomenus *albicapillus*," in the *Miles Gloriosus*) and slaves in red (*e.g.* "Si quis me quæret *rufus*," in the *Phormio*)—a custom probably derived from the typical dresses of the stock personages in the old comedy of Rome.

at first the work of borrowing was attempted under a Roman dress and apparently in the hope of attracting all sorts and conditions of Roman society. Livius Andronicus, a Greek slave brought from Tarentum to Rome in 275 B.C., represented his first play in 240 B.C. The Livian play would seem to have been a rude performance, containing but a slight advance from pantomimic dancing towards personal dialogue; for, as Mr. Simcox observes, Livius "originated the curious division of labour whereby one actor, commonly himself, danced and acted while another, whom the audience were not supposed to see, sang the words which he would have sung himself if the exertion of singing and dancing at once had not been too overwhelming. Such a device implies that the public came for the spectacle, and held the pantomime more important than the song; so it is not strange that the plays of Livius Andronicus should have been very meagre, and that the dialogue should have been very little above stage directions, just serving to explain to the audience what was going on."* But Livius was something more than a pantomimic dancer; his translation of the *Odyssey* into Saturnian verse shows that he was attempting to *popularise* Greek culture at Rome by exhibiting the Greek Muses in the coarse garb of the Italian Camenæ. In this bold attempt to assimilate

---

* Even these performances of Livius, however, would seem to have been a considerable improvement on the older spectacles. Among these, the *Saturæ* appear to have been performances of the country clowns of Latium, in which separate songs or comic stories were sung or recited, with gesticulation and dancing, to the accompaniment of a *tibia;* their subjects were more varied than those of the *Fescenninæ*. The Mimes were performed by one principal actor; while in the *Atellanæ* "only the general plot was arranged, the rest being left to improvisation." The form of the *Atellanæ* "may be presumed to have been in most cases a simple dialogue, songs in Saturnian metre being perhaps interspersed; the jokes were coarse, accompanied by lively gesticulation which was also obscene." See Teuffel's *Hist. Lat. Lit.*

the Greek to the Roman spirit rather than the Roman to the Greek, Nævius, whom Plautus, in the *Miles Gloriosus*, calls an "*un-Greek* poet," followed the example of Livius. A native of Campania, the home of the *Atellanæ*, Nævius brought out his first play at Rome in 235 B.C.; and, though his works were mainly comic translations from the Greek, his desire to *Romanise* Greek culture will be seen not only from his introduction of the *prætexta*, or drama based on Roman history, two specimens of which (*Clastidium* and *Romulus*) are known to us by name, but also from his celebrated epic on the First Punic War, written in Saturnian verse.

§ 59. But this effort to Romanise the Greek spirit was necessarily a failure. Greek literature in general, and the drama in particular, had long been the expression of an intensely individualised life; and in the comedies of Philemon, Menander, Diphilus, subtle analyses of personal character had banished the heroic types of the old Athenian stage, while the display of personal motives exactly reflected a state of society in which the ephemeral life of the individual had swallowed up all thoughts of common destiny. The development of legal status at Rome (so far as we can now recover it) proves, indeed, that the *gentile* and family life of the patricians had advanced some way towards individualism before Greek thought acquired any considerable influence at Rome. But this slow progress was now to be expedited by contact with a spirit centuries its senior in evolution. Not only, therefore, was it impossible to bring down the Greek spirit to the level of the Roman, as Livius and Nævius had hoped to do, but only Romans whose social and political eminence allowed them wider and deeper experiences than most of their fellow-citizens could appreciate the new modes of thought so unlike those of their native city. Hence it was to be expected from the first that the development of literature would fall into the hands of the upper classes as soon as Greek influences acquired their certain mastery at Rome. It was also to be expected that the drama—a form of literature which loses its vitality in proportion as it becomes the property of a class—would undergo some strange transformation in passing from its Roman cradle into the adult life of the New Comedy. Since this transformation, so far as the present writer is acquainted, is unparalleled * in the literary history of the world, and illustrates the progressive individualisation of Roman life, we shall discuss its nature at some length.

The great difficulties which Livius and Nævius had experienced in their attempts to Romanise the Greek drama had been the rude form and spirit of Roman literature in its "barbarous" state. The Saturnian measure was altogether inadequate to translate the Greek metres. Character-types, like Manducus, were altogether inadequate to express Greek personality. Were Greek metres, Greek characters, Greek ideas of place and time, to be transferred *en masse* from Athens to Rome? And, if all this had to be done, how were Roman associations to be kept from intruding when the language used was to be Latin and not Greek? These were the problems which Plautus faced and Terence solved; and it is because the plays of the former represent the transition from the Roman to the Greek

* The Japanese drama is by some supposed to have been borrowed from the Chinese; but, even granting the truth of this supposition, these Eastern dramas are not sufficiently developed, and do not reflect states of society sufficiently developed, to be compared with the dramatic relations of Rome and Greece. And if the influence of the French drama on the Russian be cited as a parallel, we must remember that this influence of the French has been modified by that of the English and German dramas.

associations that they are especially interesting to the scientific student of literature.

To touch upon the Plautine metre first, as the formal mark of this transition, all students of Plautus know that the main reason why his scansion is so difficult to ears accustomed to Vergilian and Horatian metres, is that in his plays the old accentual scansion, on which the Saturnian measure was based, modifies and occasionally overrides the Greek scansion by quantity; just as the mixture of accentual and syllabic scansion in Chaucer would seem to mark the junction of Saxon and Norman literatures. But the spirit of the Plautine comedy is even more distinctly transitional than the form. In the prologue to the *Casina* the difficulty of depicting the manners of a foreign country in such a way as to retain truth yet interest the spectators is clearly illustrated. Two slaves of the same household are seeking in marriage their fellow-slave; but, the marriage of slaves being unknown to the Romans, the difficulty must be explained. "I suppose," says the speaker of the prologue, "that some present are now talking thus among themselves: 'Faith, what's this now? Slaves' marriage? Would slaves be marrying or asking a wife for themselves? They've introduced a new thing that happens nowhere in the world.' (Novum áttulerunt quód fit nusquam géntium.) But I assert that this is done in Greece and Carthage, and here, too, in our own country in Apulia; in these places slaves' marriages are usually looked after even more carefully than those of freemen."*

---

* Professor Tyrrell, in the introduction to his excellent edition of the *Miles Gloriosus*, observes with truth that the Plautine prologues are, as a rule, spurious, containing sometimes (as in those of the *Casina, Asinaria, Menæchmi, Pseudolus*) references to Plautus of a kind which would seem to imply that he was no longer living. But, though the prologue of the *Casina* may not have been written by Plautus, the introduction of manners

Truthfulness to time and place and social character must have been forced upon the Roman playwright by this constant necessity of realising his *dramatis personæ* in the midst of conditions different from those of the audience to which they spoke. Thus, the use of the Phœnician language by Hanno in the *Pœnulus* is to be partially explained by this constant contrast which must have produced the desire of realism on a minute scale. In the Indian drama a like effect was produced by similar causes, viz. the use of different languages or dialects by the *dramatis personæ*, and the introduction of personages in character and language very different from the educated Bráhman. Just as the Plautine comedy—as is proved not only by its Greek names, characters, places, but also by its Greek phrases, words, puns—is addressed to an audience thoroughly familiar with Greek language and life, and by its nature puts the playwright on his guard against untruthful descriptions, so the Indian drama, being addressed, as is expressly stated in the prelude to *Málatí and Mádhava*, to the Bráhmans, aimed at exact truth of language and character beyond the circle of the sacred caste. Technical Indian writers on the drama, clearly expressing the influences of caste in their conceptions of dramatic propriety, note with care the exact kind of sentiments proper to each character— a propriety which plainly reduces character to what in the East it has commonly been, a type. In Plautus we have also types, side by side with real characters such as *Tyndarus* in the *Captivi;* for not only are the leno, meretrix, coquus, sycophanta, parasite, stock characters, but we have such allegorical personages as the Lar in

in the play out of keeping with social life in Rome is not affected, and the need of an apology for such an introduction, whether it was felt by the author himself or by some later producers of the play, is likewise not affected.

the *Aulularia*, Auxilium in the *Cistellaria*, Arcturus in the *Rudens*, Luxuria and Inopia in the *Trinumus*. As we shall find elsewhere, the Indian rules both on propriety of typical characters and on propriety of language altogether surpass anything Plautine comedy could enable us to conceive; and, no doubt, this Indian realism of language and character is due to causes some of which are peculiar to India—the sacred classical tongue, the great variety of dialects, the presence of caste. Still the Indian drama will aid us in realising the conditions under which Plautus wrote. For just as in the Indian drama character is more typical than personal in our European sense, so in that state of Roman society in which the patrician *gentes* and *familiæ* supplied as perfect a substitute for the Indian's castes as European history can offer, we can easily see why Plautus should have preferred types to persons whenever they would suit his Greek stage; and just as realism of language and character forced itself on Indian critics from the sharply contrasted social conditions which the dramatists sought to personify on the stage, so the perpetual contrast of Greek manners and ideas with the Roman language he employed made the Roman dramatist, at least in the *Pœnulus*, more truthful to language than dramatic art permits.

Plautus, however, is by no means quite at home in the expression of Greek thought and action through the words and phrases of Rome's language. Technical phrases of Roman law meet us sometimes in his Athenian scenes, and remind us that we are really near the *Forum*, not the Ekklêsia. But the plays of Terence, with their smooth diction and thoroughly Greek associations, show the transition from the Romano-Greek to the purely Greek spirit to be a *fait accompli*. The efforts of Livius, Nævius, and to some degree even Plautus, had failed;

the Greek drama had not been and could not have been Romanised either in form or spirit. In the hands of Terence, comedy became the expression of a polished class of Græcised Romans and gave up the attempt to be popular; at the same time, it made a quiet protest against patrician exclusiveness and the old strictness of the Roman *familia* by bringing the freedom of the Greek citizen directly before the eyes of the class whose wealth and power made them the patrons of literature.

It has been said with truth that "all the plays of Terence are written with a purpose; and this purpose is the same which animated the political leaders of free thought." When it is remembered that the aim of Terence was "to base conduct upon reason rather than tradition, and paternal authority upon kindness rather than fear," we may find a distinct reason for the repetition of certain characters in his plays. If his characters may be easily classified (as Terence himself in the prologue to the *Eunuchus* classifies them), if they look not so much like individuals as types of social and domestic relationships, these features are to be attributed to the influence of family life at Rome, and Terence's desire to remind his audience of family relations incomparably less servile than those which turned on the *patria potestas*. A Carthaginian by birth, Terence published his first play, the *Andria*, in 166 B.C., and his last, the *Adelphœ*, in 160 B.C. The six comedies which represent this short dramatic career enable us to note various important changes in the tone of Roman culture. In his metres, language, and careful exclusion of Roman associations of place, time, incident, Terence breathes the spirit of the Græcised Roman, while Plautus, in spite of Greek metres and associations, has still something of the Romanised Greek about him. The literary refinement of Terence's language, which made his comedies even more influential as works to be read than as plays to be acted, his prologues dealing critically with the form or spirit of the drama, the absence of burlesque in his characters, and even the very names of his *dramatis personæ*,* show that we have left the popular spectacle and entered the refined theatre of an educated class.

§ 60. But in these thoroughly Greek associations of the Terentian stage we may close our brief review of the progress of dramatic art in Rome. Terence, the slave from Carthage, drawing exact pictures of Greek life in the language of Rome for the edification of an audience which thinks Greek, transforms the drama into as curious a literary exotic as can be easily conceived. If such was the end of Rome's rude native comedy, in tragedy the Romans were from the first dependent on the Greeks. Without common mythology, without bonds of common religion, the divided city of plebeian and patrician could feel none of the public sentiments out of which tragedy arose at Athens. If a tragedy based

* Many names of the Plautine characters explain themselves—such are Artotrogus, "Breadeater," the parasite in *Miles Gloriosus*; Polymachæroplagides, "Macmanyswordblows," the boastful soldier in *Pseudolus*; Anthrax, "Coalman," the cook in *Aulularia*. In Terence, on the contrary, the same name, "Chremes," for example, is used for totally different characters, and of course without any meaning being conveyed by the name. The dramatic use of names intended to convey their own meaning is, in fact, a sign that character-drawing is subordinated to types; hence the constant use of such names in Aristophanes. In Mr. Ruskin's extravagant attempt to find meanings in Shakspere's dramatic names—Desdemona, δυσδαιμονία, "miserable fortune," Hamlet, "homely," Iago, "the supplanter," and so on—we have much more than a "note of provinciality in the highest excess," as Mr. Matthew Arnold has said; we have in it a complete failure to grasp the difference between characterisation through the medium of types and characterisation through the medium of individual personality, the latter and not the former being the essential feature of Shaksperian art. The characters in the *Canterbury Tales* are indeed types of social life in the England of Chaucer; but in the England of Shakspere and on the Shaksperian stage men and women possess an individuality impossible in the days of medieval guilds and serfage.

on the ethics of clan life had been started in early Rome, it would have possessed nothing to interest and everything to repel the general body of the Roman populace; and such heroes as it exhibited must have summoned up recollections which no plebeian could have felt without shame and indignation. Common sympathies of religion, patriotism, social unity, being impossible, Rome had to borrow her tragedy from the Greeks, and for the service of that Greek spirit which was at once peculiarly attractive for the upper classes and the destroyer of their traditional thought. It was not the first or the last time that possessors of property became the disseminators of ideas fatal to their own ascendency; Athens had seen much of this social suicide, the Paris of the eighteenth century was to see much more of it. But patrician bonds of social duty and clan conceptions of sympathy and obligation were now out of keeping with the widened circle of Roman life, as much as the traditional morality of the Hebrew clans was out of keeping with ideas of personal responsibility in Ezekiel's age, as much as the traditional morality of primitive Athens was out of keeping with the expanded associations of the Periclean age. The discussion of Euripides whether men owe their character to inborn nature (φύσις) or education, the repudiation of inherited sin by Ezekiel, and a famous line of Terence's *Hautontimoroumenos*—"Homo sum; humani nihil a me alienum puto"—alike mark in their respective social groups the clash between an ethic of narrow sympathies and conditions of social life too wide and too complex to be ruled by the old morality.

The line of Terence just quoted may be treated as the text of a new gospel at Rome, a gospel for which legal relaxations of old patrician exclusiveness had previously opened a way. This gospel of *humanitas*,

expressed on the legal side by appeals to the Jus
Naturale (a fusion, as Sir Henry Maine has so well
explained, of the old *Jus Gentium* of Rome with the
νόμος φύσεως of the Greek Stoics), was on the literary side
expressed by the scepticism of Ennius (209-169 B.C.),
Pacuvius (220-132 B.C.), and, in lesser degree, Accius
(170-94 B.C.). To these tragic poets Euripides supplied
the same recurring model as Menander had supplied to
the comedians. In their tragedies the strongly individualised spirit of Euripidean Athens was transferred
to the home of men under the lifelong sway of the
father's power, and women never freed from perpetual
tutelage. The friendship of Ennius and Scipio Africanus
symbolises the union of this individualised literature
with the growth of personal independence from all
restraints of *gens* or *familia*; and Ennius' translation
of Euêmerus (the rationaliser of the Greek myths) expresses almost as clearly as his denial of a guiding
providence in human affairs that purely personal conception of destiny which is fatal to every kind of social
creed. " But superstitious seers and brazen-faced soothsayers," says Ennius in one of his plays,* "lazy or mad,
or forced by poverty, men who cannot see the path for
themselves, point out the way for others, and ask a
drachma from those to whom they promise wealth." In
another fragment of the play which contains this vigorous
attack on the seers and soothsayers of the old Roman
religion, Ennius speaks thus: "A race of gods there
is, I said, and always shall declare, but I think they care
not what the human race is doing; for, if they cared,
the good should get the good things and the evil bad,
which is not so." Evidently communal morality and
slavery proved in Rome as fatal to the future life as

* The *Telamo*.

a sanction for personal conduct as they had proved in Athens. Pacuvius, in the same spirit as Ennius, finds the ruler of human life to be Temeritas or Chance; and if Accius, who lived late enough for Cicero to converse with him, displayed some tenderness for the old superstitions of Rome, this apparent relapse was probably due to the discovery that the nihilism of Greek thought could find intellectual weapons at least as readily for the communism of a Gracchus as for the literary taste of a Scipio.

Thus, in spite of its imitative character, the drama of Rome derives its true interest from Rome's social life, and reflects the evolution of that life in a manner not to be mistaken. No greater dramatic contrast can be well conceived than that between a play of Euripides or Pacuvius, full of personal destiny and veiled or open disbelief in the gods and common creed, and the Indian drama, which in its very form (as in the benediction with which it opens) bears witness to the overwhelming influence of religious and caste ideas. Yet the starting-points of the Athenian and Roman dramas, especially the former, are by no means far removed from those of the Indian. What makes the dramas of Athens and Rome, however, so much more interesting than any of the Eastern world is the social evolution which underlies their progress. In the comparatively stationary life of India or China, there was little scope for such evolution or its dramatic influences; but in the narrow range of the Aryan city commonwealth we have an opportunity for watching dramatic variations of form and spirit closely in accordance with the development of a social life not too wide to be confusing, and not so rapid in its changes as to obscure the relations of cause and effect.

BOOK IV.
WORLD-LITERATURE.

CHAPTER I.

WHAT IS WORLD-LITERATURE?

§ 61. THE fundamental facts in literary evolution are the extent of the social group and the characters of the individual units of which it is composed. So long as social and individual life moves within the narrow associations of the clan, or of the city commonwealth, the ideal range of human sympathy is proportionately restricted. It is true that the clan life of the Hebrews supplied in its *Berith* or League, in its communal associations of property and descent, the central conceptions of a national ideal. It is true that the city of the Greeks supplied the ideal of Greek centralism as of Greek local patriotism. But before the larger destinies of humanity as a whole could come home to either Hebrew or Greek minds, the associations of the clan and the city commonwealth alike required to be widened by enlarged spheres of social action. This expansion among tribal communities like the Hebrews and Arabs leads to religious cosmopolitanism, to an ideal of human unity deeply social in its character, and strictly confined within the circle of a common creed. A similar expansion in municipal communities like Athens and Rome leads to political cosmopolitanism, to an ideal of human unity within a circle of common culture whose peace is secured by centralised force and whose character is intensely individual. Between the world-religions of Israel and Islâm and the world-cultures of Alexandria and Rome there are, no doubt, very wide differences. Yet, though the former reach universality through social bonds of creed and the latter reach universality through the unsocial idea of personal culture, the outcome of both is to rise above old restrictions of place and time, and to render possible a literature which, whether based on Moses or Homer, may best be termed a " world-literature."

What, then, is world-literature ? What are the marks by which it may be known ? What is its proper place in the evolution of literature ?

The leading mark of world-literature has been already stated ; it is the severance of literature from defined social groups—the universalising of literature, if we may use such an expression. Such a process may be observed in the Alexandrian and Roman, the later Hebrew and Arab, the Indian and Chinese, literatures ; and this universalism, though differing profoundly in its Eastern and Western conceptions of personality, is alike in the East and West accompanied by the imitation of literary work wrought out in days when the current of social life was broken up into many narrow channels foaming down uplands of rock and tree. Closely connected with this imitation of early models is the reflective and critical spirit, which is another striking characteristic of world-literature. Language now becomes the primary study of the literary artist, and the causes of his devotion to words are not difficult to discover. Just as the language of Hebrew life, in its struggle with Northern and Southern invasion, and in its own internal break-up, underwent a gradual change which necessitated the production of Targûms, or Paraphrases of the Law, Prophets, and Writings, and thus led to a scrupulously exact study of the sacred texts; just as the Sanskrit, in the course of likewise becoming a dead language, roused that spirit of grammatical criticism for which India from early times has been famous; so among Greeks, Romans, and Arabs deterioration in language was met by the rise of verbal criticism. The triumph of Islâm occasioned the corruption of Arabic by making it the official tongue of the conquered, and turned later Arab literature into a pedantic study of classical words which exactly reproduces the Alexandrian spirit. Magdâni, a contemporary of the famous Harîri, collected and explained Arab proverbs precisely in the manner of Suidas; and Harîri's *Makâmât*, in their forced display of erudition, deserve comparison with the Cassandra of Lycophron. This development of linguistic criticism, among the Arabs, as a consequence of their world-wide conquests, illustrates the need of Alexandrian criticism, when the conquests of Alexander had made the Greek a world-language and proportionately increased the danger of its being corrupted into barbarous jargons. The corruption of Arabic in foreign lands also illustrates the necessity which Roman writers experienced of setting up a refined standard of speech, opposed at once to plebeian coarseness and to provincial barbarism. The need and value of grammatical studies at Rome may be estimated by the deterioration of language which set in after the Augustan age. "In the first century of the Imperial period," says Professor Teuffel, "prose begins already to decay by being mixed with poetical diction, and becoming estranged from natural expression. The decay of accidence and syntax begins also about this time. Later on the plebeian element found admission; and when the influence of provincial writers, who were not guided by a native sense of the language, and who mixed up the diction and style of all periods, became prevalent in literature, the confusion became still greater." It can be easily understood how the classical language of India, likewise, in its conflict with a great variety of local dialects, came to depend more on the verbal criticism of grammarians than on that creative originality which in our days of national languages, stereotyped by the aid of printing and widely diffused education, is rightly accounted so much more valuable than the study of words.

But, besides the universal idea of humanity and the critical study of language as the medium of sacred books or models of literary art, there is a third characteristic of world-literature which to our modern European minds is perhaps the most interesting. This is the rise of new æsthetic appreciations of physical nature and its relations to man. Among the Hebrews and Arabs, it is true, we cannot observe this characteristic of world-literature so distinctly as elsewhere. For the Hebrews the idea of Yâhveh was so closely connected with physical conceptions—sunshine, storm, rain, lightning, thunder—that the sights and sounds of Nature were scarcely realisable save through the creator-god of his peculiar people. The Allâh of the Arabs is even a closer approach to that One Unhuman Power which modern science tends to reduce into an Impersonal Force; moreover, the Arabs, while, like the Hebrews, prevented from treating Nature as distinct from the Deity, found the proper subjects of their literature within the limits of the Qur'ân's language and ideas. But in India, China, Greece, and Italy it was otherwise. Indian poetry, for example, through the medium of its polytheistic religion, could deify physical nature without offending religious feelings. The myths of early Greece had been closely connected with physical nature; and, though the city commonwealth tended to humanise and rationalise these myths, they remained, even in the days of Greek world-literature, a treasure-house from which Theocritus, Moschus, and Bion could bring forth things new and old for those who were tired of the crowded and dusty thoroughfares of Alexandria. Italy, indeed, had no real mythology of her own, and the purely practical value attached to agricultural life by the old Romans was fatal to any poetical sentiment of Nature; yet in the world-empire of Rome also we find the poet turning away from man to physical nature, and, though the inspiration of Lucretius may smack too much of the *savant*, and that of Vergil too much of manuals *de re rusticâ*, we are justified in regarding the world-literature of Rome, like that of India or Greece, as a witness to the sentiment of Nature in man.

But here we must draw a distinction between some of the world-literatures known to history and others. No doubt the habit of realising humanity as a whole accustoms the mind to the contrast between man and physical nature, and sets it the difficult task of reconciling the claims of each; but the social conception of humanity is connected with physical nature in a different manner from the individual conception. Wherever the idea of personality as distinct from all social ties has been reached, the aspects of the physical world are and must be altered. Hence the great differences between the sentiment of Nature as manifested in the Græco-Latin literature of Alexandria and Rome, and the same sentiment as manifested in the literatures of India and China. In the latter no separate relation between each individual and the physical world is observed; all is social, and differences of human personality do not obtrude themselves between the world of Man and the world of Nature.

But in the former the isolated feelings of individuals, their personal loves, their personal pains and pleasures, are brought into constant contrast or comparison with Nature's life. The Western idyll is a "picture-poem" of dramatic and descriptive character curiously differing from such abstract, social, and impersonal poetry as India offers in abundance; and, whatever the origin of the idyll may have been, its essential features—dramatic perception of individual character and picturesque description of physical nature—show how differently the individualism of the West looks upon Nature, compared with the monotheistic social view of Hebrews and Arabs and the polytheistic social view of Indians and Chinese.*

But, though it may be readily admitted that in the history of the world there have been certain social stages sufficiently similar in the literature they produced and the conditions of their literary production to warrant our use of the word "world-literature," it may be said that our order of treatment—after the literatures of the city commonwealth and before those of the nation—is not in harmony with prevailing ideas of literary development. Why not pass, it may be asked, from the city commonwealth to the nation, and from national literatures reach the universalism of world-literature? No doubt much might be said for this arrangement if the philosophy of ancient Greece, if the language, law, and religion of ancient Rome, were not so closely intertwined with the growth of our European nationalities; if their social and political progress had not been so profoundly affected by the world-wide ideas of Roman

---

* M. Victor de Laprade (*Le Sentiment de la Nature chez les Modernes*, p. 216) notes the vastness and profundity of the Indian sentiment of Nature and contrasts it in these respects with the Greek. The source of the difference is plainly to be found in the individualism of Greek contrasted with the socialism of Indian life.

law and the Christian religion. But, since it is clearly impossible to treat of national progress in Europe without allowing great weight to these powerful influences, it would be highly inconvenient to pass from the city commonwealth to those national groups whose internal and external developments have owed so much to days of world-empire and world-literature. We shall, accordingly, examine the literary characteristics of the latter before we approach the national groups.

CHAPTER II.

THE INDIVIDUAL SPIRIT IN WORLD-LITERATURE.

§ 62. THE relations of imagination and reason to forms of social life present or suggest great problems which have never received a tithe of the attention they deserve. Although it is impossible to separate these two great faculties of the human mind, although at their extremities, so to speak, they fade into one another in a manner which seems, and perhaps must always be, inscrutable, yet to distinguish them in general outline, without attempting minute distinctions, is not impossible. Perhaps the essential features of imagination are two— the building up of generalisations and abstractions out of individual facts, and the transition from the individual self to the collective conception of humanity on a more or less extensive scale. Similarly, perhaps, the essential features of reason may be stated as the analysis of generalisations and abstractions into individual facts, and the transition from the social or collective conceptions of action and thought to the individual. If we accept some such view of imagination and reason, we shall be able to explain that decadence of imagination which Macaulay, in his essay on Dryden, elevates into a general law of literary progress. Macaulay failed to observe the dependence of imagination upon social sympathies, a dependence which Chateaubriand and Shelley have alike hinted, but without any attempt at logical explanation. When the author of the *Génie du Christianisme* maintains that the principal cause of the decadence of taste and genius is unbelief, he perhaps unwittingly lays his finger on a principle which may be illustrated far beyond the range of Christian influences. A common creed, whether it be that of Christianity or any other system, rests, and must rest, on the belief of men in their fellow-men, on the sympathy of man with man, on the extension of man's pains and pleasures beyond the narrow circle of his personal being, within which he may be a god or a "glorious devil," but never the possessor of a creed. Moreover, since any literature deserving of the name must address itself to a community of human hopes and fears however narrow, the disbelief of man in his neighbour, which cuts away all sympathies, also paralyses the workings of imagination in its efforts to pass from the individual to a wider and greater world. Shelley, in his *Defence of Poetry*, has expressed this truth in words worthy of quotation, especially as coming from the pen of one whose conception of Christianity, and indeed of all creeds, was so different from that of Chateaubriand. "A man, to be greatly good," says Shelley, "must imagine intensely and comprehensively; he must put himself in the place of another and of many others; the pains and pleasures of his species must become his own. The great instrument of moral good is the imagination. Poetry and the principle of self, of which money is the visible incarnation, are respectively the God and Mammon of the world. What were virtue, love, patriotism, friendship, what were the scenery of this beautiful world which we inhabit, what were our consolations on this side of the grave and what our aspirations beyond it, if poetry did not ascend to bring light and fire from those eternal regions where the owl-winged faculty of calculation dare not ever soar? . . . These and corresponding conditions of being are experienced principally by persons of the most delicate sensibility and the most enlarged imagination; and the state of mind produced by them is at war with every base desire. The enthusiasm of virtue, love, patriotism, and friendship is essentially linked with such emotions; and while they last self appears as what it is, an atom to a universe. The most unfailing herald, companion, and follower of the awakening of a great people to work a beneficial change in opinion or institution is poetry. At such periods there is an accumulation of the power of communicating and receiving intense and impassioned conceptions respecting man and nature."

The periods which followed the fall of Athens in Greece were eminently unfavourable to this unity of social feelings which forms the groundwork of imagination and poetry. The break-up of social ties and the substitution of action from self-interest had resulted from the decay of old Athenian morality at the touch of associations far wider than early Athens had ever known; and now, when her political power was reduced, expansion of social and political ideas as a matter of theory continued. In three different directions the improvement of prose, the proper vehicle of philosophic individualism, was being carried on. The practical oratory of the law-court and assembly was being advanced to a perfection which in Demosthenes, the last great representative of practical Athenian politics, attained its highest point. The art of speech-making, in the hands of the cosmopolitan theorist Isokrates, had established the normal shape of Greek prose. In the dialogues of Plato the destructive logic of the sophists had resulted in an attempt to reconstruct the moral and political union of citizens out of universal principles in place of local and antiquated traditions. Like the political reconstructions of Isokrates, the philosophic reconstruction of social life contemplated by Plato looked to the whole range of Greek life, and did not attempt to glide back into days of narrow isolation beyond which the expansion of Greek intellect had now for ever passed. At the same time, the relations of the individual to the group, relations which the general loosening of social ties was rendering sharply distinct, became the great questions to which philosophy addressed itself. In the highly poetical and imaginative style of Plato these questions are put, directly or indirectly, again and again. Is human action to be regulated by eternal principles of justice or by personal self-interest? Is there a sanction for personal morality in a future state of personal reward or punishment? Does the government of the State properly belong to a few wisely experienced persons or to the many? Such are some of the Platonic problems in which the new Greek consciousness, social and personal, is expressed.

Perhaps the relations of the individual to the group are nowhere so curiously realised by Plato as in the social classification laid down in his *Republic*. Instead of accepting such classes as the social life of Athens might have supplied—freeman, metœc, slave—and thus anticipating the process by which English economists have built up their theories on a classification supplied by English life—landlord, capitalist, labourer; instead of adopting a plan like that of the Bráhman *redacteurs* of the Code Manu, viz. that of accepting certain existing classes, but arranging them according to religious theory; Plato sets out from an analysis of individual psychology which he applies to the classification of the State. The individual soul he regards as composed of the appetite (ἐπιθυμία), naturally wild but capable of being tamed; the spirit (θυμός), courageous though capable of both good and evil; and the guiding intelligence (νοῦς), the source of wisdom and culture. This analysis of individual being Plato transfers to social life, and finds in his State (which, to apply the expression of Milton, is simply the citizen "writ large") three classes corresponding with these three elements of individuality. The philosophers, to whom he would intrust the government of his State, represent its νοῦς; the warriors or military class, its θυμός; the mob, its ἐπιθυμία.*

Plato's ideal communism of wives and property in his *Utopia* has recently met with apologists who would reduce the former to a State control of marriage and education, and remind us of the limited range within which the latter was to be confined. But for us the really significant fact is that Plato's ideal communism clearly results from his observing how personal inequalities of property had contributed to destroy the old Greek union of citizen and city, the State and its individual units. Men who agree with Aristotle's criticism on this ideal communism will do well to remember the social conditions which suggested that ideal, especially when we find similar conditions in Hebrew society producing, not merely an ideal Utopia, but organisations, like that of the Essenes, aiming at a practical return to the communism of the old Hebrew village community.

§ 63. But while the enlargement of Athenian ideas and the development of prose were leading to the severance of science from literature in Aristotle's dry theorising and collections of facts, the heart of literature was being

---

* See *Rep.*, bk. iv. 440 E., etc. Cf. *Hist. Gk. Lit.*, Müller, vol. ii. p. 245.

eaten away by the growth of an individualism which more and more was coming to regard itself as linked with social existence solely through the fact of common government, that is, by chains not of sympathy but of force. Lyric and epic poetry had in the city commonwealth given way to the drama; and when the old morality and political freedom, upon which Athenian comedy and tragedy had been based, were weakened, almost the only scope for a new Athenian poetry lay in the direction of a new drama of some sort. Tragedy, of course, this new drama could not be; for not only had the old morality been undermined, but the hero-worship which old Athenian tragedy expressed was impossible in a society of individual units, equally assertive of their own personal merits and distrustful of any character transcending the very limited degree of greatness which their own associations rendered probable. Comedy, on the other hand, was admirably suited to such a society; not, indeed, the comedy of Aristophanes, with its extravagant political caricature, its allegorical or typical characters, through which satire on classes and individuals is conveyed, but the comedy of contemporary life and manners, in which analysis of individual character could be wrought out in a spirit of polished ridicule resembling that of Molière. It is usual to say that the "Middle" comedy of Athens, exchanging a tone of philosophic and literary criticism for the political farce of the old comedy and losing the chorus, lasts from about 390 B.C. to 320, Antiphanes, Alexis, Arâros, being its chief makers; and to date the "New" comedy of manners, with its stock characters of father, son, parasite, soldier of fortune, as beginning about 320 B.C., its chief makers being Menander, Philemon, Diphilus, and terminating about 250 B.C. But any such exact limits are artificial. Our real interest lies not in these uncertain distinctions, but in the general lines taken by the Attic drama in its decadence, and the causes of this course.

In its descent from the ideal worlds of the old tragedy and comedy, the world of heroes struggling against fate and the world of uproarious burlesque, the Attic drama of contemporary life found two great obstacles to a truly profound analysis of human character—the presence of slavery and the low intellectual status of Attic free women. In a city of twenty-one thousand free citizens reposing on the labours of some four hundred thousand slaves, a city in which out of every twenty human beings you met at least eighteen would be chattels bought and sold in open market, the variety of human character which so largely arises from free diversity of social pursuits must have been greatly limited. Moreover, these limits were narrowed still farther by the almost servile dependence of Attic free women. The speeches of Isæus, which shed many interesting lights on the Attic family relations, show us that, though an Athenian could not disinherit his son nor separate his estate from his daughter, he could choose the person whom his daughter might marry; and her position when married was not greatly superior to that of the Roman wife *sub manu viri*. And when we turn from the forensic orator to the philosophers of Greece we meet the same dependence of women. Though Plato in his caste of guards proposes the equal treatment of the sexes, his idea of temporary marriage would hardly have suggested itself save in the degrading associations of Attic womanhood. Aristotle believed that women differed from men intellectually not only in degree but also in kind, and did not "contemplate their ever attaining more than the place of free but inferior and subject personages in the household."* It is not surprising that comedy turned away from individuals of such limited freedom to another class of Attic women whose intellectual culture was purchased at the expense of their morals—the *hetæræ*, or courtesans. Among the characteristics of the New Comedy Mr. Mahaffy places "the increased prominence of courtesan life;" and among the stock characters the designing courtesan now occupies the foremost place. As an evidence of this prominence, it may be observed that out of some forty female characters in the extant plays of Plautus (whose drama is a close imitation of the New Comedy) about one-half are courtesans or *lenæ*, or their maids; while the *Captivi*, notable as the most moral play of Plautus, "ad pudicos mores facta," contains no female characters at all—a fact which would seem to imply that their presence was incompatible with a drama "ubi boni meliores fiant," the quality claimed for the *Captivi* by its *Caterva*.

§ 64. The main materials of this later Athenian comedy were supplied by domestic life, though philosophers of the day, such as Epicurus and Zeno, or even occasionally political personages, even Alexander himself, might be attacked. In truth, the individualism of Attic life could not have tolerated any drama but that of trivial personalities. Whether we accept the extant *Characters* of Theophrastus as really his or not, we have abundant evidences in the ethical and political theories of Plato and Aristotle to show that analysis of individual character had become from the conditions of Attic society a common subject of Attic thought. It was individualism, though in the very different social life of Elizabethan England, that produced such works as

* Mahaffy, *Hist. Class. Gk. Lit.*, vol. ii. p. 415. See Aristotle, *Nat. Hist.*, bk. ix. ch. 1.

Earle's *Microcosmography* * and Overbury's *Characters*. It was individualism within the circle of the "Grand Monarch's" court that produced at once the *Caractères* of La Bruyère and the comedies of Molière.

Bringing out his first comedy in the very year of Demosthenes' death (322 B.C.), Menander, the model of Terence, is a literary man who may be said to occupy the unique position of a link at once between Athens and Alexandria, and between Athens and Rome. The drama, like the written dialogue of criticism and the written speech, had now become an instrument of the literary artist rather than a public voice addressing itself to the people; and the enormous number of comedies attributed to the later comedians, contrasted with the small number of their victories, has been regarded as an evidence of their plays having been intended to be read, and fulfilling to some extent the functions of the critical press in our days. Thus the severance of literature from practical life—a severance in which some modern critics have discovered a kind of literary Arcadia—was everywhere accompanying the decadence of the creative spirit. We need not here

---

* "Microcosmographie, or a peece of the world discovered; in essays and characters. London. Printed by William Stansby for Edward Blount, 1628." In the introduction to Mr. Arber's reprint of this book, it is observed that "in these earlier days of Puritanism especially, and generally throughout the seventeenth century, there was a strong passion for analysis of human character. Men delighted in introspection. Essays and characters took the place of the romances of the former century. Dr. Bliss, to an edition of *Microcosmographie* in 1811, added a list of fifty-seven books of characters, all, with one exception, published between 1605 and 1700. Forty-four years later, writing in 1855 to *Notes and Queries*, he stated that this list in his own interleaved copy had increased fourfold." So popular was *Microcosmographie* that five editions appear to have been published in the first two years of publication. It is worth adding that the character of the "upstart country knight" (like that of Sir Giles Overreach in Massinger's play) marks the changes in landownership which the prosperity of the commercial classes was bringing about. In other characters of Earle we may similarly discern the social conditions of his day.

pause to inquire how far the plays of Menander were intended for reading rather than acting; we only notice the prominence of the former purpose as a point of similarity between the drama of cosmopolitan Athens and that of Indian world-literature. The play had, in fact, come to address itself to a cultured class who could take as much pleasure in turning over its pages with critical acumen as in witnessing its action on the stage. There are certain other respects in which the drama of Menander recalls the Indian, and indeed the Chinese, theatre. The introduction of philosophic speculation could be easily illustrated by parallels from Indian and Chinese plays. The following fragment of Menander will serve as an example of its introduction:—

> "O Phania, methought that wealthy men,
> Who need not borrow, never groan at night,
> Nor, tossing to and fro, cry out 'alas,'
> But deeply sleep a sweet and gentle sleep
> While some sad pauper makes his bitter cry;
> But no; I see the men called 'blessed with wealth'
> Distressed like any of us; is there then
> Some bond of kinship between life and pain—
> Pain that accompanies the life of wealth,
> Stands close beside the life of reputation,
> And with the life of poverty grows old?"*

How far the comedy of Menander resembled the Indian drama in its picturesque descriptions of natural scenery, we have not now the means of discovering; but another fragment given by Meineke † would at least suggest that the ephemeral span of individual existence beside the comparatively eternal life of Nature was forcing itself on the Greek mind with something of that deep pathos which only the poets of modern Europe have profoundly expressed. The fragment runs thus:—

> "This man I call the happiest of men
> Who, having seen without a touch of pain

---

* For Greek, see Meineke, vol. iv. p. 140. † *Ibid.*, p. 211.

> The show of all these splendid things—the sun,
> Common to all the world, stars, water, clouds,
> Fire—then returns to whence he came, my friend –
> For, though a man should live a few sad years,
> Yet shall he ever see this show pass by,
> And, though he were to live a century,
> No grander sight than this he e'er shall see."

§ 65. When the muse of Menander was thus uttering the last notes of that dramatic song which had risen from Athens at the birth of her literature, the separation of philosophy and science from the spirit of literary creation had been established. Science, which, save in its infancy, refuses to be the citizen of any peculiar State and rapidly grows into the cosmopolitan questioner of Nature and Humanity, had thrown off the pleasing form of Athenian conversation, so brilliantly assumed by the world-wide thought of Plato, and in Aristotle had settled down into a dry-as-dust collector of facts. Two circumstances would seem to prove that Aristotle himself realised with peculiar distinctness this separation of science from literature. The first of these is his intentional alteration of his own style from a graceful imitation of the Platonic to that crabbed but closely accurate use of words with which every student of his extant works is familiar. Not only do Cicero, Quintilian, and others speak of Aristotle as a master of style, but it is a well-ascertained fact that in his early writings he essayed to imitate the form of Plato's dialogues; and, though Aristotle's dialogues may not have been so dramatic as those of Plato, he certainly produced three of these compositions ($\pi\epsilon\rho\grave{\iota}$ $\phi\iota\lambda o\sigma o\phi\acute{\iota}\alpha\varsigma$, $\pi\epsilon\rho\grave{\iota}$ $\tau\grave{\alpha}\gamma\alpha\theta o\tilde{\upsilon}$, and $E\check{\upsilon}\delta\eta\mu o\varsigma$) closely after the Platonic model. This transition from the diction of a stylist to the harsh and often obscure brevity which has been likened to a table of contents, a transition which has been aptly compared to "passing from a sunlit garden, gay with flowers, to a dark and chilly reading-room," may be taken as one mark of the Aristotelian separation of critical from creative faculties, of science from literature, of reasoning analysis from imagination.

Another mark of the same process is to be found in the library associations which Aristotle's works contain. In his youth Aristotle had been a collector of books; while residing at Athens as a pupil of Plato his house had been designated the "house of the reader" (οἶκος ἀναγνώστου), and the sum of £200,000, given him by Alexander mainly with a view to collections for his natural history, probably contributed to swell his private library. The days of public libraries, too, and laborious study of the past had now arrived. Aristotle died in 323 B.C., shortly before the death of Demosthenes, and a few years afterwards, at the suggestion of Demetrius Phalereus, last of Attic orators, Ptolemy Soter founded the celebrated library of Alexandria, the city in which the cosmopolitan Greek spirit was henceforward to find a more congenial home than in any of the old city commonwealths. From a Latin scholium on Plautus (discovered by Professor Osann in 1830) we learn that this library (partly kept in the temple of Serapis, partly in the Brucheium adjoining the palace) contained " in the Brucheium 400,000 rolls of duplicates and unsorted books, and 90,000 separate works properly arranged, and in the Serapeum 42,800 volumes, probably the ultimate selection or most valuable books in the whole collection." Here was a reservoir for literature ; and, if literature were really of artificial making and not the outflow of social life, this famous Alexandrian library should have made up for the stagnant shallows into which the living streams of old Greek society had now spread out. But though a library may produce excellent grammarians, critics, scientists, it can do little for literature as distinct from science and criticism. It cannot make imagination live or change the dry skeletons of analysis into creatures of flesh and blood. Hence in Alexandrian erudition formal prose occupies the foremost place, critics like Zenodotus, men of science like Euclid and Archimedes, and chroniclers like Manetho and Berosus, finding it their proper instrument. Didactic "poetry," like the astronomical "epic" of Aratus, called *Prognostics of the Weather* (Diosêmeia), and the so-called "epics" of Nicander on venomous bites and on antidotes to poison, are not sufficiently removed from science to be called "literature," and as examples of imagination in the service of science rank much below Darwin's *Loves of the Plants*. If Alexandria could offer us nothing better than such productions we might pass by the great library, contented to note that literature had become so much a thing of the past, so little a reflection of living mind, that even Theocritus is believed to have made one of those tricks with written words which mark a time when literature has become a formal toy rather than a spiritual reality. The *Syrinx*, a little poem in twenty verses attributed to Theocritus, is so arranged that lines, complete and incomplete, succeed one another in couplets, "passing from the hexameter down to the dimeter dactylic metre, so as to represent the successive lengths of the reeds in a Pandean pipe." When we remember how such "half-mechanical conceits" (as Sir J. F. Davis calls them), consisting in the fantastic imitation of such objects as a knot, a sceptre, a circle, have been well known to the Chinese and Arabs, we may find in this *Syrinx* and in the practice of Simmias of Rhodes (who wrote verses "in the shapes of an egg, an altar, a double-edged axe, a pair of wings") evidences of the Oriental torpor which had fallen upon Greek poetry at Alexandria.

§ 66. Yet the name of Theocritus reminds us that in the midst of this decay a new kind of genuine poetry blossomed forth. The ephemeral life of individual men, contrasted with the apparent eternity of Nature, had profoundly affected Menander; and the contrast was now to be expressed in those "little pictures" of Theocritus, in which the shepherds in the front stand out against beautiful backgrounds of Nature's own creation. It was not, indeed, the first time that the sentiment of Nature had found a Greek voice. In the great epics, dating from a time when city life had not yet absorbed all the social interests of Hellas, we may readily cull out evidences of this sentiment. Thus in the *Iliad* * we have the simile—

"As when at night shine out in the sky by the moon in her glory
Bright stars, when not a breeze is stirring the calm of the heavens;
Watch-posts stand out clear, high headlands, and in the distance
Open glades, and the open of sky looks a break in the heavens;
And as he watches the host of the stars the shepherd rejoices;"

or, in the *Odyssey*,† the famous description of the great boar's lair—

"Here was the lair of the great boar deep in the heart of the thicket,
Here where the raging rains of the storm-clouds never had entered,
Here where the blaze of the noonday sun shot never a sunbeam,
Here where the piled-up leaves lay dark in the heart of the thicket."

Every reader of the Greek epics can recall similar passages—the description of Calypso's cave or that of the garden of Alkinous; and the *Works and Days* of Hesiod contain a picture of winter truly ancient and graphic. Moreover, in certain lyrics of early Greece a deep feeling for Nature had not been wanting. Thus Alcman's description of night, it has been said, is "more like the picture we should expect from Apollonius Rhodius or Vergil than from an early Greek poet "—

"Now sleep the mountain-peaks and vales,
Headlands and torrent-beds,

---

* *Iliad*, viii. 555-559. † *Odyss.*, xix. 439-443.

> The leafy trees and the creeping things the black earth nourishes;
> The wild beasts on the mountains, and all the swarms of bees,
>   And the snakes in the deeps of the purple sea
>   Are sleeping;
>   And all the tribes of wide-winged birds
>   Are sleeping."

Again, while philosophers like Empedocles turned from the perpetual jar of human conflicts to physical Nature, poets like the Ionic Mimnermus were beginning to sing in a strain which anticipates the tones of Menander—his confession of human sorrow, his pessimism, as we call it in these Schopenhauer days, and his contrast of man's ephemeral life with the ever-renewing powers of Nature. His pessimism Mimnermus expresses thus :—

> "We, as the leaves which the season of spring full-budding begetteth,
>   When the warm ray of the sun gloweth to glory again,
> Only a span-length time by blossoms of youth are delighted,
>   Knowing nor evil nor good sent by a being divine.
> For in the garments of mourning the Fates stand ever beside us,
>   One with the sorrows of age, one with the sorrows of death,
> Therefore the fruitage of youth grows short-lived in their presence,
>   And as a gleam of the sun so is it scattered and gone."

But the sentiment of Nature in Theocritus, Bion, Moschus, is something deeper than we can find in any of the early epic or lyric poets. Cosmopolitan Greece had now experienced the littleness of individualised life to a degree which neither rhapsodists nor lyric poets could have conceived. Men had broken loose from their old clan groups only to isolate themselves in turn from the State; and if the individual had thus become "free," it was at the expense of that greatness which, as a member of such corporate bodies, he once possessed. Therefore more than in the days of kingly heroism, more than in the days of city patriotism, men turned to Nature as symbolising that permanence which looks divine. To the glades, the springs, and the rivers Moschus turns for a voice of lamentation over Bion—to the trees of the forest and the flowers rather than to men and women, who have become too selfish to lament much over any of their short-lived fellows. The sad contrast of man's being with the life of Nature, the contrast of Homer, Simonides, Mimnermus, is thus repeated by Moschus:—

"Raise, ye muses of Sicily, raise ye the wail of the mourner!
Ah! when the mallows have withered, have withered away in the garden,
Or the green parsley dies, or dies the soft bloom of anêthum,
Yet will they rise in life and spring for the season returning;
But we, the great and the wise and the strong among men, when we perish,
Silently sleep in the earth the sleep that knows no waking."

§ 67. Theocritus is the true spokesman of this new sentiment. Like other Alexandrian poets (Philetas of Cos, Callimachus of Cyrene, who has been called "the type of an Alexandrian man of letters," Lycophron of Chalkis), Theocritus was not an Alexandrian, but either, as seems most probable, a native of Syracuse, or of Cos. His use of Sicilian Doric and the Sicilian tone of his poems would seem to confirm the general opinion that he was a Syracusan. In any case bucolic or pastoral poetry finds its home in Sicily; and, when we remember the slave-gangs of Italy and the vast estates (*latifundia*) which ruined her free yeomanry, we shall see that the home of bucolic poetry is not so secondary a matter as might at first appear. There can be little doubt that the rise of a true poetry of Nature, besides being checked by the municipal organisations of Greece and Italy, was partly prevented by the ugly associations of slavery with country life. Just as the presence of serfdom in medieval Europe would appear to have diverted the feudal singers from Nature herself to Nature seen through the medium of the seigneur's life of war and the chase, so the singers of Greece and Italy could not take that intense interest in Nature which largely arises from the personal freedom of

S

man in her presence. To discuss the influences of different forms of landownership on the sentiment of Nature would carry us too far afield; yet, if the village community of India is to be largely credited with the Indian love of Nature, the very different system of the Roman *latifundia* may be credited with an opposite effect. If Sicily, then, was the real home of bucolic poetry, we may feel assured that there was some special reason for the fact; that the relations of man with Nature were here less repulsive from servile associations than elsewhere; that his freedom and happiness were not so far removed from those of the bucolic Daphnis or Damœtas as to make the idyll a grotesque falsehood. No such idylls would ever have been suggested by the associations of an American slave-worked plantation any more than by those of a Roman *ergastulum;* and if, among all the slave-owning countries of the Alexandrian age, Sicily was the home of the idyll, we cannot help believing that, while the new poetry of Nature marks a general desire to look for poetic inspiration elsewhere than in the littleness of human individualism, it also indicates special conditions of social life in the country of the idyll.

It is the union of vivid natural descriptions with graphic pictures of simple human life and character that has made Theocritus the favourite of so many and diverse literary epochs. To sympathise truly with the dramas of Sophocles or Aristophanes, we must be largely acquainted with the contemporary spirit of social life at Athens, or even with minute points in Athenian politics. To sympathise with the odes of Pindar we must possess some of a Dissen's learning as well as a musical imagination which no learning can create. But the idylls of Theocritus present man and Nature in such simplicity that we take in all at a glance. Take, for instance, part of the twenty-first idyll as a picture in which the human interest predominates; and, though the idyll opens with the heartless sophism of wealth—

"Want, Diophantus, alone stirs men to the arts of invention" * —

the description of the "two ancient fishers" could not have been written by a man whose sympathies were bounded by the courtly life of Alexandria. Mr. Calverley here saves me the trouble of translating; his scholarly translation runs thus:—

> "Two ancient fishers once lay side by side
> On piled-up sea-wrack in their wattled hut,
> Its leafy wall their curtain. Near them lay
> The weapons of their trade, basket and rod,
> Hooks, weed-cucumbered nets, and cords and oars,
> And, propped on rollers, an infirm old boat.
> Their pillow was a scanty mat, eked out
> With caps and garments. . . .
> Their craft their all; their mistress, Poverty;
> Their only neighbour Ocean, who for aye
> Round their lone hut came floating lazily."

Elsewhere the framework of natural scenery attains to greater prominence, as in the following description at the end of the seventh idyll.

> "There we lay
> Half-buried in a couch of fragrant reed
> And fresh-cut vine-leaves—who so glad as we?
> A wealth of elm and poplar shook o'erhead;
> Hard by a sacred spring flowed gurgling on
> From the nymphs' grot, and in the sombre boughs
> The sweet cicada chirped laboriously;
> Hid in the thick thorn-bushes far away
> The tree-frog's note was heard; the crested lark
> Sang with the goldfinch; turtles made their moan,
> And o'er the fountain hung the gilded bee.
> All of rich summer smelt, of autumn all;
> Pears at our feet, and apples at our side
> Tumbled luxuriant; branches on the ground
> Sprawled, overweighed with damsons; while we brushed
> From the cask's head the crust of four long years."

Theocritus has combined dramatic pictures of human life and character with graphic description of Nature; but

* ἁ πενία, Διόφαντε, μόνα τὰς τέχνας ἐγείρει.

let it not be forgotten that the latter is only description, not what Mr. Matthew Arnold has appropriately termed *interpretation*. Theocritus cannot see, makes no effort to see, Nature as distinct from human associations. He cannot, like Keats and Guérin, speak of the physical world "like Adam naming by divine inspiration the creatures." His expressions do not altogether "correspond with the things' essential reality." Nature for him is beautiful not because she *is* Nature, but because Lycidas, "the favourite of the Muse," with shaggy goat-hide slung across his shoulder, broad belt clasping his patched cloak, and gnarled olive branch in his right hand, watches "the lizard sleeping on the wall," or "the crested lark fold his wandering wing." Nature is bountiful for Theocritus because some human singer hears "the bees that make a music round the hive," and when this singer dies all Nature may "go wrong"—

> "From thicket, now, and thorn let violets spring;
> Now let white lilies drape the juniper,
> And pines grow figs; and Nature all go wrong;
> For Daphnis dies."

§ 68. In Roman imitations of this Alexandrian poet Nature likewise owes her beauty to human associations. A Roman Daphnis sits beneath the "whispering oak" of Vergil; the Mincius has his "green banks wreathed with tender reeds," the "swarms of bees are humming from the sacred oak," and Corydon sings the delights of the summer scene; but it is the presence of man that the heart of the poet loves, it is *humanised* Nature he really celebrates. Between the Alexandrian and the Roman poetry of the empire there are, indeed, many bonds of kinship. Social conditions at the Alexandria of the Ptolemies and the Rome of Augustus were not widely dissimilar. In both courtly adulation had taken, or was taking, the place of old political freedom. In both the elegant imitation of models was choking any inspiration of genuine poetry. In both literature had become the peculiar possession of the few. In both individualism was well pleased to offer the incense of its learned refinement to any human god who was strong enough to embody the force of government and propitious to grant official reward. Perhaps there was no domain of poetry in which the Romans could breathe a little freely from the mastering spirit of Greek song save one—that of natural poetry; but the Eclogues of Vergil show us that no such freedom was to be attempted. Abounding in imitations of Theocritus—for out of the 840 lines of which they are made up we may reckon at least 150, or about one-fifth, as imitations of Theocritus more or less distinct—the Eclogues illustrate a fact in the imitation literature of Rome which is singularly significant and often singularly overlooked. This is the fact that Roman *littérateurs* sought their models less in the splendid masterpieces of the free Athenian commonwealth than in the cosmopolitan writings of Athenian decay and Alexandrian pedantry. If the models of Plautus and Terence were found in Menander, Philemon, Diphilus, and the "New Comedy" in general, Vergil is deeply indebted—more deeply than most scholars suppose—to the Argonauts of Apollonius Rhodius, the pupil of Callimachus. Aratus, the poetic scientist of Alexandria who threw the astronomy of Eudoxus into hexameter verse, was the model of Cicero's and Domitian's poetic attempts. In Callimachus and Philetas Propertius found his models; and the *Coma Berenices* of Catullus is a close translation of the courtly flattery in which Callimachus delighted. It was in imitation of Callimachus, too, that Ovid wrote his *Ibis*. In a word, Roman poetry owes so deep a debt to Alexandria that without her Rome might never have possessed a Catullus, an Ovid, a Vergil. Where shall we find the cause of this indebtedness? In similarity of social conditions, in the great truth that literature, even in its imitative work, depends on contemporary life and thought; that no number of exquisite models can make up for deficiencies in these living sources of inspiration. If it were otherwise, not only would the making of literatures be matter of chance or personal caprice, but the scientific study of literature would almost be an absurdity.

The main characteristics of Roman, as of Alexandrian, world-literature are its individualism and the colossal personality of the emperor, who, in an age when force alone held the community together, absorbed as the world-god all the divinity Roman courtiers could feel. In the satirists of Rome we have the spirit of this individualism crying aloud, a spirit which only takes permanent possession of a community when a profound belief in human selfishness has become the terrible substitute for a creed. "Satira tota nostra est," says Quintilian; and, though the satiric spirit was by no means absent from Athens, we must allow that, in spite of the moral purposes to which Lucilius, Horace, Persius, and Juvenal applied it, only the Rome of the empire could have produced such witnesses to social disintegration as the works of the last three writers. It was an error, common until Mommsen (erring, perhaps, in the opposite direction) had exposed the sham of later Roman Republicanism, to suppose that this disintegration was due to the decay of old Roman life alone. It was to a large extent the result of an organised religious, political, and moral hypocrisy which the coexistence of aristocratic rule with mock democracy rendered unavoidable. In a community based on slave-labour it was really impossible that the democratic sentiment of equality could count for much. The Roman citizen had only to walk out into streets thronged with slaves in order to realise the truth that plebeian citizenship was, after all, only an aristocracy with a larger radius than the old circle of patrician kinship. To the other ruinous results of Roman slavery—decline of production and population, discredit of manual labour, discouragement of legitimate marriage, and the like—must be added the constant evidence it afforded that high-flown language of social reformers, as in appeals to the "Law of Nature," were but expressions of an organised hypocrisy. When it is also remembered that old Roman religion long before the time of the emperors had become such a farce that Cicero wondered how two augurs could meet without bursting into laughter in one another's face, it need not surprise us that Roman literature produced its most original works in satires which exposed the political, religious, and moral hypocrisy upon which the decaying republic as well as the empire depended for social stability. In such works the rage of an Archilochus or the misanthropy of a Swift can do great things, because they are built out of unsocial antipathies, personal piques, and all that little meanness which is fatal to the truly constructive imagination nothing but wide and deep social sympathies can create.

§ 69. But over and above this individualism, which must have sadly chilled any original imagination of the Roman poets, there was another cause which, from the rise of the empire, turned the makers of Roman literature to cosmopolitan and courtly Alexandria for guidance. This was the centralisation of all power in the person of the emperor. The adulation of Callimachus, who found among the stars the stolen tresses of Berenice, was now to be outdone. In his first Eclogue Vergil does not shrink from calling Augustus his god—

"For he shall be to me ever a god, and his altar be reddened
Oft with the blood of the tenderest lamb to be found in the sheepfolds."*

So Horace addresses Augustus as a god to whom altars are being raised—

"Præsenti tibi maturos largimur honores,
Jurandasque tuum per nomen ponimus aras,
Nil oriturum alias, nil ortum tale fatentes."

And gradually this worship of the emperor became not merely a piece of courtly flattery or vulgar servility, but the last substitute for a common creed between Romans of wealth and birth, the proletariate, and the provincials.

If we wish to observe the influence of this divine imperial personage on literature, we cannot do better than turn to the pages of the Roman Thucydides—Tacitus, the man of all others opposed to the new divinity. The cessation of the *Comitia*, the conversion of the Senate into a mere registering machine for imperial decrees, the dependence of the law-courts on the emperor's despotism, had now checked any farther development of Latin prose —if, indeed, under any circumstances it could have been carried higher than the point in which the eloquence of Cicero had culminated. Moreover, the extension of Latin, for administrative purposes, over a vast extent of conquered territory was beginning to affect Roman literature much as a similar cause some centuries later produced the mixture of pure Arabic with Persian and other languages of peoples subjugated to Islâm. As yet, however, prose, the proper medium of Roman literature (for, except the rude Saturnian, Roman metres were only Greek exotics), showed little sign of decay. It is not any weak-

* "Namque erit ille mihi semper deus; illius aram
Sæpe tener nostris ab ovilibus imbuet agnus."

ness in his prose, certainly as vigorous and graphic as Rome had yet known, that makes Tacitus an exponent of imperial times. It is the fact that, in spite of his Republican Conservatism, he is forced to make the Imperator the central figure in his Histories and Annals. While his dominant idea, like that of Lucan, is a mistaken belief in the old Roman oligarchy which had been a manifest failure a hundred years before the battle of Actium, it is the personal character of the Cæsar that not only gives their unity to his historic writings, but supplies a false explanation of Roman decline as due to the depravity of the emperors. Extreme individualism had, in fact, reached such a height in Rome that even the historic theorist could only picture the unity of the Roman world in the person of the emperor, and insensibly transferred to it all the dark traits of the selfish units into which Roman society had been broken up. Closely connected with this effect of individualism is another literary characteristic which Tacitus shares with all Roman historians—preference for biography over any description or explanation of social life. So Sallust's *Catiline* and *Jugurtha*, and Suetonius' lives of the Cæsars, remind us how an aristocratic and courtly society, in many respects resembling that of Paris a century ago, showed the aptitude for memoir-writing which long characterised the literature of France. Another mark of the individualising spirit shared by Tacitus with such writers as Saint Simon and De Retz is the satirical tone often heard in the Histories and the Annals, but perhaps most distinctly in the *Germany*—a work which even loses some of its antiquarian credit from its clear intention to contrast the vices of civilisation with the virtues of barbarians.

But, besides these marks of Roman decadence, the prose of Tacitus contains an element which is at once the secret of its strength and an evidence of literary decay. The condensed brevity with which he writes is not, like the brevity of Thucydides, a mark of undeveloped prose, not, like that of Aristotle, an effort to be scientifically accurate in the use of words, but rather like the epigram itself the outcome of an age which thinks it knows all that men can know, and seeks to make up for the triteness of its ideas by packing them in small bundles, weighty yet portable, and in themselves complete. It is possible for communities, no less than individuals, to exhaust their old stock of ideas without acquiring new; and such an age of exhaustion, reduced to the elegant or brief expression of small witticisms, is marked by the epigrams of Martial, the contemporary of Tacitus.

§ 70. Beyond Martial (who died between 102 and 104 A.D.) we need not pass. The world-literature of Rome, which had from the first been an imitative toy made and intended to be appreciated by a narrowly exclusive class of cultured men, never heartily sought the only fountains of true literary inspiration—popular life and the life of nature. There was now not much to inspire song in the life of Rome—that cascade of contempt which we may conceive as perpetually falling from the wealthy patrician to the poor patrician, from the poor patrician to the plebeian, from the plebeian to the provincial, and from all these to the slaves. Such was the miserable state of social life which drew forth from Pliny the remark that "there is nothing more proud or more paltry than man." A society of such limited sympathies and unlimited selfishness was unsuited to the production of song, save such as "the flock of mockbirds" (as Apollonius Rhodius, Quintus Calaber, Nonnus, Lucan, Statius, Claudian, are termed by Shelley) could produce by imitation. Perhaps the making of oratorical prose (which, by the way, was largely due to contact with popular life) was the true mission of that language which, as Heine says, "is the language of command for generals, of decree for administrators, an attorney language for usurers, a lapidary language for the stone-hard people of Rome "—" the appropriate language of materialism" which Christianity has "tormented itself for a thousand years in the vain attempt to spiritualise." Not even in Nature herself had the cultured Romans a refuge from the paralysing spectacle of Roman society. It is true that the Roman poets occasionally give us descriptions of Nature. Such, for example, is Vergil's picture of the gathering and bursting tempest in the first book of the *Georgics;* such is Ovid's description of the fountain on Mount Hymettus, or Lucan's sketch of the ruined Druidic forest in the third book of the *Pharsalia.* But the gloomy spectacle of slavery would seem to have checked the development of a truly imaginative Nature-poetry, and to have thrown back Roman genius on those scenes of social life in which the unsympathetic characters of Roman citizens were enough to freeze the most vigorous imagination.*

Thus did the broken bonds of social sympathy, a disruption terribly confessed in Diocletian's famous edict on prices, and inevitably avenged by the disappearance of the Roman empire before barbarians who reintroduced the devotion of man to man, react upon the sentiment of Nature. If, as Professor Blackie has said so truly, the

* It is worth observing that the landscape painting of Rome (so far as may be judged from excavations at Herculaneum, Pompeii, and Stabia) would seem to have consisted of pictures which "were often mere bird's-eye views, resembling maps, and aimed rather at the representation of seaport towns, villas, and artificial gardens, than of Nature in her freedom. That which the Greeks and the Romans regarded as attractive in a landscape seems to have been almost exclusively the agreeably habitable, and not what we call the wild and romantic."—Humboldt, *Kosmos,* vol. ii. p. 77 (Colonel Sabine's translation). Cf. Ruskin, *Mod. Painters,* vol. iii., on the "subservience of classical landscape to human comfort."

writing and appreciation of poetry depend on kindly and genial sensibility, if imagination itself depends on the existence of some genuine sense of human brotherhood, be it wide as the world or narrow as the clan, we must admit that the social life of Imperial Rome was such as must destroy any literature. The Stoic maxim, "to watch the world and imitate it," may seem to us a fine thought finely expressed; but the world of the Roman had become a microcosm too small and selfish to suggest anything of that universe by participation in which we rise out of our individual littleness. The philosophy of self-culture could do little but aggravate the miseries of such an age. No renovation of a perishing society was to be expected from that isolating individual culture which had breathed its poison into Roman literature in its Greek fosterage, and now

> "Shut up as in a crumbling tomb, girt round
> With blackness as a solid wall,
> Far off she seemed to hear the dully sound
> Of human footsteps fall."

CHAPTER III.

THE SOCIAL SPIRIT IN WORLD-LITERATURE.

§ 71. THE story of a literature's decline and fall, as exemplified by Alexandrian and Roman cosmopolitanism, is curiously like and unlike that of Israel's decadence. Hebrews, like Athenians, before the destruction of their political independence had lost much of their old communal sympathies. Perhaps no better exemplification of the principle that the movement of progressive societies is from communal to individual life can be found all the world over than the contrast between the inherited guilt of the Decalogue and the strenuous assertion of personal responsibility by Ezekiel. "Behold," says the nâbî, "all souls are to me thus—as a soul the father and as a soul the son; thus are they to me; the sinning soul, *it* shall die. . . . The sinning soul, *it* shall die; son shall not bear the father's sin, nor father bear the son's sin; the righteousness of the righteous shall be on himself, and the iniquity of the iniquitous shall be on himself." * Between the period at which the Hebrew castes of priests had collected the customs of the allied tribes and the age of Ezekiel we may thus infer that a great social change had taken place. Clan life among the priestly and landowning aristocracy of Israel, as

* Ezek. xviii. 4, 5, 20

afterwards in the town life of Athens and Rome, had been broken up and the spirit of self-interest and personal responsibility had been developed. No doubt the Hebrew village communities still remained as the social organisation of the 'am-hââretz, or "common folk of the land." But, just as the village communities in India became subordinated to the Bráhmans, so the Hebrew clansmen seem to have sunk perhaps even into serfdom under the rule of their priests and nobles.

But, though communal ideas might have lost something of prestige by thus becoming the peculiar property of impoverished if not degraded freemen, they remained the great ideals of Hebrew thought; and side by side with Ezekiel's priestly and aristocratic individualism we have clear signs of this old Hebrew social spirit. If in his utterances personal responsibility is, as we have seen, stated with startling distinctness such as no earlier nâbî approximates, in none also can we find the same social conception of national unity under the figure of an ideal clan communion. As in days of Spartan decline the idea of a fresh distribution of lands became a kind of echo from old Doric communal life, so does the mind of Ezekiel recur to the primitive allotments and village communes of early Hebrew life. Even in this return, however, there is a mark of the cosmopolitan spirit which the associations of Babylon were stirring in the Hebrew soul; the "stranger" is also to have his lot among the clansmen of the chosen people. "So you shall divide this land into lots for you, for the tribes of Yisrâêl; and it shall be that you shall allot it by portion to yourselves and to the resident strangers (gêrim) among you, who have begotten children among you, and they shall be for you as native among the sons of Yisrâêl. . . . And it shall be that in the tribe where the stranger resides you shall assign his portion." † Thus are the cosmopolitan and personal spirits found in company among the Hebrews, as among the Greeks and Romans, and the twofold process of social expansion and individual emancipation from clan restraints again meets us.

It is this union of the individual with the social spirit which makes Ezekiel perhaps the most interesting figure in Hebrew literature. In him we have a link between the oldest forms of Hebrew life and that spirit of Greek philosophy which the conquests of Alexander and his successors were to introduce into Israel. In him we have a thinker and poet and priest who explains at once the narrowness and the breadth of which the Hebrew mind has proved itself capable. From him, as in two streams, we may watch the learned individualism which was to terminate in Sadducean materialism and the puerilities of the Talmud, and the life-giving spirit of social sympathy which was to expand into the morality of Christ, taking their rise as from a common source. But, unlike some of his Greek contemporaries, Ezekiel does not appear to be conscious of the grave ethical problems raised by individualism. Pindar has learned the value of an individual future life of reward or punishment as the great sanction of personal morality. But the shadow-world of Ezekiel is little more than the Odyssean Hades. For Ezekiel Sheôl is indeed a place far wider, far more grandly vague than the subterranean home of the clan; the shadow-world has expanded into the gathering-place of whole nations, and the idea of Sheôl has become world-wide. In Ezekiel's "land of the underparts," which he contrasts with "the land of life," are fallen nations " with their graves all round "— Ashur and his company, Elam and her multitude, Edom,

† Ezek. xlvii. 21-23.

her kings and princes; and at the sight of the fallen mighty, " who have descended to Hades with their weapons of war and laid their swords under their heads," Pharaoh and all his host are comforted.* Throughout this remarkable picture there is no glimpse of *personal* punishment or reward in a future state; it is the picture of a shadow-world in which the dead in nations lie disfigured shades of their mangled bodies, a pale subterranean battle-field in which national or group distinctions are alone noticed. When Vergil in Hades sees Deiphobus with mangled body and gashed face, the idea is as materialistic as Ezekiel's; but Vergil's Hades is peopled with individuals, and contains the Pindaric ideas of personal reward and punishment; it is far removed from the clan age and clan associations. Dante's descriptions of the City of Dis, where are the tombs of the heretics burning with intense fire, has been compared with Ezekiel's picture; but the sepulchres of Dante are not the gathering-places of *nations*, they are abodes of torture for individuals such as Farinata degli Uberti; indeed, Dante's Hades exactly reflects the strongly individualised life of the Italian republics, Florence in particular. In Ezekiel the absence of this personal future of reward or punishment is all the more remarkable because of his open repudiation of the old clan morality. He is, therefore, in the position of a man who has discarded the traditional morality without finding any sanction to put in its place; the wicked may now prosper and the righteous perish without even the clan justice of inherited evil or good.

§ 72. How this ethical position of Ezekiel was likely to lead to pessimism the Book of Qôheleth (or Ecclesiastes, as we call it) only too sadly indicates. Individualism in

* See Ezek. xxxii.

the age of Simonides and Bacchylides, while belief in personal immortality was still an esoteric doctrine, had spoken thus :—

> "For mortal man not to be born is best
> Nor e'er to see the bright beams of the day;
> Since, as life rolls away,
> No man that breathes was ever alway blest."

The mournful voice of the Semitic "Preacher" speaks in this key, too, because over him, too, there broods an age full of individualised feelings, but without that eternal conception of human personality which in a manner places the individual on a par with the corporate life of groups or even humanity itself. Like the sun in his daily round, or the wind in his circuits, or the rivers returning to the place from whence they came, moves the life of man; and there is no new thing under the sun, for the "Preacher," like the Alexandrian *savants*, possesses, or thinks he possesses, universal knowledge. Before this dull round, this fatal law of human cycles, all differences between individuals disappear; an impersonal Fate destroys the distinctions between good and evil bound up so indissolubly with personal morality, and even reduces man, individual and social, to the level of the brute. "For the fate (*miqreh*, lit. 'what meets') of the sons of man and the fate of the beast are one, as the death of the one so the death of the other; for one spirit is to all, and the advantage of man over the beast is nothing, for all are vanity; all go to one place, all are of the dust and to the dust all return. Who knows whether the spirit of the sons of man goes upwards, but the spirit of the beast descends downwards to the earth? . . . All are alike; one fate for the righteous and the wicked, for the good and the pure and the unclean, for him who sacrifices and him who sacrifices not; like good, like sinner. . . .

This is the evil in everything done beneath the sun that all have one fate." * In this life, divorced from all moral restraints, is a pessimism which surpasses that of Greek or Roman. The sprightly Greek had reserved his melancholy for old age, with its lost vitality and outlook on the grave.

"But when at length the season of youth has vanished behind us,
Then to have perished at once truly were better than life,"

says Simonides; and even the gloomy Tacitus, when, at the opening of his Histories, he declared that "never by more ruinous disasters of the Roman people had it been proved that the gods care nothing for our safety but only for taking vengeance on us," admitted the existence of avenging deities, and shrank from the moral nihilism which Qôheleth avows. No wonder the Oriental pessimist finds the life of man altogether insufferable, and envies the blessings of the unborn: " So I praised the dead who long since died more than the living who are yet alive, but better than either of these I praised him who has never been, who has never seen the evil deeds which are done beneath the sun." †

Qôheleth thus takes us some way on one of the two streams which part from Ezekiel downwards—the stream of Hebrew melancholy which the unhappy times of Antiochus did so much to increase. The study of early Hebrew literature, fostered by the hope of national independence and the gradual alteration of popular speech into Aramaic, had produced a literate class which soon lost the idea of literary creation in a minute verbal study aimed at nothing higher than the interpretation of the Tôrah, or Law. In Ezekiel the Hebrew idea of literature had reached its widest circumference; it was then no longer circumscribed by the narrow limits of the priestly

* Eccles. iii. 19-21; ix. 2, 3.   † Eccles. iv. 2, 3.

hymnal, or the legal books, or chronicles of the priestly caste; and the rythmical address of the nâbî, primarily intended to be heard rather than to be read, had in Ezekiel's hands, as in those of Jeremiah, become an instrument for the pen as much as for the voice. A critical age,* bookish and surfeited with study, was, however, to reduce Hebrew ideas of literature into narrower bounds. No doubt the era of Hebrew captivity may be credited with an outburst of Hebrew genius; for new ideas were then breaking in upon the old exclusiveness of the Hebrew mind. But the Hebrews seem to have soon learned that if they intended to maintain any national sentiments in spite of their political weakness, they must forego cosmopolitan ideas and restrain themselves within national traditions. Thus the literary class, which now tended to take the place of an aristocracy, was checked in its sympathies. Little remained for the patriotic Hebrew but to anticipate the Arab's deification of his Qur'ân by setting up the Tôrah for verbal worship; and the alphabetical psalms and arrangement of Lamentations † show how the creative imagination of the nâbîs was giving way to literary tricks reminding us of the

* Dean Stanley (*Hist. Jewish Church*, vol. iii. p. 16) observes that while the public life of the people disappeared with the fall of Jerusalem, while "the prophets could no longer stand in the temple courts or on the cliffs of Carmel to warn by word of mouth or parabolic gesture, there is one common feature which runs through all the writings of this period, and which served as a compensation for the loss of the living faces and living words of the ancient seers. Now began the practice of committing to writing, of compiling, of epistolary correspondence;" as Ewald says, "never before had literature possessed so profound a significance for Israel." Thus Jeremiah throws his prophecies into the form of a letter to the exiles, a literary form which has been compared with the Epistles of the New Testament; and the arrangement of Ezekiel's prophecies in chronological order is another sign of critical times.

† The twenty-two verses of the first, second, and fourth chapters begin with each letter of the alphabet in succession, while the sixty-six verses of the third chapter are likewise arranged, only repeating the same letter at the beginning of three verses successively.

Alexandrian *Syrinx*. The name by which Ezra is known, "the scribe" (hassôphêr), and the intermixture of Aramaic with Hebrew in his language, indicate the age of verbal criticism and the redaction of the canon—the Alexandrian period of Hebrew literature.

Still the exiles at Babylon learned to spiritualise Hebrew sentiments and to expand their range beyond the circle of Hebrew associations—learned, in fact, the two great lessons of personal responsibility and universal sympathy taught in India about this time by the famous Gautama Buddha (543 B.C.). In the Book of Daniel, with its international tone and mystic forecast of the world's history, that book which, for its perception of successive epochs in human development, has been called the first attempt at a philosophy of history, "the first forerunner of Herder, Lessing, and Hegel," we have this expanded Hebræism displaying itself in literature as late as 168-164 B.C. Other influences, however, triumphed, and the "murmurs and scents of the infinite sea," which the night-wind of Babylonian conquest had for a moment swept into the narrow channels of Hebrew literature, died away on the stagnant shallows of a verbal criticism more deadly than those of Alexandria herself.

§ 73. But Alexandria and Greek intellect were to be much more closely connected with the Hebrew spirit than by way of parallel decadence; and in this living connection we find united those two streams of Hebrew feeling we have observed in Ezekiel—the social, typified by his national picture of clan life, and the personal, marked by his repudiation of communal morality. While exiles and returned captives were spiritualising the ritual of Israel; while the worship of the synagogue was growing up and prayer taking the place of sacrifice; while, later on, the scribes were by their traditions "making a hedge about the Law" and gliding into an exclusiveness recalling old Hebrew life, the conquests of Alexander had brought Greek language and thought among the Semites. Malachi, last of the nâbîs, describes the state of social life in Israel before this new influence reached the Hebrews. Priestly traditions have "caused many to stumble at the Law;" and the declaration of a coming judgment on "false swearers, and those who defraud the hireling in wages, the widow, and the fatherless,"* reminds us of that social injustice against which Isaiah and Amos had formerly preached. The social spirit of the old Hebrew village communities was being again shocked by action from individual self-interest without a thought of common sympathy. "Have we not all one Father? Hath not God created us? Why do we deal treacherously every man against his brother, profaning the covenant of our fathers?"† But if the old political idea of a Hebrew League or Covenant (Berith) thus meets us as an ideal of social sympathy, the dominant idea of Malachi, that God is "robbed in tithes and offerings," proves that the materialising spirit of Levitical rites rather than moral self-culture was at work.

Perhaps the earliest direct evidences of Greek influence in Hebrew literature are to be found in the Greek names of the musical instruments mentioned in the Book of Daniel.‡ Classical Hebrew was now dying out, as this very book, by its intermixture of Hebrew and Aramaic, clearly shows. But, though the social teaching of the nâbîs might thus seem to be perishing among narrow-minded descendants who were losing the very power of understanding their language, Greek influences were destined to produce an expansion of the old Hebrew social spirit, and a deepening of the weak Hebrew sense

* Mal. iii. 5.   † Mal. ii. 10.   ‡ ch. iii.

of personality beyond anything which even an Ezekiel might have anticipated. The cosmopolitan spirit aroused in Ezekiel by the world-wide associations of Babylon had been checked by the necessity of stopping, even at the cost of a relapse into narrow Hebræism, that merger of Hebrew in Aramaic language and thought which was insidiously progressing. Side by side with the scribes learned in the Tôrah had arisen an inferior class of interpreters, whose business was the rendering of the archaic Hebrew into the popular Aramaic. Moreover, something worse than Aramaised language was resulting from Hebrew contact with their Semite kinsmen; conceptions more or less opposed to monotheism were creeping in under cover of reverence for angels. It has been observed that the Book of Malachi indicates the craving for "messengers," or intermediate spirits, between that Yâhveh whose very name had become "incommunicable" and his people. Psalms written after the return * place the "angels" or "messengers" of Yâhveh at the head of the creation. In Ezekiel and Zechariah the innermost circle of angels is "dimly arranged in the mystic number of seven." In the Book of Daniel for the first time we have two names of angels, Michael and Gabriel. In the Book of Tobit a third, Raphael, is added; Uriel follows next; and then, "with doubtful splendour," as Dean Stanley says, Phaniel, Raguel, and the rest. Such were the dangers to which Aramaising influences were exposing Hebrew language and thought.

But no such dangers were, at first at least, perceptible on the side of Hellenism. Greek language and thought might well seem too widely separated from Hebrew to allow any popularisation of Hellenic influences. From the Greeks, accordingly, philosophic borrowing might

* Cf. Ps. cxlviii.

be made without any apparent danger of undermining
Hebrew unity; and while there was less fear in this
respect to be entertained of a people so different from
themselves, the condition of Hebrew thought supplied
special reasons for the preference. We have seen how the
development of individual freedom, unaccompanied by
ideas of personal immortality, had in Qôheleth terminated
in one of the most despairful pictures of human origin
and destiny which the literature of any age has ever produced. The vague Aramaic spirit-world of angels was,
however, preparing the way for Platonic teaching; and
when Hellenised Hebrews, acquainted with the ethics of
Socrates and Plato, began to compare their own Ezekiel
or Qôheleth with such philosophic inquirers, they must
have observed that the thinkers who, against the individualism of the sophistic age, had endeavoured to teach
the doctrines of conscience and personal immortality, had
been engaged in solving, or attempting to solve, the very
problems which had perplexed the master-minds of Israel.
If the literature of Greece came upon the Romans as an
anticipation of all they could hope æsthetically to effect,
a treasury of models in verse and prose which they could
not do more than imitate with some success, upon the
Hebrews, whose idea of literature had always been
didactic and whose language was too inflexible for
æsthetic purposes, it came as a great philosophic awakening, an evidence that other peoples in the world beside
the sons of Israel had met the same great moral questions,
and had far surpassed all Hebrew efforts towards their
solution. To men whose highest spiritual guides had so
often appealed to social justice between man and his
neighbour (as had the Hebrew nâbîs), with what force
Platonic discussions on "What is Justice?" must have
come home! To men whose spiritual guides had been

sorely perplexed by the ethics of inherited guilt (as had Ezekiel), how profoundly interesting must the Greek ideas of personal conscience have proved! Above all, how deeply must such an essay as Plato's *Phædo* have affected men who, like Qôheleth, had experienced the emptiness of an individual life, with no outlook save on a stream of humanity ever flowing in the same circle, and ever returning to the earth from whence it rose!

§ 74. If we contrast the Book of Wisdom with that of Qôheleth, we shall have an insight into these Greek influences. The Socratic identification of knowledge with virtue, of wisdom with justice, was sure to commend itself to the Hebrew mind, so long accustomed to mingle ideas of intellectual and moral excellence. Accordingly, the author of the Wisdom of Solomon makes Sophia or Wisdom the spirit of intellectual and moral power. Sophia will not enter "into a soul of evil arts" (εἰς κακότεχνον ψυχήν), nor dwell "in a body subjected to sin" (ἐν σώματι κατάχρεῳ ἁμαρτίας). She is a "humane spirit" (φιλάνθρωπον πνεῦμα), and stands altogether apart from and superior to that spirit (ruach) common to man and beast of which Qôheleth spoke. While we have here the humanising ideas of the Greek, ideas which found it equally hard to absorb the life of man into the general life of animals or of the physical world, Sophia is a direct rebuke to the pessimism of Qôheleth. "God did not make Death, nor is He pleased with the destruction of the living. For He created all things for existence (εἰς τὸ εἶναι), and the races of the world are worthy to be preserved (σωτήριοι); the poison of destruction is not in them, nor is the kingdom of Death (ᾅδου βασίλειον) upon earth. For justice is immortal; but impure men by deed and thought have summoned Death to themselves, thinking him a friend have been consumed, and have made a compact with him because they are worthy to take part with him. For, reasoning wrongly with themselves they said, 'Short and painful is our life; there is no healing in the end of man, and never was there known a man who escaped from Hades. For we came into life by a chance (αὐτοσχεδίως), and hereafter we shall be as though we had never been, because the breath in our nostrils is smoke, and reason (ὁ λόγος) is a spark in the motion of our heart, which being extinguished, our body shall return to ashes and our spirit dissolve like empty air. In time our name shall be forgotten and no one remember our deeds; our life shall pass away like tracks of cloud, and be scattered like a mist dispelled by rays of the sun and overcome by his heat. . . . Come, then, let us enjoy the good things that exist, and use the possession of them, like youth, with energy. Let us satiate ourselves with costly wine and perfumes, and let not the flower of Spring pass us by. Let us crown ourselves with rosebuds ere they be withered; let none of us lose his share of jollity; everywhere let us leave behind tokens of enjoyment, because this is our portion and this our lot. Let us force down the poor just man; let us not spare the widow nor reverence an old man's grey hairs. Be Might (ἡ ἰσχυς) the law of right, for weakness is proved useless.' . . . This was their calculation; and they went wrong; for their own wickedness blinded them. They knew not God's mysteries, nor expected wages of righteousness, nor discerned a reward of blameless souls. For God created man for immortality (ἐπ' ἀφθαρσίᾳ), and made him an image of His Eternal Self.* But by Satan's envy Death entered into

* εἰκόνα τῆς ἰδίας ἰδιότητος, lit. "an image of the Idea of His Personality"—a thoroughly Platonic phrase.

the universe (κόσμος), and they who are on his side find it." *

If the web of this remarkable passage is Hebrew, the woof is Greek. The Hebrew pessimism of Qôheleth meets the Greek horror of old age; the old Hebrew conceptions of social justice and respect for old age are found in the company of action from self-interest, supported by the iron rule of Force, and that contempt of old age which students of Alexandrian literature have frequently observed. But, above all, the Greek realisation of personality and the Platonic sanction for personal morality in a future state meet and correct the despairing nihilism of Qôheleth. In this juncture consists the abiding interest of Alexandrian Judæism; the personal ideas of the Greek are now united with the social ideas of the Hebrew. For neither the old clan morality, nor the ideal brotherhood of social life which had started within the narrow circle of the clan, could disappear even among educated Hebrews writing in the flush of Hellenic inspiration. Side by side with the Greek conceptions of individual punishment or reward in a future state, we have survivals from the old mundane morality of punishment or reward within the present life. "'The ends of the unjust race," says even the Platonic author of the Sophia, "are hard; the children of the wicked shall vanish; for, though they be long-lived, they shall be counted for nothing, and, at the end, their old age shall be dishonoured."

§ 75. If communal sentiments thus survived in the Hellenised culture of the educated Hebrew, how much deeper must the sentiments of early Hebrew social life have been cherished in the hearts of the Hebrew poor? From the pages of Ezra and Nehemiah we may gather

* Wisdom of Solomon, i. 13–ii. 24.

that the body of the returned exiles retained the old clan organisation; and, however this system may have been broken down by the individualising spirit among scribes and priests, there can be little doubt that the Hebrew village community not only lasted far on into Roman times, but (as the Russian Mir to the contemporary communism of Russian reformers) supplied a constant model of social reform and an ideal of Hebrew brotherhood which only needed the touch of the Greek spirit to become cosmopolitan. Such an effort at social reform may be seen in the Essenes, a sect which, retiring from the outward ceremonial of the temple, practised community of property. Josephus, in a peculiarly interesting chapter of his *Wars of the Jews*,* gives us an account of this remarkable sect, which shows that it united the character of social reformers with the deepest personal morality. Basing their social reforms on a return to clan communism—" those who come to them," says Josephus, " must let what they have be common to the whole order, insomuch that among them all there is no appearance of poverty or excess of riches, but every one's possessions are intermingled with every other's, and so there is, as it were, one patrimony among all the brethren "—the Essenes in their conception of the soul and their self-discipline were culturists in the highest sense of the word. " Their doctrine," Josephus observes, " is that bodies are corruptible, and that the matter they are made of is not permanent; but that the souls are immortal and continue for ever, and that they come out of the most subtle air, and are united to their bodies as in prisons, but that when they are set free from the bonds of the flesh they then, as released from a long bondage, rejoice and mount upward." The resemblance

* Bk. ii. ch. viii.

of these ideas to certain opinions of the Greeks is carefully noted by Josephus; and the famous passage of the *Phædo*, which contains the same simile of an imprisoned soul, will come to the mind of any Greek scholar.

But the true interest of the Essenes lies not so much in their adoption of Greek conceptions of personality as in their combining this individual culture with socialism of an advanced type. If in Ezekiel we have individualism struggling to get free from clan ethics, if in Qôheleth we have it freed from such ethics but bound up with pessimism, if in the Sophia of Solomon we have it ennobled by Greek conceptions of immortality, in the Essenes we have this eternal conception of individuality joining with the old social spirit of the Hebrews no longer confined within the limits of nationality. Spiritualised socialism and spiritualised individualism thus meet in the Essenes; and in Christianity they meet in a world-creed. But, it may be asked, was their meeting of any significance to *literature?* Are we justified in regarding that union of Hebrew and Greek thought which ultimately issued in Christianity as lying within the domain of comparative literature? And, if this question be answered in the affirmative, are we justified in regarding the social as the dominant aspect of Christian world-literature?

In answer to the first of these questions—whether the union of Hebrew and Greek thought issuing in Christianity lies within the domain of comparative literature—it will be conceded that the cosmopolitan tendencies of the Alexandrian Greeks and those of Post-Babylonian Hebrews are sufficiently similar and dissimilar to form an interesting study in literature treated comparatively. Athens and Jerusalem, taking their origin alike in those miniature social groups which we have preferred to call by the general name of clan, passed out upon two ideal worlds of spiritual influence—the world of individual self-culture and the world of social brotherhood. Unlike the vigorous human life of Athens—the life of the Ekklesia, the law-courts, the theatre—the city of Jerusalem owed its dignity to a religious centralism which recalls the Delphic Amphiktiony or the Koreish and Mecca. Here there was little scope for the development of the purely individual spirit compared with the varied field of Athenian activities. Surrounded by agricultural communities based on the clan organisation, and with its own hierarchy formed on the same model, Jerusalem could never become a congenial home for individualism; whatever steps it made within the circle of the priesthood and landowning nobility (chôrim), individualism must have always presented an invidious aspect to Hebrew associations. Hence, when we find in Christianity the meeting-place of two such divine spirits, each the master-spirit of its own sphere, are we not warranted in maintaining that no more profoundly interesting problem is to be found in the whole range of human thought than the progress of that Hebrew and Greek cosmopolitanism through which the social and individual spirits sought reconciliation? No doubt it may be replied that this is matter of ethical rather than literary interest; that the function of literature is to collect and build with the most beautiful ideas irrespective of their moral significance. But it is one thing to resolve literature into didactic prose or verse, and another to maintain that the "best ideas" which literature seeks to discover and express must be valued after standards which involve either an ideal of individual self-culture or an ideal of social happiness; must, in other words, represent either the Greek or the Hebrew spirit, or possibly endeavour to combine both. Any literature which really mirrors human life, any literature which is something greater and nobler than a graceful imitation of classical models, must ultimately derive its inspiration from individual or social being, or (the most life-giving of all sources) from that conflict between these aspects of human existence which has raged so fiercely in certain epochs of man's development.

Yet another question remains to be answered—are we justified in regarding the social as the dominant aspect of Christian world-literature, are we justified in treating the teaching of Christ and his disciples as the most splendid example of the social spirit in world-literature? No doubt the Christian idea of personal immortality is widely removed from the clan ethics of inherited guilt, and would seem at first sight to be conceived in a purely Greek spirit of individualism. But the kernel of Greek individualism—action from self-interest—is not to be found in the Christian literature. Far from this, the fundamental doctrines of Christianity—inheritance of sin by every member of the human race, and the vicarious punishment of Christ—are the ethics of early Hebrew life universalised; and ideas of social brotherhood, besides being practically expressed in early Christian communism, meet us everywhere in extant accounts of the great social Reformer. It is true that Christianity, as a grand social reformation, is far from having yet produced the fruits which it seems destined to bear. It is true that in the conditions of the Roman empire— its cruel slavery of man, its intense selfishness, its accepted materialism—the sufferings of the early Christians and the hopelessness of social reform turned away Christian thought from the realisation of the human ideal society to an ideal beyond the range of space and time.

But none the less evident are the marks of the old Hebrew social idealism on the Christian, none the less clear is it that the ideal community of Ezekiel is spiritualised and universalised in the Christian brotherhood, and that, however the conditions of the Roman empire, or the temporal power Christianity afterwards acquired, or the industrial development of modern Europe, have thrown the social spirit of Christianity into the background, the creed whose individual side was expressed by Dante was above all things the mighty utterance of man's social spirit.

CHAPTER IV.

WORLD-LITERATURE IN INDIA AND CHINA.

§ 76. IF Israel and Hellas have respectively offered us examples of world-literature in which the social and individual spirits predominate, the characteristics of Indian literature may be found in its apparently peaceful union of these conflicting spirits, accompanied by a sentiment of the beautiful in nature equally removed from the humanising nature-poetry of the Greek and the monotheistic feelings of the Hebrew, who heard the voice of Yâhveh in the thunder, and saw his arrows in the lightning shot forth on the wings of the wind. But in its earliest beginnings Indian literature contained little indication of the widely philosophic course it was to pursue, or the union of the individual and social spirits it was to attain.

Taking a bird's-eye view of Indian development—for it is a mere error of ignorance to suppose that the East in general, and India in particular, have always been the home of social stagnation—we may divide it into certain periods derived either from social or linguistic facts. In the earliest, or Vedic,* age (so called from the collection

---

* "Veda" is from the same root as "videre," Fεἴδω, "wit," "wisdom:" for the Brâhmans taught the divine inspiration of the Veda as the "wisdom of God."

of hymns believed to represent it) we find the Indian
Aryans making their settlements in the Panjab. The
earliest memorial of these settlements, the Rig-Veda,
is a hymnal of unknown age, though from astronomical
dates it has been inferred with some probability by
European scholars that about 1400 B.C. its composition was still going on. Containing 1017 short hymns,
consisting in all of 10,580 verses, the Rig-Veda displays
a picture of social life in many respects different from
any we might imagine from later Indian literature.
Among the Aryans, now on the banks of the Indus, the
agricultural village community has not yet completely
supplanted the "cattle-pens" of an older pastoral life;
and, as in Homeric, early Hebrew, and early Arab times,
the chief symbol of wealth is cattle. Divided into
various tribes, sometimes at war with themselves, these
conquering Aryans occasionally unite against the "black-
skinned" aborigines whom they call Dasyus, or "enemies,"
and Dásas, or "slaves." But though they pride themselves on their fair complexion, and though the Sanskrit
word for "colour" (varna) is destined to mark this old
difference between the fair-skinned Aryan and his dusky
foes by becoming a synonym for "race" or "caste," the
system of caste in its later sense is still unknown. "Each
father of the family," says Dr. Hunter, whose valuable
works on Indian history and social life should be in the
hands of every student of Indian languages and antiqui-
ties, "is the priest of his own household. The chieftain
acts as father and priest to the tribe; but at the greater
festivals he chooses some one specially learned in holy
offerings to conduct the sacrifice in the name of the
people." Thus the Bráhman priesthood, destined to
become the great organisers of caste, have as yet no fixed
place in the social order. Moreover, kingship seems to

be elective; and not only do women enjoy a high position (marriage being held sacred, husband and wife being alike *damputí*, or "rulers of the house," and the burning of widows on their husbands' funeral piles being unknown), but even "some of the most beautiful of the hymns were composed by ladies and queens."

Among these Indian Aryans, as everywhere in early communities, the rude beginnings of literature are found in close union with religion; and here at the very outset we meet one of the great characteristics of Indian literature—the love of Nature. The divinities of the Aryan housefathers—at once priests and warriors and husbandmen—are, as Professor Monier Williams has observed, idealised and personified powers of Nature—the wind, the storm, the fire, the sun—on which, as an agricultural and pastoral people, their welfare depended. Such deities of Nature are Dyaush-pitar (Diespiter or Jupiter of Rome, Zeus of Greece), or the sky-father; Varuna,* or the encompassing air; Indra, or the aqueous vapour that brings the rains, to whom many of the hymns are addressed; Agni, the god of fire, whose name is the Latin Ignis; Ushas, the dawn, the Greek Eôs; Vaya, the wind; Mitra the sunshine; and the Maruts, or storm-gods. As a specimen of the hymns we may select one to the Maruts and Indra which is peculiarly interesting from its rudely dramatic form. The translation, it should be added, is by Professor Max Müller, to whom all students of Sanskrit are so deeply indebted.

"Prologue. *The Sacrificer speaks;* 1. With what splendour are the Maruts all equally endowed, they who are of the same age and dwell in the same house? With what thoughts? From whence are they come? Do their heroes sing forth their (own) strength because they

* The Ouranos of Greece.

wish for wealth? 2. Whose prayers have the youth accepted? Who has turned the Maruts to his own sacrifice? By what strong devotion may we delight them, they who float through the air like hawks?

"Dialogue. *The Maruts speak;* 3. From whence, O Indra, dost thou come alone, thou who art mighty? O lord of men, what has thus happened to thee? Thou greetest (us) when thou comest together with (us), the bright Maruts? Tell us, then, thou with thy bay horses, what thou hast against us!

"*Indra speaks;* 4. The sacred songs are mine, (mine are) the prayers; sweet are the libations! My strength rises, my thunderbolt is hurled forth. They call for me, the prayers* yearn for me. Here are my horses, they carry me towards them.

"*The Maruts speak;* 5. Therefore in company with our strong friends, having adorned our bodies, we now harness our fallow deer with all our might; for, Indra, according to thy custom thou hast been with us.

"*Indra speaks;* 6. Where, O Maruts, was that custom of yours, that you should join me who am alone in the killing of Ahi? I, indeed, am terrible, strong, powerful —I escaped from the blows of every enemy.

"*The Maruts speak;* 7. Thou hast achieved much with us as companions. With the same valour, O hero, let us achieve then many things, O thou most powerful, O Indra! whatever we, O Maruts, wish with our hearts.

"*Indra speaks;* 8. I slew Vrita, O Maruts, with (Indra's) might, having grown strong through my own vigour; I, who hold the thunderbolt in my arms, have made these all-brilliant waters to flow freely for man.

"*The Maruts speak;* 9. Nothing, O powerful lord, is

* Similar personifications might be easily quoted from our European mystery-plays.

strong before thee; no one is known among the gods like unto thee. No one who is now born will come near, no one who has been born. Do what has to be done, thou who art grown so strong.

"*Indra speaks;* 10. Almighty power be mine alone, whatever I may do, daring in my heart; for I, indeed, O Maruts, am known as terrible; of all that I throw down, I, Indra, am the lord.

"*Indra speaks;* 11. O Maruts, now your praise has pleased me, the glorious hymn which you have made for me, ye men!—for me, for Indra, for the powerful hero, as friends for a friend, for your own sake and by your own efforts.

"*Indra speaks;* 12. Truly, there they are, shining towards me, assuming blameless glory, assuming vigour. O Maruts, wherever I have looked for you, you have appeared to me in bright splendour; appear to me also now!

"Epilogue. *The Sacrificer speaks;* 13. Who has magnified you here, O Maruts? Come hither, O friends, towards your friends. Ye brilliant Maruts, cherish these prayers and be mindful of these my rites. 14. The wisdom of Mânya has brought us to this, that we should help as the poet helps the performer of a sacrifice: bring them hither quickly, Maruts, on to the sage these prayers the singer has recited for you. 15. This your praise, O Maruts, this your song comes from Mândârya, the son of Mâna, the poet. Come hither with rain! May we find for ourselves offspring, food, and a camp with running water."

§ 77. Such a hymn as this shows the beginnings of a studied ceremonial sharing in that dramatic character which is more or less common to all rituals, and which in the Medieval Mass directly contributed to the creation of our European theatres. Religion is becoming something more than a spontaneous worship offered up by the father of the family, who is at once its prophet, priest, and king; the poet helps the performer of the sacrifice, the singer recites the poet's studied prayer; and the prologue —which reminds us of the religious prologues to the much later Indian dramas—the dialogue, and epilogue, even if they are quite unconnected with the development of the Indian theatre, are at least signs of a literary class. The rise of this literary class forms the second great period into which the evolution of Indian life may be divided.

The earliest Vedic hymns exhibit the Indian Aryans still to the north of the Khaibar Pass, in Kábul; the later bring them as far as the Ganges, and " their victorious advance eastwards through the intermediate tract can be traced in the Vedic writings almost step by step." In the train of conquest came the development of a higher social organisation than that of the pastoral communities which had been attracted by the steady water-supply of the Panjab, and had settled in scattered groups of husbandmen. In these old Aryan colonies of the Panjab division of mental and manual labour had been wanting; "each housefather had been husbandman, warrior, and priest. But by degrees certain gifted families, who composed the Vedic hymns or learned them off by heart, were always chosen by the king to perform the great sacrifices. In this way probably the priestly caste sprang up." Fortunate warriors or companions of the king, too, like the *comitatus* of German tribes, received grants of conquered territory which the non-Aryans cultivated as serfs; hence the warrior-caste, called Rájputs or Kshattriyas—the latter term meaning "of the royal stock"— and the Sudras or non-Aryans reduced by conquest to serfdom. Moreover, the agricultural settlers, Vaisyas, who in the early Vedic period had included all Aryans, came to be distinguished alike from the warriors and the serfs; and so there came to be four castes, three of Aryan descent, known as the "Twice-born," and one non-Aryan.

How far this social classification was the work of the Bráhmans, or priestly caste, during or after their struggle for supremacy with the Kshattriyas, it is clearly impossible now to decide with precision—especially since the very idea of caste in modern India has been rendered exceedingly complex by countless varieties of castes due, not to these facts of ancient Indian history, nor to direct Bráhmanic creation, but merely to the hereditary character of trades and occupations. But, since the Bráhmans have ever been the makers of Indian literature, the problem of the "natural" *versus* the artificial development of caste need not here be discussed. Whatever different causes, however, have contributed to create the Indian caste-system—ancient clan life, the village community, differences of race and occupation, priestly law-books and ritual—it is plain that the influence of a social fact and idea which must so profoundly affect the conception of individuality cannot be overlooked in any view of Indian literature however brief. But before we trace some Bráhmanic influences on Indian literature we shall turn aside for a moment to compare the beginnings of literature in China with the Vedic hymns.

§ 78. The ancient collection of Chinese odes known as the Shih King offers the most striking contrasts in form and spirit, in social and individual characteristics, to these ancient hymns of India. China, like India, was destined to give birth to a literature which, reflecting human life on a vast scale and deeply imbued with sentiments of Nature, was to expand its horizon beyond national destinies and become a world-literature full of philosophic efforts to explain the past, the present, and the future of the human species. But China, like India, had her day of small things, of local distinctions, of feudal states; and from this early period the Shih, or at least some of its odes, would seem to date.

The Shih, consisting of 305 pieces, the most recent of which are assigned to B.C. 606-586, the oldest to the period of the Shang dynasty 1766-1123 B.C., is divided into four parts. 1. The *Kwo Făng*, "Manners of the different States," or, as Dr. Legge prefers to translate, "Lessons from the States," are 160 short pieces descriptive of manners and events in the feudal states of Kâu. 2. The *Hsiâo Yâ*, or "Minor Odes of the Kingdom," are 74 pieces, "sung at the gatherings of the feudal princes and their appearances at the royal court." 3. The *Yâ Yâ*, or "Major Odes of the Kingdom," are 31 pieces, "sung on great occasions at the royal court and in the presence of the king." 4. Lastly, the *Sung* consist of 40 pieces, 31 of which belong to the sacrificial services at the royal court of Kâu, the rest to those of the marquises of Lû and the kings of Shang. Chinese authorities speak of the *Sung* as "songs for the music of the ancestral temple," and "songs for the music at sacrifices;" and Dr. Legge, uniting these definitions, would call them "odes of the temple and the altar."

It would seem that some at least of these odes were collected in the capital from the music-masters of the various states; and their repetitions or refrains indicate a spirit at once secular and musical, which, like the four-syllabled lines in which they are for the most part composed, contrasts remarkably with the difficult metrical forms and highly religious tone of the Indian hymns. The subordination of the sacrificial to the secular aspect, moreover, is supplemented by a wide difference in the spirit of the pieces which are professedly religious compared with the Indian hymns. It is the ancestral worship of the family which is celebrated in the Sacrificial Odes of the Shih, a worship destined to afford no scope for the development of caste or Bráhman priesthood; and, though some of the odes are in worship of Nature, they remind us rather of the utilitarian mythology of early Rome than the splendid adoration of Nature in the Vedas. Not that Nature is less prominent in the Shih than in the Indian hymns; for there is scarcely an ode of the Shih which does not turn upon some aspect of Nature— "the ospreys with their *kwan-kwan* on the islet in the river," "the yellow birds flying about the spreading dolichos." Almost every ode is decked with phrases borrowed from physical or animal life—"the swallows flying about with their wings unevenly displayed," "the wind that blows with clouds of dust," "the dead antelope in the wild wrapped up in the white grass." But in these and similar expressions we have rather simple family life enjoying the sights and sounds of Nature than any of that majestic imagery and profound reverence for Nature's life which the Sanskrit poems reveal. The same homely sympathy with Nature is to be found in certain specimens of ancient Chinese poetry, which have been assigned (but on questionable grounds, in Dr. Legge's opinion) as high or even higher antiquity than the Shih King. Among these may be quoted the "Song of the Peasants in the time of Yaou:"—

"We rise at sunrise,
We rest at sunset,
Dig wells and drink,
Till our fields and eat—
What is the strength of the emperor to us?"

And from the same specimens the "Prayer at the

Winter Thanksgiving," "Shun's Song of the South Wind," the "Song of the Fern-Gatherers," and the "Cowfeeder's Song," beginning—

"On the bare southern hill
The white rocks gleam"—

might be cited as also illustrating ancient Chinese sympathies with Nature as a good friend rather than a great God.

In fact, the religious sentiments of the Chinese were with their social evolution assuming a different channel from that of the Indian Aryans; and though we have early Chinese songs to the powers of Nature as productive agents, the most profound sentiments of Chinese religion were turned away from Nature to the ancestors of the human family, the centre of all Chinese passions and emotions. Accordingly, while the Bráhmans were building up their sacred hymnal to Nature in her grandest forms, the ancestral spirits were in China receiving the mead of sacrificial song. With a specimen of such song * we shall conclude this brief contrast of early Indian and Chinese poetry.

"Ah, ah, our meritorious ancestor!
Permanent are the blessings coming from him,
Repeatedly confirmed without end :—
They have come to you in this place.

"The clear spirits are in our vessels,
And there is granted to us the realisation of our thoughts.
There are also the well-tempered soups
Prepared beforehand, the ingredients rightly proportioned.
By these offerings we invite his presence, without a word,
Nor is there now any contention (in any part of the service).
He will bless us with the eyebrows of longevity,
With the grey hair and wrinkled face in unlimited degree.
With the naves of their wheels bound with leather, and their ornamented yokes,
With the eight bells at their horses' bits all tinkling,

---

* From Dr. Legge's *Chinese Classics*, vol. iv. pt. 2.

(The Princes) come and assist at the offerings.
We have received the appointment in all its greatness,
And from Heaven is our prosperity sent down,
Fruitful years of great abundance.
(Our ancestor) will come and enjoy (our offerings),
And confer (on us) happiness without limit.

"May he regard our sacrifices in summer and winter,
(Thus) offered by the descendant of Y'ang."

§ 79. During the growth of the Bráhman caste in India, the old ritual-book of the Rig-Veda was supplemented by the addition of three other service-books. The Rig-Veda had been the hymns in their simplest form; by degrees were added the Sáma-Veda, or hymns of the Rig-Veda, to be used at the Soma sacrifice, the Yajur-Veda "consisting not only of Rig-Vedic hymns, but also of prose sentences to be used at the great sacrifices, and divided into two editions, called the Black and White Yajur," and the Atharva-Veda, consisting of the least ancient hymns at the end of the Rig-Veda and of later poems. To each of these four Vedas prose works were in time attached, called Bráhmanas, explaining the sacrifices and duties of the priests, and forming with the Vedas the *sruti*—"things heard from God"—or revealed scriptures of the Hindus. "The Vedas supplied their divinely inspired psalms, and the Bráhmanas their divinely inspired theology or body of doctrine." Afterwards were added the Sútras—"strings of pithy sentences"—on laws and ceremonies, for the Bráhmans, like the Hebrew priests, were not only the holy guardians of religious ritual, but, like the Irish Brehons, interpreters and co-ordinators of law never in India very distinctly separated from religion. Later on, the Upanishads, treating of God and the soul, exemplified that development of philosophy out of religion which can be easily illustrated elsewhere than in India; the Aranyakas, or "tracts for the forest recluse," marked the rise of that ascetic spirit which Christian monasticism has made so familiar to Europe; and, long afterwards, came the Puránas, or "traditions of old." These writings, however, as distinct from the Vedas and Bráhmanas, are not *sruti*, or divinely inspired; they are only *smriti*—" things remembered"—that is, sacred traditions.

How did the Bráhmans manage to retain a monopoly of this politico-religious literature ? How did they prevent any such popularisation of their legal knowledge as, for example, followed the publication of the XII. Tables at Rome? They prevented publication by preferring to hand down their learning by memory within the sacred circle of their caste, even though as early as 250 B.C. two alphabets or written characters were used in India. "Good Bráhmans had to learn the Veda by heart, besides many other books. This was the easier, as almost all their literature was in verse (slokas). In the very ancient times, just after the Vedic hymns, a pure style of prose, simple and compact, had grown up. But for more than two thousand years the Bráhmans have always composed in verse; and prose-writing has been a lost art in India."

The Bráhman period of Indian literature reaches backwards and forwards into very different social and linguistic conditions of Indian life in general and of the Bráhman priesthood in particular. In the earlier period the Bráhmans are struggling into independence from the control of the military class, and with difficulty establishing their priestly ceremonial over the local worships of the House-fathers. As yet "Sanskrit," as the peculiar language of the educated, is unknown; for the language destined to become the sacred language of the Bráhmans is still the Aryan vernacular speech, the true maker of the "simple and compact prose" which (as Albrecht Weber, in his *History of Sanskrit Literature*, observes) had been gradually developed in the Vedic period. The scientific student of literature should note some of the causes which checked the growth of Indian prose.

The development of prose is to a certain extent necessarily democratic—it is the everyday speech of some social group; for example, the explanation of the prominence of Arabic prose in Arabic literature is to be found in its close correspondence with the polished speech of the Koreish. Critics have shown how Athenian conversation, in public or private, is the true source of that splendid instrument of thought we call Attic prose; and any one who takes the trouble to trace the beginnings of prose in England, France, Germany, will soon discover the powerful influences of the language actually *spoken* at court, or in the public assemblies, or in the private meetings of the educated classes. The Bráhman caste clearly lacked the freedom and variety of social status which in the West contributed so largely to the growth of prose. Moreover, prose must be *written;* for, if there is any point in which students of early literature are at length tolerably unanimous, it is the impossibility of making and retaining a prose work by the aid of the memory alone. But here the exclusiveness of Bráhman learning, the desire to prevent popularisation by writing, threw a serious obstacle in the way of prose development. Again, in the extended conquests of the Aryans—as was afterwards to happen to Latin and Arabic —the purity of the old Aryan tongue was being impaired by contact with barbarian languages, and the need of a uniform standard in Aryan speech was more and more experienced; and so the Bráhmans, as the keepers of the most ancient records, possessed a monopoly not only of religious and political knowledge, but also of the purer literary language. Hence, by degrees, popular Prákritic dialects arose out of the ancient Indo-Aryan vernacular, and marked differences began to manifest themselves between these spoken dialects and the language of the educated class or "Sanskrit." The latter gradually ceasing to be a spoken language, and becoming the peculiar property of a class which desired as little as possible to entrust its knowledge to a written form in which it might cease to be a monopoly, it is easy to see why the prose-form, of days when the speech of the educated and uneducated had been the same, was abandoned, and (as Weber says) "a rhythmic one adopted in its stead, which is employed exclusively even for strictly scientific explanation." Indian prose, indeed, we have in the grammatical and philosophical Sútras, but a prose "characterised by a form of expression so condensed and technical that it cannot properly be so called. Apart from this, we have only fragments of prose, occurring in stories which are now and then found cited in the great epic; and, farther, in the fable literature and in the drama; but they are uniformly interwoven with rhythmical portions. It is only in the Buddhist legends that a prose style has been retained. . . . Anything more clumsy than the prose of the later Indian romances and of the Indian commentaries can hardly be conceived; and the same may be said of the prose of the inscriptions. . . . Works of poetry, of science and art, and works relating to law, custom, and worship, all alike appear in a poetic form; and while, on the one hand, the poetic form has been extended to all branches of the literature, upon the other, a good deal of practical prose has entered into the poetry itself, imparting to it the character of poetry with a purpose" (Weber).

§ 80. It is evident that a language which had thus fallen into the possession of a priestly caste is not likely to enshrine a literature in any sense of the word *popular*. But in dealing with the literature of India we must remember that it is really an error to transfer our European conceptions of "people" and "popular"— conceptions which are not strictly applicable to the slave-supported municipalities of Greece and Rome, and which even in modern Europe mark the last links in a long line of development from the serfdom and *communes* of the Middle Ages—to the many races, languages, and caste-distinctions of that vast country which we briefly name "India." Without some language standing apart from the many varieties of daily speech and some privileged caste to keep watch and ward over its treasures, it is difficult to conceive how India, especially in the face of Greek, Scythic, and Mohammedan conquests, could have produced or retained a literature at all. If, indeed, the monopoly of the Bráhmans had received no serious checks, if no development of new sects and no introduction of foreign thought by conquest had left them sole masters of the religious, political, and literary traditions of India, it is probable that Sanskrit literature might never have advanced much beyond ritual books like the Vedas, law treatises full of Bráhman interests, and chronicles combining myth and history in incalculable proportions. But for Bráhman exclusiveness an *aufklärung* was reserved.

In 543 B.C., at the age of eighty, died a reformer worthy of being placed beside, if not above, the greatest our Western world has known. Gautama Buddha—"the Enlightened"—had renounced his royal rank as only son of a king, passed through years of hermitage and penance, and, from his thirty-sixth year, entered upon that public teaching which, unlike the exclusiveness of Bráhmans, sought disciples not merely among the sacred caste but in all ranks and conditions of men. In the spirit of that old Hebrew prophet who, rising above the formalism of Israel's priests, asked "to what purpose is the multitude of your sacrifices?" Buddha put in the place of the Bráhman sacrifices three great duties—control over self, kindness to other men, and reverence for the life of all sentient creatures. Just as the formalism of Hebrew priest-lawyers had reposed upon an ethical creed in which the individual's responsibility had been merged into collective, just as prophets like Jeremiah and Ezekiel, nearly at Buddha's own date, were preaching personal responsibility against the worn-out clan morality of inherited guilt, so Buddha, preaching salvation equally to all men without the intercession of the Bráhman, insisted on individual responsibility, and taught that man's state, in this life, in all previous and in all future lives, must be the result of his own acts.

But if Buddha's teaching resembles the spiritual teaching of Isaiah, if it resembles the individual ethics of Ezekiel, it also contains something of the pessimism of Qôheleth. Human life, in Buddha's view, must always be painful, more or less; "the object of every good man is to get rid of the evils of existence by merging his individual soul into the universal soul." "Two souls," says Faust, "dwell within my breast; the one would fain separate itself from the other. The one clings to the world with organs like cramps of steel; the other lifts itself energetically from the mist to the realms of an exalted ancestry." Buddha, like Goethe, like Qôheleth, is living in an age when the contrast of the individual with the group, of the microcosm self with the macrocosm not-self, has forced itself on human thought. But his reconciliation of the conflicting principles is not found in that despairful materialism in which the Hebrew thinker watches with anguish all individual distinctions, nay, even the differences between men and brutes, disappear; it is found in a pantheistic moral ideal—that Nirvana, "Cessation," absorption of the individual into the universal soul, which is only to be reached by a personal life of moral excellence. M. Guizot has remarked that the general acceptance of feudalism in Europe is the best evidence of its necessity; perhaps a similar remark may be made on the rapid extension of Buddhism, which at least shows that Bráhmanism in its early exclusive form had worn out the prestige of its pretensions. Buddhism, about 257 B.C., became a State religion; and though, after 800 A.D., Bráhmanism again gradually became the ruling religion, five hundred millions of Buddhists in Asia venerate to-day the memory of Gautama, "the Enlightened."

§ 81. It was during the domination of Buddhism that Sanskrit literature displayed its nearest approach to a popular form in its drama. But before we touch upon this form of Sanskrit literature we must briefly review another—the epic. Perhaps the earliest traces of the Indian epic may be carried as far back as the Veda; certain it is, as Professor Monier Williams has said, that not only is the germ of many legends in Hindu epic poetry to be found in the Rig-Veda, but such poetry is there foreshadowed in hymns and songs laudatory of Indra and other gods supposed to protect the Aryan from the non-Aryan races. In fact, when we remember the dramatic shape of the hymn quoted above, it is allowable to say that lyric, epic, and dramatic elements are all to be found in the Rig-Veda. But, dismissing the question of the exact process by which Indian epic poetry grew up as one too intricate for the space at our disposal, we shall turn to the two most famous Indian epics, and the points of comparison or contrast to similar European poetry which they suggest.

Of these two epics, the Rámáyana contains the story of the Aryan advance into India, while the Mahábhárata may be regarded as metrical romance-chronicles of the Delhi kings. The oldest of these epics, the Rámáyana ("the adventures of Rama," from the Sanskrit *Ráma* and *ayana*), is said to have been composed by the poet Válmíki. "For centuries," says Professor Williams, "its existence was probably oral; and we know from the fourth chapter of the first book that it had its minstrels and reciters like the Greek ῥαψῳδοί." The antiquity of Sanskrit, like Hebrew, literature cannot be fixed with certainty, and depends on internal evidences contained in its various works; but internal evidences would seem to show that a great part of the Rámáyana as now known to us was current in India as early as the fifth century B.C. Ráma, though mentioned in the Veda, may be regarded as the first real hero, belonging to the Kshattriya or warrior caste, of the post-Vedic age; and, as evidences confirmatory of the date just named, Professor Williams mentions the simplicity of style in the Rámáyana, its want of allusions to Buddhism as an established fact, and the marks it contains of that independent spirit of the northern military tribes, and that tendency to sceptical inquiry even among Bráhmans which, working southwards, led to the great Buddhist reformation.

The story of the Rámáyana, though often interrupted by episodes having little bearing on the plot, is more continuous than that of the Mahábhárata, the latter being written in celebration of the lunar race of Delhi kings, as the Rámáyana is of the solar race of Ajodya or

x

Oudh. Divisible into three principal parts corresponding with the chief epochs in the life of Ráma, the Rámáyana treats (1) of Ráma's youthful days, education at the court of his father, Dasaratha king of Oudh, marriage to Sítá, and inauguration as heir-apparent or Crown Prince; (2) the circumstances leading to his banishment, and the description of his exile in the forests of Central Asia; (3) his war with the demons of the South for the recovery of his wife Sítá, carried off by their chief Rávana, his victory over Rávana, and his restoration to his father's throne. In the first two portions extravagant fiction is sparingly used; in the last the wildest exaggeration and hyperbole prevail.

The Mahábhárata is an immense collection of legends, so wanting in unity that the episodes occupy three-fourths of the entire poem, the size of which may be imagined from the fact that it contains 220,000 lines, or, reckoning the *Iliad*, the *Æneid*, the *Divina Commedia*, and *Paradise Lost* as together containing 50,000 lines, considerably more than four times the bulk of all the great European epics put together. In fact, the central story of the Mahábhárata, which contains 50,000 lines, or about a fourth of the whole "poem," may be said to equal all these European epics in bulk. In truth, it is not one "poem" at all, but "a compilation of many poems; not a *kávya* by one author, but an *itihása* by many authors."

Both the Rámáyana and the Mahábhárata consist of many stories grouped round a central story; but the central story of the Mahábhárata is a slender thread upon which many unconnected legends are strung; while the many episodes of the Rámáyana "never break the solid chain of one principal subject which is ever kept in view." The subject of the central story in the Mahábhárata is a struggle between two families, alike descended from the royal Bharata, and brought up under the same roof. King Pándu, smitten by a curse, has resigned his kingdom to his brother Dhrita-ráshtra, retired to a hermitage and there died, leaving the five Pándavas, his sons, to the care of his brother now ruling in his stead. Dhrita-ráshtra has himself one hundred sons, named Kauravas, from an ancestor Kuru; but, acting as the faithful guardian of his nephews, he chooses the eldest of the five Pándavas as heir to the family kingdom. His own sons resent the act; hence the quarrel of the hundred Kauravas with the five Pándavas which forms the central story of Mahábhárata.

The period to which this story refers is not later than 1200 B.C.; but the composition of the Mahábhárata bears internal marks of later date than that of the Rámáyana. Though the later epic includes in its post-Vedic mythology many myths which have their germs in the Veda, its religious system is "more popular and comprehensive than that of the Rámáyana;" and when it is remembered that Bráhmanism never gained in the more martial north that ascendancy which it acquired in the neighbourhood of Oudh, we are prepared to find that the Rámáyana, to which this neighbourhood gave birth, "generally represents one-sided and exclusive Bráhmanism," while the Mahábhárata, celebrating the Delhi kings, is less inspired by the exclusiveness of the sacred caste, and (as Professor Williams observes) "represents the multilateral character of Hinduism." In the Mahábhárata the individualising spirit of Buddha is marked by the introduction of more human and popular personages and less mythical allegory than are to be found in the Rámáyana—a *humanising* process which may be compared with that which has been previously observed in the Athenian drama, and which will hereafter be noticed in the relation of miracle-plays to the modern European drama. So, also, the Mahábhárata contains "many more illustrations of domestic and social life and manners than the more ancient epic."

But while such differences as these present themselves in a comparison of the two great Indian epics, differences to be regarded as indicating literary sympathies gradually widening beyond the narrow circle of Bráhmanic interests and expanding towards a width sufficient for the creation of a drama under royal patronage, the European scholar will probably contrast with greater interest the Indian with our own European epics, especially the *Iliad* and *Odyssey*. A vast range of human interests, diversities of language and race, varieties and sharp contrasts of caste, consciousness of intricate distinctions in social life, will account for the disorderly universalism of the Indian epics compared with the far greater uniformity but also narrowly local interests of the Greek. If in the *Iliad* time, place, action, are restricted within comparatively narrow limits, if even the wider circle of the *Odyssey* is insignificant compared with the almost unbounded range of the Mahábhárata, the social and physical differences under which the Indian and Greek poets lived are amply sufficient to explain their diverse treatment of time, place, and action, a diversity which we shall find repeated in the Greek and Sanskrit dramas. Just as the similes of the Indian epics are taken from the movements of Asiatic animals— the tiger, the elephant—or from the peculiar aspects of Indian plants, the Sanskrit dictionary itself marking the profusion of Indian flowers by the number of its botanical terms, so graphic and picturesque descriptions of scenery, alike in the epics and dramas of India, reflect not only "the whole appearance of external nature in the East, the exuberance of vegetation, the wealth of trees and fruits and flowers, the glow of burning skies, the freshness of the rainy season, the fury of storms, the serenity of Indian moonlight, and the gigantic mould in which natural objects are generally cast," but also a state of social life in which the primary units are not the city and the citizen, but the agricultural village and its communal brethren redolent of Nature's life. We may say, then, that the great differences between the Indian and Greek epics are the fantastic intermixture (not merely, as in the *Iliad*, the juxtaposition) of gods, heroes, men, and the vast extension of space and time in the former, characteristics also accompanied by a profound sympathy with physical nature which, in spite of a few well-known passages, may be said to be singularly absent from the Greek epics.

Whether the cause is to be found in the unsuitableness of the Chinese language for a long poem, or in conditions of social life in China, or in both, nothing resembling an epic has been discovered in Chinese literature by European scholars. The Indian epics have thus no Chinese analogue to be here noticed, and we may pass on to another species of Indian literature. The individualising spirit of Buddha's age and the humanising tone of the Mahábhárata, contrasted with the Bráhmanic narrowness of the older epic, have already called our attention to that expansion of social sympathies and deepening of individual conscience which in India, as in Greece, preceded and accompanied the rise of the drama; and, since the differences between the Greek and Indian epics just noticed are much the same as those between the Greek and Indian theatres, we may take the present opportunity to pass on to the Sanskrit drama.

§ 82. Shelley, in his *Defence of Poetry*, maintained

that "the connection of poetry and social good is more observable in the drama than in any other form; and it is indisputable that the highest perfection of human society has ever corresponded with the highest dramatic excellence, and that the corruption or extinction of the drama in a nation where it has once flourished marks a corruption of manners and an extinction of the energies which sustain the soul of social life; for the end of social corruption is to destroy all sensibility to pleasure." How far these observations are true, and what is the kind of social life which produces the best drama, we need not here inquire. We shall at least admit with Shelley the peculiarly close relations of the drama with social life, and agree with Professor H. H. Wilson when he says, in his admirable *Theatre of the Hindus*, that "there is no species of composition which embraces so many purposes as the dramatic. The dialogue varies from simple to elaborate, from the conversation of ordinary life to the highest refinements of poetical taste. The illustrations are drawn from every known product of art as well as every observable phenomenon of Nature. The manners and feelings of the people are delineated, living and breathing before us, and history and religion furnish most important and interesting topics to the poet."

But we must be prepared at the outset to allow for certain peculiarities of the Indian drama which, although by no means rendering the Hindu theatre a monopoly of the sacred caste, prevent it from being a perfect mirror of Indian life. In one respect the Indian theatre differs from that of any other people. Every play is for the greater part written in Sanskrit, although that language, probably never the vernacular of the whole country, ceased to be spoken at an early date; and so, since none of the dramatic compositions at present known can claim a very high antiquity, "they must have been unintelligible to a considerable part of their audiences, and never could have been so directly addressed to the bulk of the population as to have exercised much influence on their passions or tastes." This, however, as Professor Wilson himself adds, is perfectly in harmony with Hindu social life, in which the highest branches of literature as well as the highest offices in the State were reserved for the Bráhmans and Kshattriyas; and, though the sacred character of the representation, as well as of the Sanskrit language itself, is regarded by Wilson as a poor substitute for really popular interest, we must not forget that such dramatic spectacles required considerable relaxation of Bráhmanic exclusiveness, that the diversities of spoken dialects would have given a local tone to any drama employing one of these dialects, and that the pedantry of Latin plays like those of Ariosto (with which the Indian have been compared) offends, not so much as an affectation of scholarship, but rather as the wilful preference of a dead language to a polished national speech. Had India possessed any national speech, we might be justified in comparing her drama with the Latin plays of modern Europe; but, in the absence of uniform speech, it is not easy to see how a drama could have been produced without the aid of some such instrument as Sanskrit. Dramas in the vernacular dialects and of an inferior character have, indeed, left traces of their existence "in the dramatised stories of the *Bhanrs*, or professional buffoons, in the *Játras* of the Bengalis, and the *Rásas* of the western provinces." Of these, the first are representations "of some ludicious adventure by two or three performers, carried on in extempore dialogue usually of a very coarse kind, and enlivened by practical jokes not always very decent. The *Játra* is generally the exhibition of some of the incidents in the youthful life of Krishna, maintained also in extempore dialogue, but interspersed with popular songs. The *Rása* partakes more of the ballet, but it is accompanied also with songs, while the adventures of Krishna or Rama are represented in appropriate costume by measured gesticulation." A theatre really worthy of the name needed the dignity of that language which contained the treasures of India's lyric and epic poetry and wore a look of permanence and universality to which none of the spoken dialects could pretend.

The Sanskrit dramas, like those of Athens, are primarily written for but one specific performance, which, since their length often extends to as many as ten acts, must have occupied, not the two hours' traffic of the Shaksperian stage, but probably from five to six hours. Resembling the Athenian in their sacred character and not written, like the plays of modern Europe, for permanent theatrical companies with their professional ends, these dramas seem to have been acted only on solemn occasions which may be compared with the spring and autumn festivals of Bacchus in the Athenian theatre. "According to Hindu authorities," says Wilson, "the occasions suitable for dramatic representations are the lunar holidays, a royal coronation, assemblages of people at fairs and religious festivals, marriages, the meeting of friends, taking first possession of a house or a town, and the birth of a son; the most ordinary occasion, however, was the season peculiarly sacred to some divinity." While this association of the Indian drama with sacred festivals may remind us of our European miracle-plays, or the Persian *tazyas*, or passion-plays, represented in the first ten days of the month Moharrem, as described by Count Gobineau, the infrequency of the Indian spectacle, together with the use of Sanskrit, will guard us against the error of Sir William Jones, who supposed that "the Indian theatre would fill as many volumes as that of any nation in ancient or modern Europe." While the list of dramatic pieces composed by Chinese dramatists of the Youen dynasty reaches a total of five hundred and sixty-four, it is doubtful whether all the Sanskrit plays to be found, together with those mentioned by writers on the drama, amount to more than sixty. Only three plays are attributed to each of the great Indian dramatists, Bhavabhúti and Kálidása—a number to be contrasted not merely with the two hundred and sixty comedies attributed to Antiphanes or the two thousand plays of Lope de Vega, but with the substantial dramatic contributions of Aristophanes, Plautus, or Shakspere. But, though the number of Indian plays is small, they supplied, in the decay of dramatic art, a rich field for that verbal criticism in which Oriental intellect delights. System-mongers, taking the place of dramatic poets, laid down a *technique* and dogmatical precepts, and "set themselves to classify plays, persons, and passions until they wove a complicated web out of very spider-like materials." Seeking no initiation in the mysteries of this criticism, we shall now turn to the main characteristics already noticed as common to the Indian epics and the Indian drama—the prominence of physical Nature and the disregard of "the unities."

§ 89. Although the prominence of Nature in the Indian drama is by no means to be estimated solely from descriptive passages, the constant use of similes and figures taken from Nature's life really supplying more convincing evidences of this prominence than any number of such passages, it is easier to select some of the latter than to give the read any idea of that perfect mosaic of

Nature-language which these dramas contain. Perhaps, however, the following translation of Maitreya's observations in the fourth act of *Mrichchhakati*, or the "Toycart," may convey some impression of this Nature-language, while two passages from the fifth act of the same play will illustrate the descriptions of Nature with which Indian plays abound. The translations, it must be added, are the work of that profound and elegant scholar, the late Professor Horace Hayman Wilson, to whom all Sanskrit students are so deeply indebted, and whose words have already been frequently quoted.

"A very pretty entrance," says Maitreya; "the threshold is neatly coloured, well swept and watered; the floor is beautified with strings of sweet flowers; the top of the gate is lofty, and gives one the pleasure of looking up to the clouds, while the jasmine festoon hangs tremblingly down, as if it were now tossing on the trunk of Indra's elephant. Over the doorway is a lofty arch of ivory; above it again wave flags dyed with safflower, their fringes curling in the wind like fingers that beckon me 'come hither.' . . . Bless me! why, here is a line of palaces, as white as the moon, as the conch, as the stalk of the water-lily. Oh, ho! this is a very gay scene: here the drums, beaten by tapering fingers, emit like clouds a murmuring tone; there the cymbals, beating time, flash as they descend like the unlucky stars that fall from heaven. The flute here breathes the soft hum of the bee; some damsels are singing like so many bees intoxicated with flowery nectar; others are practising the graceful dance, and others are employed in reading plays and poems. . . . The arched gateway is of gold, and many-coloured gems on a ground of sapphire, and looks like the bow of Indra in an azure sky. . . . A very lovely scene! The numerous trees are bowed down by delicious fruit, and between them are silken swings constructed for the light form of youthful beauty; the yellow jasmine, the graceful *málatí*, the full-blossomed *mallíká*, the blue clitoria, spontaneous shed their flowers and strew the ground with a carpet more lovely than any in the groves of Indra; the reservoir glows with the red lotus-blossoms, like the dawn with the fiery beams of the rising sun; and here the *asoka* tree, with its rich crimson blossoms, shines like a young warrior bathed in the sanguine shower of the furious fight."

The fifth act of the same play opens with the following speech of Chárudatta:—

" A heavy storm impends; the gathering gloom
Delights the peafowl and distracts the swan
Not yet prepared for periodic flight;
And these deep shades contract with sad despondence
The heart that pines in absence. Through the air,
A rival *Kesava*,* the purple cloud
Rolls stately on, girded by golden lightning
As by his yellow garb, and bearing high
The long white line of storks. . . .
From the dark womb in rapid fall descend
The silvery drops, and glittering in the gleams
Shot from the lightning, bright and fitful, sparkle
Like a rich fringe rent from the robe of heaven;
The firmament is filled with scattered clouds,
And, as they fly before the wind, their forms,
As in a picture, image various shapes,
The semblances of storks and soaring swans,
Of dolphins and the monsters of the deep,
Of dragons vast and pinnacles and towers."

---

* *Crinitus*, a name of Krishna, perhaps alluding to his graceful tresses, as Professor Wilson notes. Although descriptive passages such as the above and following are strictly without parallel in the Shaksperian drama, the student of Shakspere will be reminded of the lines in *Antony and Cleopatra* (Act. IV. sc. xii.):—

" Sometime we see a cloud that's dragonish:
A vapour, sometime, like a bear, or lion,
A tower'd citadel, a pendant rock,
A forked mountain, or blue promontory
With trees upon 't, that nod unto the world,
And mock our eyes with air: thou hast seen these signs;
They are black vesper's pageants."

Then follow lines peculiarly interesting for their allusions to the story and persons of the epic Mahábhárata; the Dhritaráshtra mentioned here has above been already referred to in our notice of the epic, while Duryodhan is one of the Kauravas, and Yudhishthira the eldest son of Pándu. Chárudatta continues:—

> "The spreading shade, methinks, is like the host
> Of Dhritaráshtra shouting loud in thunder;
> Yon strutting peacock welcomes its advance
> Like proud Duryodhan vaunting of his might;
> From its dread enmity the *koïl* flies
> Like luckless Yudhishthira by the dice
> Bereaved of power; and scatter wild the swans
> Like the proscribed and houseless Pándavas."

In the same act of the "Toy-cart" occurs a famous description of the rainy season in a dialogue between Vasantasena, the *Víta*, and an attendant. The *Víta*, it must be added, like the *Vidúshaka*, or Buffoon, is a stock-character of the Hindu theatre; this personage must be accomplished in poetry, music, singing, may be the companion of a man or a woman, is on familiar terms with his associate, and may be compared with the Parasite of the Greek and Latin plays. The passage is here quoted at length as one of the best specimens of Natural description in the Indian drama.

> "*Atten.* Lady, upon the mountain's brow the clouds
> Hang dark and drooping, as the aching heart
> Of her who sorrows for her distant lord;
> Their thunders rouse the peafowl, and the sky
> Is agitated by their wings, as fanned
> By thousand fans with costly gems enclosed.
> The chattering frog quaffs the pellucid drops
> That cleanse his miry jaws; the peahen shrieks
> With transport, and the *Nípa* freshly blooms.
> The moon is blotted by the driving scud,
> As is the saintly character by those
> Who wear its garb to veil their abject lives;
> And, like the damsel whose fair fame is lost
> In ever-changing loves, the lightning, true
> To no one quarter, flits along the skies.
> *Vas.* You speak it well, my friend; . . .

Let the clouds fall in torrents, thunder roar,
And heaven's red bolt dash fiercely to the ground,
The dauntless damsel faithful love inspires
Treads boldly on, nor dreads the maddening storm.
    Vita. Like an invading prince, who holds his court
Within the city of his humbled foe,
Yon mighty cloud, advancing with the wind,
With store of arrowy shower, with thundering drums,
And blazing streamers, marches to assail
In his own heavens the monarch of the night.
    Vas. Nay, nay, not so; I rather read it thus;—
The clouds that, like unwieldy elephants,
Roll their inflated masses grumbling on,
Or whiten with the migratory troop
Of hovering cranes, teach anguish to the heart.
The storks' shrill cry sounds like the plaintive tabor
To her who muses on her lord's return.
    Vita. Behold, where yonder ponderous cloud assumes
The stature of the elephant, the storks
Entwine a fillet for his front, and waves
The lightning like a *chouri* o'er his head.
    Vas. Observe, my friend, the day is swallowed up
By these deep shades, dark as the dripping leaf
Of the *taurála* tree, and, like an elephant
That cowering shuns the battle's arrowy sleet,
So shrinks the scattering ant-hill from the shower. . . .
In sooth, I think the firmament dissolves:
Melted by Indra's scorching bolt, it falls
In unexhausted torrents. Now the cloud
Ascends—now stoops—now roars aloud in thunder—
Now sheds its streams—now frowns with deeper gloom,
Full of fantastic change, like one new-raised
By fortune's fickle favours.
    Vita.   Now the sky
With lightning flames, now laughs with whitening storks,
Now glows with Indra's painted bow that hurls
Its hundred shafts—now rattles with his bolt—
Now loud it chafes with rushing winds, and now,
With clustering clouds that roll their spiry folds
Like sable snakes along, it thickens dark
As if 'twere clothed with vapours such as spread
When incense soars in circling wreaths to heaven."

To exhaust such descriptive passages, even in such Indian plays as have been translated into European languages, would be a long and rather monotonous task. At the end of Act V. in this same play two similar descriptive passages are put into the mouth of Chárudatta. In *Vikrama and Urvasí* (or "The Hero and the Nymph"), attributed to Kálidása, the first act opens on the Himálayan Mountains, and, a troop of *Apsarasas*, or nymphs of heaven, entering, the opportunity for such passages may be readily conceived. As a brief specimen from this play, we may select the closing words of the second act spoken by King Parúravas:—

> "'Tis past mid-day. Exhausted by the heat,
> The peacock plunges in the scanty pool
> That feeds the tall tree's root; the drowsy bee
> Sleeps in the hollow chambers of the lotus
> Darkened with closing petals; on the brink
> Of the now tepid lake the wild duck lurks
> Among the sedgy shade; and even here
> The parrot from his wiry bower complains,
> And calls for water to allay his thirst."

In the third act of the same play a description of the rising moon is put into the mouth of Parúravas; and in the fourth act, the scene of which lies in the forest of Akalusha, the lyrical descriptions of Nature are too numerous to admit of easy illustration. From other plays examples of natural description might readily be collected, such as the lines of Vasantí, beginning, "The sun, with glow intense," etc., in the second act of the *Uttara-Rama-Charitra*, the scene of which is the forest of Janasthána, along the river Godáverí. But, instead of uselessly multiplying examples from these and other Indian plays, we shall turn aside to observe a similar prominence of Nature in the Chinese and Japanese dramas.

§ 84. If the Hindu critic attributes the legendary origin of his drama to an inspired sage, Bharata, or even to the god Bráhma, the less ambitious Celestial is content to refer the origin of his theatre to the Emperor Hiouentsong, of the T'ang dynasty, founder of an Imperial Academy of Music and of the Chinese drama (cir. 736 A.D.). Among the Chinese neither music nor literature was destined to be monopolised by a caste of priests; and this difference in social development has left its marks in certain differences of the Chinese and Indian dramas. The prologue of the Indian play, *Málatí and Mádhava*, shows how the Indian dramatist, addressing himself to a cultured audience acquainted with Sanskrit, valued artistic qualities such as fertility of imagination, harmony of style, diversity of incident. But the purpose of the Chinese drama is not artistic but moral; it is "to present the noblest teachings of history to the ignorant who cannot read;" "to present upon the stage," as the Chinese penal code puts it, "real or fictitious pictures of just and good men, chaste women, affectionate and obedient children, which may lead the spectators to the practice of virtue." In the *Pi-pa-ki* (or "History of a Lute"), a Chinese drama in twenty-four scenes represented at Peking in 1404 A.D., there are indeed some signs of artistic criticism—variety of incidents and greater individuality of character, for example; but the Youen Collection of Chinese plays, an anthology which belongs to the thirteenth century, altogether subordinates art to didactic moralising. So important, indeed, is this didactic purpose that it has produced a feature of the Chinese drama not to be found in any other theatre of the East or West—the singing personage. "In all Chinese plays," says Sir John Davis,* "there is an irregular operatic species of song which the principal character occasionally chants forth in unison, with a loud or soft accompaniment of music as may best suit the sentiment or action of the moment." "It was not enough for the Chinese," says M. Bazin,† "to have laid down moral utility as the end of their dramatic representations; they must also discover

* Introduction to the *Sorrows of Han*.
† *Théâtre Chinois*, Introduction, p. xxx.

the means of attaining that end. Hence the *rôle* of the singing personage, an admirably ingenious conception, a characteristic essentially distinguishing the Chinese from all known theatres. This singing personage, with figurative, showy, and lyrical diction, his voice aided by a musical accompaniment, is a link between the poet and the audience, like the chorus of the Greek theatre, only with this difference, that he remains no stranger to the action. On the contrary, the singing personage is the hero of the piece, who, when the catastrophe occurs, always remains on the stage to rouse the sorrow of the spectators and draw forth their tears. It will be observed that this personage, like the rest, may be taken from any class of social life; in the *Sorrows of Han* he is an emperor; in the *Maid's Intrigues*, a young servant. When the chief personage dies in the course of the play, his place is taken by another character of the drama, who sings in his turn. In fact, the singing personage is the leading character that instructs, cites the maxims of the wise, the precepts of philosophers, or appeals to famous examples from history or mythology."

The passages in which descriptions of Nature, or figures taken from the sights and sounds of Nature's life, occur most frequently are sung by this curious personage; it is to be remembered, however, that, as in the Indian drama, the prominence of Nature is marked quite as much by the use of similes as by actual descriptions. Such a simile, for example, is contained in the very name of the play, *Han-koong-tseu*, literally, "Autumn in the Palace of Han"—a name translated the "Sorrows of Han," because in Chinese "Autumn" is emblematic of sorrow, just as "Spring" is of joy. Throughout this play, the subject of which is the tragic fate of a Chinese lady, who throws herself into the river

Amoor rather than wed the Khan of the Tartars, there breathes an air of autumn delicately in keeping with the simile from Nature just observed in the name. The prominence of Nature in the Chinese drama may indeed be readily conceived from the fact that Chinese critics, dividing the subjects of dramatic composition into twelve classes, specify as the second and ninth of these classes, " Woods, springs, hills, and valleys," and " The wind, the flowers, the snow, the moon." A few illustrations may be selected from the plays of the Youen Collection translated by M. Bazin.*

In *Tchao-meï-hiang* (" A Maid's Intrigues ") the following words, partly sung, partly spoken, are put into the mouth of one of the female characters. " With gentle sound our gemmed sashes wave in the wind; how softly trip our little feet like golden creepers o'er the grass! Above, the moon shines brightly as we tread the dark green moss. . . . Lady, see, how crimson are the flowers; they show like pieces of embroidered silk. Look on the green

* The Chinese drama is at present known to European readers chiefly through the translations of Sir J. F. Davis, M. Stanislas Julien, and M. Bazin, made from the *Youen-jin-pé-tchong*, or "Hundred Plays composed under the Youen," princes of Genghis-Khan's famous family. Earliest among European translations from this dramatic anthology came the *Orphan of the Tchao Family*, made in 1731 by Father Prémare, a Jesuit missionary, and published in 1735. Voltaire, twenty years later, adapted the subject of this Chinese play to the French stage; but three quarters of a century were to elapse before European scholars manifested any zealous interest in the theatre of China. At length the *Heir in Old Age* and the *Sorrows of Han* were translated by Sir J. F. Davis; and, in 1832, the *History of the Chalk Circle*, and (in 1834) a new and full translation of the *Orphan of the Tchao Family*, were added by M. Julien. But not till 1838 was any considerable knowledge of this Eastern drama placed within reach of European readers. In that year M. Bazin published his *Chinese Theatre*, which not only contained four plays never before translated, but was accompanied by an excellent preface, describing the general character of the Chinese stage under the Youen dynasty. In 1841 M. Bazin put students of Chinese literature under new obligations by publishing his translation of the *Pi-pa-ki*. The study of the Chinese drama in Europe does not, however, seem to have made any farther progress.

Y

hues of the willows—afar one might have thought them clouds of mist all balanced in the air. . . . The flowers and willows seem to sigh at our approach; the breeze, the moon, are fuller still of sympathy; 'tis they that bring to life the varied colours that we love. A poet in such moments of delight might feel constrained to pour out in sweet verse the feelings of his soul. No *han-lin* by his talent could describe the charms of this fair scene, no painter with rich colours represent them. . . . The perfumed plants are veiled in floating mist; our lamp throws a still flame within its covering of blue gauze; yonder the willows like green silks are hanging, from whence drip pearls of dew, and fall, like rain of stars, into the limpid pool—gems, one might call them, softly dropped within a crystal basin. And, look, the rising moon shines at the willow's edge, like that sky-coloured dragon who of old carried the mirror of *Hoang-ti*."

Other examples of the sentiment of Nature in the same play might be quoted; for example, in the third act Fan-sou sings, "The moon is silvery, the breeze fresh, and the flowers spread out thick clouds of perfume —the moon floats on the water's face; with gentle breeze the willows wave, and veiled in summer mists the palace lies." But we prefer to vary our examples. In the next play translated by M. Bazin, *Ho-han-chan*, or "The Tunic compared," Tchang-i, the Youen-waï (a title of merchants and proprietors), watching from within his house (known by the sign of the Golden Lion) a fall of snow, partly speaks, partly sings, as follows: "My son, 'tis true the flakes of icy snow are very beautiful. Clouds that look like reddish mists stretch out and mass together from all sides; big snow-flakes whirl and eddy in the air; the north wind blows with fury, and the view loses itself in a silvery horizon. . . . Now are we just at the season when the cold begins, and so you say the winter comes; but as for me I say it is the spring; if it were otherwise, how could these pear-blossoms be tumbling leaf by leaf? How could the willow-blossoms fly in whirls? The blossoms of the pear-tree crowd together and make a silvered ground; the blossoms of the willow lift themselves skywards like to a waving dress and fall again to earth." *

Beside this highly imaginative description of the falling snow, we may place the character of the deceitful courtesan drawn in *Ho-lang-tan*, or the "Singing Girl," a play detailing the ruin of a Chinese family by a courtesan, and excellently illustrating that inculcation of family virtues to which we shall presently advert as one of the striking characteristics of the Chinese drama. "You love," says the matron Lieou-chi to her husband, who has determined to make a second wife of Tchang-iu-ngo the courtesan, "you love those looks in which the streams of autumn seem to play;† you worship those eyebrows painted and delicately arched. But know you not that you ruin your character? Bethink you that this forehead, wearing the splendour of the *Fou-yong* flower, brings ruin upon households; that this mouth, with its carnation-hues of peach and cherry, devours the souls of men. Her perfumed breath exhales the odours of the clove tree; but much I fear that all her

* The second act of the same play contains some lines which remind us of Pope's famous simile, so much admired by Johnson, ending—

"Hills peep o'er hills, and Alps on Alps arise."

Tchang-i, in pursuit of his son, sings, "My outlook darkens more and more. The river here is deep, the mountain-heights vanish among the clouds; e'en so, among my grievous sorrows, I am checked by watery wastes and by that limited horizon which robs me of all view."

† The lustre of beautiful eyes is compared by Chinese novelists to "the pure waters of a fountain in autumn, over which there floats a willow-leaf."

flowers shall scatter, and a whirl of wind bear them away."

Again, the opening verses of *Teou-ngo-youen*, recited by the lady Tsaï, remind us of those in which so many poets, from Homer to Menander, from Theocritus to Lamartine, have expressed the contrast of Nature's everlasting life with man's individual decay and death—a contrast in which the origin of the pastoral elegy of Bion and Moschus, imitated by English poets, from Milton in his *Lycidas* to Matthew Arnold in his *Thyrsis*, is to be truly found. The Chinese verses run thus: "We watch the flowers spring ever forth afresh—but man grows young again like them no more. What need to hasten after wealth and rank? Rest and rejoicing are the immortals' lot." The central scene of this play offers a peculiar evidence of the close relations conceived by Chinese mind to exist between human justice and the physical forces of Nature. Teou-ngo, condemned to death by a corrupt judge,* is about to be executed on the stage; she forewarns the court of the prodigies which are to prove her innocence, and which remind us of the fire that fell on the prophet's sacrifice, and the three years' drought that came on Israel. " My lord, we still are in that season of the year when painfully men bear excessive heat. 'Tis well! If I be innocent, then shall the heaven let fall, when I shall cease to live, thick flakes of chilling snow to cover o'er the body of Teou-ngo. . . . Know you why, of old, three years was blessed rain kept from the earth? Because the district of Tong-haï had incurred the just revenge of a woman filled with filial piety. Now it is the turn of your district of Chan-

---

* The Chinese drama was evidently used occasionally as a vehicle of satire. In the *Chalk Circle* an unjust judge is also satirized; and in the *Pi-pa-ki* there is an entire scene parodying the Chinese Official Examinations.

yang. All this comes from the magistrates abandoning justice and humanity. . . . Clouds that float in the air for me, darken the sky! Winds that murmur and moan for me, whirl down in tempest!" Snow in the heats of summer and a three years' drought attest the innocence of the unjustly executed Teou-ngo; and if for the epic poet of England the seasons change at the sin of Adam, for the Chinese dramatist they change at the condemnation of the innocent.

Many other examples of this prominence of Nature in the Chinese drama might be cited—for example, the description of the Yellow River in the first act of *Si-siang-ki*, translated by M. Stanislas Julien; but we shall prefer to observe the same feature in the lyrical drama of Japan. The characters and names of the Japanese plays translated by Mr. Chamberlain, in his *Classical Poetry of the Japanese*, show want of individual characterisation, and predominence of allegorical or abstract ideas and natural description. In the *Robe of Feathers* the *dramatis personæ* are a fairy, a fisherman, and the chorus; in *Life is a Dream* (an allegorical piece suggestive of Calderon's *autos sacramentales*) and the *Deathstone* individuality is likewise wanting. Here, however, we are only concerned with the prominence of Nature in these plays; it may be illustrated by an outline of the *Robe of Feathers*, as translated by Mr. Chamberlain. The play opens with a long recitative, in which the fisherman and chorus describe the beauties of Miho's pine-clad shore at dawn on a spring morning. The fisherman steps on shore and the action of the piece begins. "As I land on Miho's shore," says the fisherman, "flowers come fluttering down, strains of music re-echo, and a more than earthly fragrance fills the air. Surely there is something in this." Suddenly he sees a fairy robe hanging from the branches of a pine tree, and determines to take it back with him to the old folks in his village. But now the fairy owner of the robe claims it—without her robe of feathers "never more can she go through the realms of air, never return to her celestial home." The fisherman refuses to restore the robe; and a situation arises reminding us somewhat of Philoctetes and Neoptolemus in the drama of Sophocles. The chorus pity her, and sing, in a spirit full of natural sentiment—

"Clouds, wandering clouds, she yearns and yearns in vain,
Soaring like you to tread the heaven again."

Presently the fisherman relents. On one condition he will restore the robe—that the fairy shall dance one of the fairy dances of which he has heard so much. The fairy consents to dance "the dance that makes the Palace of the Moon turn round," and, singing

"Now the dancing maiden sings,
Robed in clouds and fleecy wings,"

commences one of those dances which occupy so prominent a place in the Japanese drama. Meanwhile the chorus sings of the cause that "gave the blue realms of air their name of firmament," the fairy now and then joining in their song. The fairy continues dancing to the end of the play, the chorus in imagination watching and describing her disappearance from their sight towards heaven in the following ode, which well deserves a place alongside the descriptive passages of the Indian and Chinese dramas.

"Dance on, sweet maiden, through the happy hours;
Dance on, sweet maiden, while the magic flowers
Crowning thy tresses flutter in the wind,
Raised by the waving pinions intertwined. . . .
But, ah, the hour, the hour of parting rings!
Caught by the breeze the fairy's magic wings

Heavenward do bear her from the pine-clad shore,
Past Ukishíma's widely stretching moor,
Past Ashidaka's heights, and where are spread
Th' eternal snows on Fusiyama's head—
Higher and higher to the azure skies,
Till wandering vapours hide her from our eyes."

It is to be noted how strongly this prominence of Nature distinguishes the Oriental from the Western dramas. The scene of Æschylus' *Prometheus Bound* lies on the Caucasus, in the midst of that savagely sublime scenery which Lermontoff, the Russian Byron, was to depict in his *Demon*; but the Athenian dramatist makes no use of the opportunity for description, his own interest and that of his audience being centred on humanity, not physical Nature—a striking contrast to Shelley's *Prometheus Unbound*, in which we have humanity subordinated to Nature. Again, in the *Persians* how an Indian dramatist would have delighted in giving a full and graphic description of the Hellespont; in Sophocles' *Philoctetes* and *Œdipus at Colonus*, how widely would he have extended the brief notice of the hero's cavern and of the sacred grove! Nor is this domination of human interest by any means confined to the classical drama of the West. Beyond the description of the starry night in the *Merchant of Venice*, and a few glimpses of Nature such as that of the sea in *Lear*, we shall find few passages descriptive of Nature in Shakspere's plays, and not many more in the plays of his contemporary dramatists. Moreover, the mysteries and miracle-plays of England, France, and Germany are curiously deficient in description of Nature. The same characteristic is presented by German dramatists, who can by no means be accused of slavishly following Greek models. Schiller's *Wilhelm Tell*, for example, though elaborated from ideas first roused in the mind of the poet's friend Goethe by Swiss scenery, confines description to the scenic notices at the commencement of each scene—notices which an Indian dramatist would certainly have worked out as poetry in the body of the play, expending, too, his highest art on these very parts which the Western dramatist cannot allow into his drama at all. If we are asked the causes of this marked difference between the dramas of the East and those of the West, we shall be content to name the absence of individuality in the former contrasted with the latter—weak character-drawing being thus supplemented by natural description—and the prominence of town-life in the Western contrasted with that of the village and country in the Eastern civilisation; but to answer the question at all fully would carry us far beyond the limits of the present work.

§ 85. Closely connected with this prevalence of natural description is a vivid realisation of sights and sounds likewise common to the Indian and Chinese theatres. In the Indian play *Mrichchhakati*, for example, the following graphic speech is put into the mouth of Karnapúraka. " Only hear. Your ladyship's fierce elephant ' Post-breaker ' killed his keeper and broke his chain; he then scoured off along the high-road, making a terrible confusion. The people shouted and screamed, ' Carry off the children, get up the trees, climb the walls ; the elephant is coming ! ' Away went girdles and anklets ; and pearls and diamonds were scattered about in all directions. There he was, plunging about in Ujjayin, and tearing everything to pieces with his trunk, his feet, and his tusks, as if the city had been a large tank full of lotus-flowers." Again, every reader of *Sakuntalá* will remember the graphic description with which that play opens. After the Bráhman has pronounced the usual benediction, and the actress, at the manager's request, has sung "the charming strain," the play opens with the forest scene. King Dushmanta, in a chariot, is pursuing an antelope with bow and quiver. " The fleet creature," says the king to his charioteer, " has given us a long chase. Oh! there he runs, with his neck bent gracefully, looking back now and then at the pursuing chariot. Now, through fear of a descending shaft, he contracts his forehand and extends his flexible haunches; and now, through fatigue, he pauses to nibble the grass in his path with half-opened mouth. See, how he springs and bounds with long steps, lightly skimming the ground and rising high in the air." At the king's order the reins are loosened and the chariot driven over the stage, first at full gallop and then gently, the charioteer and the king making speeches descriptive of their rapid imaginary course. " The horses," says the former, " were not even touched by the clouds of dust which they raised; they tossed their manes, erected their ears, and rather glided than galloped over the smooth plain." " Soon," responds Dushmanta, " they outran the swift antelope. Objects which, from their distance, appeared minute, presently became larger; what was really divided seemed united as we passed, and what was in truth bent seemed straight; so swift was the motion of the wheels that nothing for many moments was either distant or near." If space permitted, it might be shown that the Chinese dramatists possess a like talent for graphic description; but we shall prefer to illustrate that neglect of the unities which we have already observed as a common characteristic of Indian epic and dramatic poetry, and which in the Chinese drama is no less marked.

To illustrate the Indian disregard of the temporal unity—in the *Toy-cart* the time of action is four days; in the *Ratnávalí*, the same; in the *Málati and Mádhava*, a few days; and in the *Uttara-Rama-Charitra*, though the time of each act is that of its representation, an interval of twelve years occurs between the first act and the remainder of the play. The violations of the temporal unity in the Chinese drama are much greater, and that for a special reason. Here didactic purposes have made the dramatist peculiarly fond of historical personages and events; and it is almost needless to say that wherever any form of the historical drama, religious or secular, has prevailed, the temporal unity has been neglected. Thus, in *Ho-han-chan*, eighteen years elapse between the second and third acts, the unborn infant of the former having become the young hunter, Tchin-pao, of the latter; in *Ho-lang-tan*, the third act opens with the words of Youan-yen, "Alas, the days and months glide away with the speed of the arrow," for thirteen years have elapsed since the purchase of the child formally detailed in the second act; and, in *Teou-ngo-youen*, the father of Teou-ngo says, "'Tis now full sixteen years since I left my daughter"— the event dramatised in the first act. Far from any apologies such as the chorus in *Winter's Tale* and in *Henry V.* offers, the Chinese dramatist does not even see the need of always recollecting the lapse of time. In *Ho-han-chan*, for example, when the old couple are again brought upon the stage (Act. III. sc. vi.), eighteen years have not accustomed them to beggars' habits. Tchang-i is still lamenting his losses as if they had happened but yesterday; both he and his wife are still mendicants fresh at the trade, feeling bitterly "the disgrace of asking alms in the street;" nay, even the snow-flakes are still falling and the winds still roaring as on the dismal day of the conflagration in which he lost his wealth.

Unity of place is equally disregarded by Indian and

Chinese dramatists. The vast range of Indian and Chinese life, contrasted with the petty circle of the Greek city commonwealth, prevented fixity of place from being attended to. Thus, to take some Indian examples, in *Vikramórvasí* the scene of the first act is on the peaks of the Himálayan Mountains, that of the second and third the palace of Parúravas, that of the fourth the forest of Akalusha, while the fifth shifts again to the palace. So in the *Uttara-Rama-Charitra* the scene of the first act is in the palace of Ráma at Ayodhya, that of the second act in the forest of Janasthána along the Godáverí, while in the rest of the piece the scene lies in the vicinity of Valmíki's hermitage at Bithúr, on the Ganges. To select some Chinese examples, the scenes of the *Sorrows of Han* shift from the palace of the emperor to the Tartar encampment and the banks of the Amoor; those of *Ho-han-chan* from the Sign of the Golden Lion to the Yellow River, thence to the house of the brigand Tchinhou, next to the monastery of Fô, to the pagoda of the Golden Sand, to the valley of Ouo-kong, finally again to the pagoda; and those of *Pi-pa-ki* constantly change from the capital to the native village of the family whose fortunes form the subject of the piece.

§ 86. But if there are striking resemblances in the Indian and Chinese theatres, such as natural description and the neglect of the unities, there are differences no less striking. We have already referred to the singing personage of the Chinese drama and the didactic purposes to which this character, and indeed the entire play, is applied; and we have contrasted this didactic moralising with the artistic aims of the Indian theatre. This didactic purpose of the Chinese drama tends to prevent profound analysis of individual character and to concentrate attention on the incidents of the story. But there is another and far deeper reason for want of individuality in Chinese plays—the family system upon which the social life of China rests. It might even seem at first glance that the Chinese, like the early Roman, family should have been fatal to the rise of any drama of character. But the *old* Roman *familia*, with its *patria potestas*, children under power, perpetual tutelage of women, presented for a long time more serious obstacles to the development of personal freedom and individuality of character than the Chinese system, modified as it was by the principle of election to public offices as well as by State examination. But, though the Chinese family did not prevent the rise of a drama, it has certainly left its marks deep on almost all Chinese plays. Such marks are to be seen in the constant injunction of family virtues and the limitation of character-drawing to the virtues or vices of family life. To select a few examples, the plot of *Tchao-meï-hiang* turns upon the proper celebration of marriage rites; that of *Ho-han-chan* upon the fortunes of a family wrecked by an ungrateful impostor; that of *Ho-lang-tan* upon the ruin of a family by the intrigues of a courtesan; that of *Pi-pa-ki* upon the filial devotion of a daughter-in-law in days of famine. Indeed, so perpetually are we reminded of the formal and spiritual presence of the family in Chinese plays, that the *dramatis personæ* are always careful to announce the name of the family to which they belong. One effect of the Chinese family upon the drama deserves particular attention. The ancestral worship of the family, in which the representation of deceased ancestors by living persons was itself an infant drama, seems to have materialised and familiarised the associations of the spiritual world to a degree we can but faintly realise. The *Koueï-men* ("Ghosts' Gate") of the Chinese stage—the door through which the ghosts make their entrances and exits—marks the frequent presence of spiritual (but by no means immaterial) personages in the theatre; even amusing parodies on ancestral worship might be quoted—for example, from Act IV. sc. vi. of *Ho-han-chan.* Indeed, the Chinese dramatist displays an easy familiarity with the world of spirits worthy of the roughest maker of medieval mysteries. The *Revenge of Teou-ngo,* for example, is a drama in which ghost-life— if we may use such a phrase—is denuded of all that solemn horror which shrouds the Æschylean Darius or the Shaksperian Banquo; even the tragic poets in the *Frogs* maintain the ghostly proprieties better than Teou-ngo. This is not because the Chinese play intermingles comedy and tragedy, as is usual with the Chinese dramatists; it is because we see the ghost in plain daylight, pleading in a court of justice, arguing its case with consummate coolness, and confronting, nay, actually *beating* its false accusers. We may look upon the mutilated form of Vergil's Deïphobus—

"Lacerum crudeliter ora,
Ora manusque ambas, populataque tempora raptis
Auribus, et truncas inhonesto vulnere nares"—

or the scornful face of Farinata degli Uberti—

"Come avesse lo 'nferno in gran dispitto"—

without starting at the materialism of the thought; but this is because we are for the time in Hades, a long way from the upper world. But to imagine the effect of Teou-ngo on our Western stage we must picture Polydorus' ghost accusing Polymêstor in the presence, not only of Hecuba, but a full Athenian court, or "the majesty of buried Denmark" walking arm in arm with Hamlet and even beating the astonished Claudius.

But, if the marks of family life and family worship meet us everywhere in Chinese plays, the social system of caste—a system directly opposed to anything like Chinese election and examination—has left its marks scarcely less distinctly on the Indian drama. Thus, the prologue of the Indian plays (partly imitated in the *Vorspiel* of Goethe's *Faust*) is really a piece of religious ceremonial conducted by the Bráhmans, and is without parallel in the thoroughly secular drama of China. The hereditary system of caste has not only led Indian critics to assign minutely the proper characteristics of personages taken from different social grades, but has even left its mark on the language used by the *dramatis personæ*. Heroes and principal personages speak Sanskrit, while the women and inferior characters use the modifications of that language comprehended under the term Prákrit. "According to the technical authorities," says Professor Wilson, "the heroine and principal female characters speak Saurasení; attendants on royal personages, Mágadhí; servants, Rajputs, and traders, Arddha or mixed Mágadhí. The *Vidúshaka*, or Buffoon, speaks the Práchí or Eastern dialect; rogues use Avantiká or the language of Ougein;" and altogether, as Professor Wilson himself adds, if these and other directions were implicitly followed, "a Hindu play would be a polyglot that few could hope to understand; in practice, however, we have rarely more than three varieties, or Sanskrit and a Prákrit more or less refined." An interesting example of this appropriation of language to social status may be observed in the second act of the *Mudrá Rakshasa*. Here Viradhagupta, an agent of Rakshasa, enters disguised as a snake-catcher, and, in keeping with the social status of the character he has for the moment assumed, addresses the passers-by in Prákrit, but when they have gone recovers, as if at one stroke, both his status and his language, and soliloquises in Sanskrit. But the social system of China permits no such attempts to fix the characteristics of *dramatis personæ* after hereditary models, or to vary their language in accordance with caste. Chinese critics have indeed classified the subjects and characters of their dramas, but the classification does not represent social distinctions. The diction of Chinese plays contains wide differences—the *kou-wen* or antique style, *siao-choué* or familiar style, in which dialogue is commonly written, the *hiang-tan* or patois of the provinces, used in modern pieces and especially in low comedy; but such variations of diction take their origin from the nature of the subject, and are no more connected with a system of caste than the erroneous English of good Mistress Quickly of Eastcheap.

But it is time to close not only our brief comparison of the Chinese and Indian dramas, but the very imperfect review of Chinese and Indian literatures which space has permitted. Constantly reminded of the littleness of individual life by the vast masses of men and women among whom they lived, the makers of Indian and Chinese literatures turned to the life of Nature and to questions of human origin and destiny before which individualism can never maintain itself. To detail the manner in which the castes and village communities of India, the family system and sentiments of China, aided by physical conditions, prevented the growth of that individualised life which has become in Europe the main source of literary as well as scientific ideas, would be a task far beyond the limits of a work like the present. We have merely selected a few specimens from an immense field of inquiry, and rather stated than solved some of the problems they suggest. With one other remark we shall close this inadequate notice of a literary field so boundless in its wealth of interest.

Compare the Indian or Chinese poetry of Nature, dramatic or otherwise, with that of modern Europe, and you discover a striking difference. The cuckoo brings to Wordsworth "a tale of visionary hours"—the recollection of his personal past never to return again—the memory of that "golden time" when the cuckoo's voice was "a mystery," and earth appeared "an unsubstantial fairy place." In the Oriental poetry this passionate sense of *personal* being is merged in one of social life. Only as a representative of his species does the Indian poet describe the seasons, only as such does the Chinese poet or philosopher describe or speculate. The Oriental knows not that concentrated personal being which looks on Nature as peculiarly connected with itself alone, and is for ever pacing round the haunts of its childhood, "seeking in vain to find the old familiar faces." Individual life, among the castes and village communities of India, or under the family system and paternal government of China, has attained no such social or artistic significance as in the West; and so in the Eastern dramas the face of Nature, too great and eternal to be brought into direct contrast with the ephemeral units of our Western stages, looks out fitly on the castes and families of the East.

BOOK V.
NATIONAL LITERATURE.

CHAPTER I.

WHAT IS NATIONAL LITERATURE?

§ 87. WHAT is a "nation"? The question has been discussed for a variety of purposes, political and philosophical, without apparently leading to any satisfactory definition. Mr. Freeman, for example,* admitting the difficulty of definition, tells us that the word " suggests a considerable continuous part of the earth's surface inhabited by men who at once speak the same tongue and are united under the same government." This unity of territorial possession, language, and government, together with the vague requirement of a "*considerable* part of the earth's surface," affords an easy mark for captious criticism. At least Mr. Freeman's conception of nationality shows that historical accuracy compels us, while assuming some normal type of nationhood and treating it as if it were permanent, to admit that no definition of nationality can express more than a limited range of truth. Such a definition cannot cover the entire course of national life, for the beginnings of a nation are lost in countless little channels whose union has afterwards formed the full stream; and if we pursue this stream far enough we come out upon an ocean in which distinctions of clan, city commonwealth, nation, are alike lost in cosmopolitanism.

* *Comparative Politics*, pp. 81, 83.

The word "natio" points to kinship and a body of kinsmen as the primary idea and fact marked by "nationality." "Nation," like *dêmos*, carries us back to the groups of kinsmen in which social communion all the world over is found to begin. But the "nations" of modern Europe have left these little groups so far behind that their culture has either forgotten the nationality of common kinship, or learned to treat it as an ideal splendidly false. Old ideas of common descent have been weakened in European progress by many causes. As the barbarian invaders settled down, ties of communal brotherhood tended to be displaced by ties of locality, just as among the Hebrews "Sons of Israel" had given way to the "Sacred Land." Sir Henry Maine, in his *Early History of Institutions*,* has admirably described this process by which "the land begins to be the basis of society instead of kinship;" and in a familiar passage of his *Ancient Law* he has traced a corresponding development of territorial from tribal sovereignty. Feudalism, linking personal obligations with the ownership of land, played a prominent part in this development. Moreover, the feudal seigneurs in another way aided in weakening the old sentiments of kinship; like the Roman patricians, they united ideas of privilege and descent, and prevented conceptions of common kinship from being popularised. Feudalism, indeed, based as it was upon the life or death or coming of age of an *individual*, could not but undermine corporate ideas of clanship and kinship. Christianity, again, but in a very different manner from feudalism, weakened European ideas of national kinship, turning the hopes of the scholar and the serf alike to that great democracy of Christian brotherhood before which all earthly distinctions of national as well as

* pp. 73, *sqq.*

personal descent were but filthy rags in the light of the eternal sun. Thus, if feudal exclusiveness narrowed ideas of descent in a manner likely to chill popular sympathies as soon as "the people" should arise out of isolated *bourgs* and the serfs, the universal ideas of Christianity also tended to weaken national kinship by counting every individual, irrespective of land or race, as a spiritual unit and nothing more. Finally, the growth of the towns, upon which the growth of national sentiments, as distinct from the localism of feudal life and the universalism of Christianity, was so largely to depend, laid the foundations of a comparative and historical inquiry not to be far pursued without discovering the hybrid character of European nations.

But, though community of blood is disproved by the history of each European nation, vague feelings of common kinship, no doubt supplemented by love of native land, still form the groundwork of national sentiments for the masses. In cultured minds the place of such feelings has been taken by respect for common language and the long line of literary and scientific achievements embodied in that language, and by sympathies with the historical doings and sufferings of those men and women who from age to age have borne the nation's name. To unity of country and government— a material rather than an ideal unity—we must add, as an element of nationality, respect for the monuments of national literature. National literature is an outcome of national life, a spiritual bond of national unity, such as no amount of eclectic study or cosmopolitan science can supply. So thought Goethe, when he said that the Germans of his youth, though acquainted with all the kinds of poetry in which different nations had distinguished themselves, lacked "national material"—"had handled few national subjects or none at all;"* and yet Goethe is the admirer of world-literature.

National literatures, then, require a vigorous and continuous national life; and if we seek for perfect types of national literature, we shall find them only under such conditions. In Italy, neither a language delightfully musical nor an early development of individualism of character within her cities could make up for the loss of such a life; nationality was here paralysed by the over-lordship of the German emperor, the presence of a world-religion visibly centred in that ancient capital which might have been the heart of an Italian nation, the strife of city commonwealths strangely like and unlike those of ancient Greece. In Germany the isolation of the feudal princes and of the towns aided the cosmopolitan ideas of the Holy Roman Empire in checking the progress of nationality. Russia, long the prey of Asiatic invaders, and exposed as a kind of rude barrier for the security of quiet culture in the West, was equally slow in manifesting signs of national life. In short, we may say that only in England, France, and Spain do we find truly national groups; and, when we remember how the burst of national life in Spain under Charles V. and Philip II. was succeeded by three centuries of comparative stagnation, we may add that, if continuous development be one grand mark of nationality, England and France, especially from a literary standpoint, are the only perfect types of nationhood yet known to history. But they are types to be contrasted as well as compared; and the contrast will enable us to distinguish two aspects curiously different under which national literature has revealed itself.

§ 88. A. W. Schlegel, discussing the progress of the

* *Wahrheit und Dichtung*, bk. vii.

Italian drama, notices the opinion of Calsabigi, that the decline of dramatic poetry in Italy was caused by "the want of permanent companies of players *and of a capital.*" In Italy and Germany, says Schlegel, "where there are only capitals of separate states but no general metropolis, great difficulties are opposed to the improvement of the theatre." * These observations of an Italian and a German critic suggest the most vital distinction in the literary development of England and France—the different degrees of literary centralism reached by the two countries.

In the literature of France, since the firm establishment of centralised monarchy in the seventeenth century, we everywhere feel the presence of that centralising spirit which in the Académie Française found a local habitation and a name. Mr. Matthew Arnold, in his essay on the literary influence of academies,† has shown how much may be said for literary centralism. The improvement of the French language, as the statutes of the Academy bear witness, was the great aim of the institution; and opponents of such institutions must admit the usefulness of this aim and the success of the Academy in this direction. In a democratic age, moreover, when, as De Tocqueville observed, accuracy of literary style is liable to be lost in the temporary predominance of inferior work, a central tribunal may maintain an ideal of style which in the rush of trade-literature is likely to be trampled underfoot. Still, Mr. Arnold's conception of provincialism cannot be accepted either as in harmony with English literary development in the past, or as a prophetic forecast of its future. A critic, himself thoroughly imbued with the spirit of French criticism,

* *Dramatic Art and Literature*, lect. xvi.
† *Essays in Criticism*, pp. 42, sqq. (ed. 1884).

would plant on English soil an exotic as indigenous to Paris as it is unsuited to the atmosphere of English national life. Another critic—Macaulay, in his essay on the *Royal Society of Literature*,—takes a very different view of learned academies and their literary influences. It is in literary academies, he tells us, that "envy and faction exert the most extensive and pernicious influence." The history of the French Academy, in particular, has been "an uninterrupted record of servile compliances, paltry artifices, deadly quarrels, perfidious friendships." Governed by the court, the Sorbonne, the philosophers, "it was always equally powerful for evil and impotent for good"—sought to depress Corneille, long refused to notice Voltaire, and even under the superintendence of D'Alembert was the home of the basest intrigues. There is some exaggeration in this view; yet Macaulay expresses the national spirit of English literature. Local and individual independence from the control of any central corporation is the peculiar characteristic of English literature—an independence equally removed from the dictation of a tribunal like the French Academy, and that total absence of any literary centre which Schlegel and Calsabigi deplore.

Mr. Arnold's transference of the French centralism into the life of English literature is capable of its best defence from the standpoint of cosmopolitan culture. From this standpoint national centres like Paris and its Academy become the best substitute for a world-centre which differences of language and national character cannot permit. "Let us conceive the whole group of civilised nations," says Mr. Arnold,[*] "as being, for intellectual and spiritual purposes, one great confederation bound to a joint action and working towards a

[*] Preface to Wordsworth's Poems.

common result. This was the ideal of Goethe, and it is an ideal which will impose itself upon the thoughts of our modern societies more and more." Yes; the ideal of world-literature, which Herder's *Voices of the People* did so much to foster in Germany, is attractive, especially to men who have never known true national unity. But, however deeply national literature may be indebted to an international exchange of ideas, however splendid may be the conception of universal principles in literary production and criticism, the true makers of national literature are the actions and thoughts of the nation itself; the place of these can never be taken by the sympathies of a cultured class too wide to be national, or those of a central academy too refined to be provincial. Provincialism is no ban in truly national literature. The influence of London has indeed been continually expressed by Chaucer, by Shakspere, by Milton, by Dryden, by Addison and Pope and Johnson. Perhaps the flavour of London life has been sometimes too strong in English literature.* But provincial language as well as spirit have found a ready place in the literature of England.

Here, then, we have two types of national literature —the English, blending local and central elements of national life without losing national unity in local distinctions such as Italy and Germany have known too well; the French, centralising its life in Paris, and so tending to prefer cosmopolitan ideals. Montesquieu tells us that he would subordinate his personal interests to those of his family, those of his family to those of his nation, those of his nation to the good of Europe and of the world. † In

* It has been said of Hogarth (1697-1764) that he depicted the manners of the London populace rather than those of the English people; the remark might be applied to a good deal of English literature in the eighteenth century.
† *Œuvres de Montesquieu,* Pensées diverses, t. ii. p. 456.

the development of national literatures we must picture something of the same kind, only allowing for the early influence of Christian world-religion, and not forgetting that special causes have given to some national literatures of Europe a more cosmopolitan aspect than to others. To watch the internal and external development by which local and national differences give way in turn to national and cosmopolitan ideals—this is one line of study open to students of national literatures; another is the deepening and widening of personal character which accompany such social expansion; a third is the changing aspect of physical nature which this social and individual evolution likewise involves. But to chronicle the rise of new forms, new spirits, of verse and prose in each European nation, and the gradual separation of science from literature; to trace such growth to its roots in social and physical causes; finally, to compare and contrast these causes as producing the diverse literatures of England and France and Germany, of Italy and Spain and Russia; this, truly, were the task of a literary Hercules. We shall here but briefly illustrate the evolution of individualism in national literatures and the effect of such evolution on man's views of physical nature.

CHAPTER II.

MAN IN NATIONAL LITERATURE.

§ 89. AT first sight it might seem that the individual and not the social spirit laid the foundations of national literature throughout Europe. In such early extant specimens of Saxon, German, and French poetry as *Beowulf*, the *Lay of the Nibelungs*, and the oldest *Chansons de Geste*, the note of communal song is subordinated to that of personal glory. Whatever choral odes or hymns the clans and village communities of Teuton and Celt may have possessed, we have now but scanty indications of their existence; and such glimpses of communal literature as we do find are to be observed only through a dense growth of individualised poetry.

At this fact, however apparently inimical to our view of literary development, we need not be surprised; for the most powerful causes united to obscure the social beginnings of modern European literatures. Clan songs and hymns, full of pagan worship and unchristian conceptions of clan duties, like Blood-revenge and a Shadow-world such as the gathering-place of the Hebrew kinsmen, could have little to attract the class to which we are indebted for almost all we know of European barbarism —the Christian clergy. Moreover, contact with Roman life and habits of military service in the imperial armies must have done much to weaken clanship and strengthen the power of the chiefs long before the inroads of the barbarians commenced. This aristocracy of chiefs had as little interest in treasuring up the folk-songs of their tribesmen (which could not but contain many a reminder of the social equality typified by the story of the Vase of Soissons) as the monks; and, even if they had the desire to perpetuate such songs, they lacked the requisite degree of education. Thus on all sides causes combined to obscure the very existence of any rude literary beginnings save those which the individualising life of the chiefs and, later on, the seigneurs permitted, or the laborious learning of the monks attempted in their Latin world-language in the belief that it alone was the proper instrument of literature. Local isolation and feudal individualism could not create national languages or sentiments; the universal religion of Christ had its world-language already made; it seemed for a time as if no social maker of national literature were to arise.

We cannot now enter upon that vast field at present attracting the labours of antiquarians, jurists, historical economists—the changes undergone by the clans of barbaric Europe in their degradation into the serfs of feudal lords. Even a general picture of these changes could not fail to introduce features more or less untrue in certain places, and suggesting a transition in some cases too rapid, in others too slow. In Northern Italy, for example, town life and the municipal system, upon which Rome's empire had been based, were so strong that the barbarians readily adopted city organization, and feudalism as known elsewhere was checked in its development. In Southern France, also, the municipal system continued to hold its own; and here, as among the Italian towns, arose by degrees an individualism of the old Greek and Roman stamp.

and quite different from that of the feudal castle. Elsewhere, however, the old domination of city life was overthrown, and a lasting preponderance of the country over the town established. It was during this preponderance of country life that the villagers, dependent on feudal lords and their men-at-arms, fell into a serfdom frequently more oppressive than pagan slavery. Unbound to their masters by any ties of sentiment or kinship, held together solely by the force of their local despot, hopeless for the future, ignorant of the past, shut out from each other and made the enemies of each other by their lords' raids, these villages, whether descended from provincials of Rome or barbarian clans, could feel none of that free enthusiasm in life which makes the flesh and blood of song. Before the life of men in groups could again become a song-maker, some degree of social happiness, some width of social sympathy, some sense of a free equality which slaves attached to the land or person of a lord could not feel, needed to be developed. This development was the work of the towns throughout Europe; it is with their struggle into independence from feudal control that social sentiments, the earliest makers of song, rise as in resurrection from the grave in which they had been buried with the old clan communities of Celt and Teuton.

§ 90. Thus from the fifth to the twelfth centuries, from the fall of Rome to the rise of the cities, two individualising types of human character prevail—the monk and the baron; and the Christian resignation of the former as well as the brutal or chivalrous prowess of the latter need not here be illustrated from Latin chronicle or early chanson. For neither of these types can any deep sense of personality be claimed. The man of mail, you may see from his songs, thinks of personality as so much blood, bone, and muscle, whose duty it is to joust or war, if possible, in the romanceful twilight of love and chivalry, but in any case to war. The man of prayer, if his sense of personality be less material, clothes his spiritual self and his entire spirit-world in sensual shapes, and would treat as a heretic any who might hint an objection against such earthly dress. Warrior and saint alike touch but the surface of personality; if it be so objective for the former as to be identified with animal strength, it is for the latter the sensual prop on which his " Realism " is supported. How is the growth of the cities connected with these types of weak personality? If these show themselves in monkish chronicle or baronial " epic," do not the *commune* and the *bourg* reflect themselves in a literary form of their own?

It is no mere accident that brings together the rise of the modern European drama and that of towns; a brief contrast of feudal and town life will prove this. The lord in his fortified castle, surrounded by his family and armed retinue—such is the centre of each feudal molecule. Beyond the castle walls a group of serfs cultivates the lord's lands; and, though the village church may stand as a reminder that there is an ideal of human unity before which even the gulf which separates serf and lord disappears, the castle chapel has its own caretaker of souls who is himself of knightly parentage, loftily patronises the village priest, and reminds the villagers that the Christian ideal of human equality is indeed only an ideal. Between this outer circle of the feudal group and the lord's family there is, in fact, no tie save that of force, no spiritual link save the ceremonial of Christian worship. This ceremonial is, indeed, a drama in miniature; but so long as there is only one gigantic personality of force (that of the lord), so long as bonds of social sympathy are wanting, sacred story alone can supply the personages or incidents of a dramatic spectacle.

Let us change the scene to a medieval town. Insurrection, or aid from the king, or commerce, has been here at work; that servile circle of the feudal camp which had been hewers of wood and drawers of water now lives within stone walls, and can stand a siege or make a sally as well as the best of armoured knights. The burghers have little feeling of fellowship with other towns; their group is rather an offensive and defensive alliance against all comers than any forecast of national burghership and the modern rule of the European *bourgeois*. But though their social sympathies are narrow, they are also intensely real; moreover, an infantine subdivision of labour and trade is going on; the magistracy and the clergy are being organised; new types of character, far different from knight and squire and man-at-arms, are being developed. If modern prose is being roughly hammered into shape in the townsmen's assemblies and their preachers' pulpits, the elements of a drama are also at hand. How does the communal life of the medieval *bourg* display itself in the townsmen's drama?

The relation of Mysteries, Miracle-plays, Moralities, to the growth of towns all over Europe is a subject which has not received the attention it deserves; and the consequences have been that neither has the peculiar nature of this early drama been understood as reflecting contemporary social life, nor has the growth of the drama of personal character out of these old spectacles been explained as accompanying the evolution of society. We must at the outset get rid of a fallacy which blinds the eyes of many students to the influences of the towns upon the early drama of modern Europe—the fallacy of finding in the Biblical incidents and personages of the Mysteries and Miracle-plays the key to all their characteristics. The abstract, allegorical, impersonal characters of these spectacles cannot be attributed to the nature of the Christian faith; for in the early days of that faith profound problems of personal being—personal immortality, responsibility, and the like—had formed, with subtle speculations on the subject of the Trinity, the great questions of Christianised Greek intellect. The truth is that a new communal life was giving a new prominence to the impersonal, the allegorical, in religion and philosophy and poetry. Men again, but under very different conditions from those of the clan, had merged their sense of personality in that of group life, content to leave to feudal lords those sentiments of individualism which, in the ears of serfs or townsmen but lately freed from serfdom, sounded of the lord's tyranny and the tortures of hell, devoutly believed and hoped to be reserved for such strongly marked personalities. No doubt there are wide differences between a body of feudal serfs fighting their way to burghership and clan corporations of kinsmen. No doubt there are differences almost as wide between a *commune* of France, or a chartered town of medieval Spain, Germany, England, and the city commonwealths of Greece before they began to lose the clan feeling of identity between the citizen and his city group. Yet in one fundamental point the characteristics of the city commonwealth and the clan are repeated in these European organisations—in the subordination of the individual to the corporation of which he is a member. It is here that we discover the social maker of the medieval drama's abstract and allegorical and impersonal characteristics.

§ 91. The communal authorship of the Mysteries and Miracle-plays recalls that clan ownership of early song to which we have elsewhere alluded. "*Le Mystère du Vieil Testament*," for example, "n'est-pas une œuvre personnelle dont il y ait lieu de rechercher l'auteur; c'est une œuvre collective, qui a dû s'elaborer lentement pendant le cours du xve siècle." * Whatever importance the clergy possessed as the first makers of rude plays, both the making and acting, sooner or later, passed into the hands of guilds —either the trade-guilds of the town, or bodies of literary craftsmen who (like the Homêridæ or the Hebrew musician-clans) assumed the familiar organisation of the guild. Thus, the Chester Mysteries, performed for the last time in 1574, were acted by trading companies of that city. In France it was out of the Town-Guilds that the *Confrèrie de la Passion* was formed—a fraternity which, chiefly composed of tradesmen and citizens of Paris, played Mysteries from 1402 to 1548. At Coventry particular parts of the Mystery were assigned to particular trading companies; thus, the Smiths' Company acted the Trial and Crucifixion, the Cappers' Company acted the Resurrection and the Descent into Hell. † In Germany Master-Singer Guilds for the composition and recitation of verse were established at Mayence, Ulm, Nürnberg, and other towns, the old "Singing School" at Nürnberg being maintained as late as 1770. The famous scene of the Tower of Babel in the *Mystère du Vieil Testament*, in which the carpenter *Gaste-Bois* (Spoil-wood), the mason *Casse-Tuileau* (Break-tile), and the rest, are medieval guildsmen doing duty as Nimrod's workmen, graphically illustrates the dramatic workmanship of these literary guilds. But the impersonal view of human character taken by these corporations is a more interesting evidence of communal feeling than this impersonal

* Baron James de Rothschild's *Introduction*, p. iv.
† Cf. *History of Early English Guilds*, Early English Text Society, 1870.

2 A

authorship, just as the gradual disappearance of sacred and allegorical characters before the growth of individualism in the towns is a still more interesting evidence of the dependence of literature on social evolution. Let us take a bird's-eye view of this dramatic evolution from communal to individual life.

I. The sacred spectacle, exhibited by the clergy in town or monastery, either written completely in Latin, or intermixed with French or German, as the case may be, presents divine personages who, like the heroes of the early Attic stage, present at once an abstract and historical character. The first great Miracle-play of German origin (*The Rise and Fall of Antichrist*, an Easter play of the tenth century, found in the Convent of Tegernsee in the Bavarian Highlands) is in Latin, and contains such personages as Paganism and the Jewish Synagogue (introduced as women), Mercy, Justice, Hypocrisy, Heresy. In the old French Miracle-play, *The Wise and Foolish Virgins*, " Christ speaks, or rather sings, in the words of the Latin Bible; but he then repeats what he has said in Provençal verse, which is also used by the Virgins." In fact, the Latin Mysteries were easily elaborated out of the *Officia* of the Church; and old remains of *Officia* used for this dramatic purpose have been discovered at Freising in Bavaria, at Orleans, Limoges, and Rouen. "From the time of Gregory the Great the Mass itself became an almost dramatic celebration of the world-tragedy of Golgotha. It embraced the whole scale of religious emotion, from the mournful cry of the *Miserere* to the jubilee of the *Gloria in excelsis*."

II. Though the personages of the Latin Mysteries were already rather allegorical and abstract than individual and concrete, the use of vernacular languages and the consequent influx of prevalent ideas so much increased this tendency, that in most literary histories attempts are made to distinguish the Mysteries, with their sacred personages, from the Moralities, with their allegorical characters, Virtue, Vice, Pity, and the rest. But we cannot distinguish these spectacles by any fixed line; we can only say that the popularisation of the drama which is marked by the use of the vernacular languages is accompanied by an increased love of abstractions and allegories; and the student of contemporary social life cannot fail to observe how this love of impersonal being reflects that tendency towards corporate or guild life which is the most striking characteristic of the growing towns. It must not be forgotten that nameless characters (such as L'Evesque, Le Prescheur, L'Ermite, in the *Miracles de Notre Dame*) are not individuals properly so called, but types of classes, and as such deriving their interest from a social life which (like that of the German towns even in the days of Hans Sachs) could be marked off into trades almost as distinct as Eastern castes. The prevalence of allegorical thought and ideas of men in classes or types can, indeed, be illustrated from all kinds of medieval literature as well as the drama; the satirical allegory of *Piers Ploughman*, or Rabelais, or *Das Narrenschiff* of Sebastian Brandt, with its hundred and ten classes of fools, might be readily traced to conditions of social life. So, too, in Chaucer's famous tales, Knight and Squire, Prioress and Monk and Friar, the Shipman, the Doctor of Physic, and the rest, in spite of individualising touches, are primarily types of social classes; while in the Haberdasher, Carpenter, Webbe, Dyer, Tapicer, all "clothed in one livery of a solemn and great fraternity," we have the guild directly introduced. Every reader of medieval literature knows the popularity and perpetual allegory of the *Roman de la Rose*, echoed in the *Faux-Dangier*,

Déplaisir, Espérance, of even the lyric poet Charles d'Orleans; so, too, in the chivalrous allegory of Spenser we may find these corporate modes of thought decked in feudal trappings, and meeting that individualising spirit of the Elizabethan age, which, in the drama of Marlowe and Shakspere, displaced the abstract and typical by the individual and concrete.

III. But the names of Marlowe and Shakspere suggest a third stage of the early European drama, in which we approach the analysis of personal character more closely than in the sacred or allegorical spectacle, yet not so closely as some enthusiastic worshippers of the great English dramatist would have us believe. When we find historical personages in such Miracle-plays as *Robert le Diable* or *Guillaume du Desert* side by side with allegorical personages, we may be sure that the historical drama is not so closely connected with profound analysis of individual character as has been sometimes assumed. When it is remembered that the Mysteries were primarily sacred histories (certain English Mysteries, for example. presenting a picture of the world's progress from the Creation and anticipating its future to the Day of Judgment), the secular history and the sacred spectacle cannot be separated by a very wide gulf. Let it also be remembered that one of the marked features of the Chinese drama—in which analysis of individual character is, as already explained, peculiarly deficient—is the frequent use of historical incidents and personages. The historical drama and subtle analyses of character are, in fact, rather opposed than, as some maintain, closely connected. No doubt there are wide differences between what may be termed an antiquarian historical drama, such as modern dramatists have sometimes attempted, and "histories" in the Shaksperian sense. No doubt Shakspere, in some of his historical plays, was as little hampered in his creative imagination as the Attic dramatists, when they used the heroes of old Greek story as a canvas on which almost any variety of character might be depicted. Still, we must admit that the truly *creative* conception of dramatic art is opposed to the necessary restrictions of historic fact, and must look upon the early "histories," with their improprieties of time and place and character, rather as secular imitations of the sacred story detailed in the Mysteries, than as a sign that the drama had now passed out of its religious tutelage and the region of moral abstractions into the sphere of artistic "realism." For dramatic "realism" means something more than the copying of historic fact; it means the putting together of a character in such a way that it shall wear the look of an individual reality without being an exact reproduction of any personage we already know; it means that the dramatic personage must be at once an individual *and something more*, an abstract type *and something less*—in a word, a double-faced entity containing both an individual and a general element, and so reproducing in art the most profound truth of human experience—that individual being is only realisable as a contrast between self and not-self.

IV. This dramatic realism is only possible where social conditions foster sufficient personal freedom in action and thought to allow a vivid realisation of personal as distinct from corporate being; it is only possible where socialism is not carried into such an excess as to merge individuality in group life, and where individualism is not carried into such an excess as to make personality insignificant by destroying all bonds of social thought and action. Dramatic realism needs personal freedom from communal restraints, various types of personality, and, coexisting with this freedom and variety, a fund of social sympathies and a belief in the dignity and mysterious greatness of individual being. In Elizabethan England and the Spain of Charles V. and Philip II., a variety of causes had supplied these elements of dramatic art. In both countries the individualism of the feudal lords had been forced to live in peaceful relations with the corporate life of the towns by a strong centralism holding in its hands the reins of local government. In France, too, a like growth of central authority was drawing together these types of ultra-corporate and ultra-individual life. Indeed, it is at this confluence of the feudal with the corporate spirit that we reach the full stream of national literature in each European country; and perhaps the best point from which we may view the meeting of the waters is supplied by a dramatist whose fatherland was destined to bitterly experience the want of a central arbitrator between the nobles and the towns.

§ 92. Hans Sachs, born at Nürnberg in 1494, stands on the borderland which divides the old allegorising drama, with its acting guilds and impersonal authorship, from the drama of personal authorship and individualised character. Sachs, as Dr. Karl Hase [*] observes, "attempts no subjective development of character, but simply causes his personages to translate into action, or more often into dialogue only, the event which he wishes to represent." Like the writers of Mysteries, also, he places Christianity and heathendom closely together. "Next to God the Father and God the Son appear Jupiter and Apollo; at the Last Judgment the bark of Charon bears the departed souls; with the Judgment of Solomon appears the Choice of Paris." But, though proprieties of time and place are

[*] *Miracle-Plays and Sacred Dramas*, by Dr. Karl Hase; translated by A. W. Jackson, and edited by Rev. W. W. Jackson (Trübner, 1880).

ignored, the life of the great German free towns being
transferred to Hebrew and Christian story, though tragedy
and comedy are still combined as in the Mysteries or in a
Chinese play, the subdivision of labour in towns is, in the
theatre of Hans Sachs, individualising the types of the old
spectacle, and Sachs' conception of the burghers and the
nobles, as divided by God Himself into castes, marks
the union of two spirits—that of the hereditary feudal
seigneurs and that of the town corporations.

Sachs' comedy, *Eve's Unlike Children*, introduced by
the usual herald of the Mysteries, illustrates this union of
town and castle, feudal lord and trading burgher. The
division of labour is attributed to God, who, having come
down from heaven to examine Cain and Abel in Dr.
Luther's Catechism, is shocked by the contemptuous
ignorance of Cain, whose time is spent in running wild
about the streets (clearly a reminiscence of the German
town rather than the plains of Asia), and who, with his
wicked brothers, four in number, ranged before the Lord,
expresses "a passionate dislike for the examination." The
Lord laments their impiety, which is to bring down an
inherited curse in the shape of hard labour.

> " Therefore on earth shall be your place
> As a poor, rough, and toiling race,
> As peasants, woodmen, charcoal-burners,
> Herdsmen, hangmen, knackers, turners,
> Grooms, broom-makers, beadles, tailors,
> Serfs, shoemakers, carters, sailors,
> Jacob's brethren, rustics coarse,
> Hireling men with one resource—
> A labouring life and little gain."

Dr. Hase notices as a remarkable fact that Hans Sachs,
not only here but elsewhere, has adopted "the harsh aristocratic theory which would derive the scions of every
noble house from a pious and divinely favoured ancestry,
and the pith of the nation, which supports the upper

classes, from a race under the divine ban." But when it is remembered how the medieval trades tended to adopt a spirit of caste in their guilds, and how the towns had sprung for the most part out of hereditary serfs, this peculiar version of the old clan ethics of inherited sin need not surprise us. Sachs afterwards rearranged this play under the name *How God the Lord blesses the Children of Adam and Eve;* and here we again meet the doctrine of a divine fate in the social status of men. Eve brings her four favourite children to Adam as the most likely to please the Lord. Adam praises them, but inquires for the rest of his children who ought also to receive God's blessing. Eve replies that they are too ugly and dirty to be shown; "some are hidden in the hay in the stable, some are asleep behind the fireplace." Adam thinks differently, but agrees to bring forward the four better-looking children. The Lord comes, and at Eve's request blesses these four children. The first shall be a great king, and as such receives the gift of a sceptre; the next shall be a warrior, and is presented with shield and sword; the third shall be a burgomaster with judicial staff, and the fourth a wealthy merchant, whose portion is a set of weights and measures. Every one shall remain in his own station—an idea thoroughly in keeping with the spirit of medieval guilds. The Lord then takes the children for a walk in Paradise. Meanwhile Eve, left to herself, regrets that she had not brought forward the other children also; and, though the sun has almost set, the Lord waits for Eve to present the four boys whom she now takes out of the hay. They, however, have not learned to pray properly; and Eve receives from the Lord a reprimand in consequence. Still the Lord is not unwilling to bless them. The first shall be a shoemaker, and his gift is a last; the second receives a weaver's shuttle; the third, a shepherd's pouch; the fourth shall be a peasant, and to him is given a ploughshare. Eve, astonished, asks—

> " O, thou most gracious Lord of heaven,
> Why is thy blessing so uneven?
> Since sons they are of Adam born,
> All equal, why hold four in scorn?
> Since some as great men thou hast blest,
> Why common folk should be the rest—
> Shoemakers, weavers, herdsmen, hinds?"

But the Lord replies that each has been selected according to his *natural* fitness, and points out the dependence of each rank of society on the other.

> " One class is even as another,
>   Each rank of service to its brother. . . .
>   Be each man on his calling bent,
>   And every man shall be content."

§ 93. But, while the individualism of the feudal lords and the socialism of corporate life were thus meeting under the shadow of central government, there was one part of Europe in which, from an early date, the conflict of the individual with the group had made its appearance. The Lombard League, victorious in its conflict with the world-empire of Barbarossa, had allowed the city commonwealths of Italy to develop within their walls an individualising spirit which could ill brook the reins of the Christian world-religion. The conflict between this individualising life of the Italian republics and the spiritual brotherhood of Christianity inspires the chant-like song of Dante, on whose inexpressibly mournful face the deadliest struggle of which human nature is capable— the struggle of intensely individual with intensely corporate feeling—seems graven as in scars. But in the *Divina Commedia* individualism is victorious, and in the Italian cities wealth and faction displaced the social spirit of Christianity by one of personal passion scarcely to be paralleled save in the decaying republics of ancient Greece. At first glance the Italian towns would seem the veritable home of a drama full of individual characterisation. But excessive individualism is almost as fatal to dramatic progress as a corporate life in which all differences of personality are lost. Innumerable units, raised out of individual littleness by no bond of corporate union, become too ephemeral to attract the analyses of the artist, who will soon prefer to turn to physical nature or to Fate. Individual being, which only comes out distinctly on a great background of social sentiments, could not alone supply the Italian republics with an original drama. Moreover, the similarity of the Italian dialects to Latin turned men's attention to classical models, in which they found a spirit like their own already expressed; and, when the plays of Seneca were supplemented by the recovered masterpieces of Greece, it was clear that any indigenous Italian drama was doomed.

Thus their social conditions and the peculiar nearness of classical associations united to make the Italian drama an imitation of classical models. Such, for example, was the *Rosmunda* of Rucellai, represented before Leo X. at Florence in 1515—a play which retains the classical chorus, and contains direct imitations of the *Antigone;* such, also, is the *Sophonisba* of Trissino, which (though not published till 1524) suggested the former, and is written on the Greek model, being divided, not into acts, but only by choral odes. It is significant that Trissino found his model in Euripides, the tragedian of Attic individualism. The declamatory tone, which had been one of the marks of decadence in the Athenian drama, and (as has been pointedly observed) " fixes the attention of the hearer on the person of the actor rather than on his relation to the scene," soon disclosed itself in the Italian theatres; and even such poets as Ariosto and Tasso failed to create a real and lifelike drama within the shell of the classical form. In half a century the appearance of the Pastoral drama, based on the Theocritean dramatic idyll, and in less than a century that of the Opera, showed how poets were turning (as Agathon and Chœremon had turned) from the dramatist's function—creation of individual character—to physical nature and the embellishments of music.

But though the Italian drama was not destined to do great things in its own country, its influences on other countries were powerful. In England and Spain, indeed, corporate and individual being met and produced dramatic originality as striking as the same conscious conflict had struck out in Athens. Here the development of the drama from the social figures of the early spectacles to subtle displays of individual personality was unbroken. In Shakspere himself the marks of the old spectacles are evident. Beside his many real fictions, which so wonderfully unite the breadth of a general type with the deepest individual personality, we find figures such as Rumour in the Induction to the *Second Part of Henry IV.*, reminding us of many a symbolical character in the Mysteries; the half-mythical, half-divine Hymen in *As You Like It* stands side by side with characters so carefully individualised as Rosalind and Celia; Shakspere's clowns clearly present a transition from typical personages like the old Vice to such a marked individuality as that of Touchstone; moreover, the allegorical personage Time, who, "as chorus" at the opening of Act IV. in *Winter's Tale*, apologises for sliding over sixteen years, reminds us that Shakspere's disregard of the "unities," as well as his mixture of tragic with comic scenes, was largely due to the influence of Mysteries and Moralities.* Individualism is indeed the dominant note in Shakspere's drama, but it maintains its profound interest because of the multitude of voices above which it is clearly heard; the secret of the master lies not in his having "incarnated feudalism in literature" (as Walt Whitman says), not in his having championed the cause of the nobles (as Rümelin tells us), but in his combining, as Æschylus and Sophocles before him had combined, the conflicting spirits of corporate and individual life now walking side by side through the streets of Elizabethan London. Here, for a time at least, was no place for classical and Italian restrictions; the remonstrances of Sidney (*Defence of Poesie*), against "our tragedies and comedies observing rules neither of honest civilitie nor of skilful poetrie," knew not that a more vigorous life than even that of Periclean Athens was producing for itself its own dramatic principles.

But if Elizabethan London did not supply an audience sufficiently polite and erudite to appreciate the classical and Italian restrictions, the courtly centralism of Paris, opposed to strong emotions as breaches of etiquette, easily submitted its theatre to classical imitation. In 1552, only five years after the Parliament of Paris had suppressed the Fraternity of the Passion, Jodelle, father of the regular French drama, exhibited his tragedy of *Cléopatre* before Henry II. The play is simple, devoid of action and stage effect, full of long speeches, with a chorus at the end of every act; but, as if anticipating the future destroyer of national drama in France, the troop of performers, whose Mysteries had been so lately interdicted, "availed themselves of an exclusive privilege

* Milton's original plan of *Paradise Lost* as an allegorical drama, with abstract personages and a chorus, would have curiously blended the manner of the Mysteries with classical form. Even in *Samson Agonistes*, as is well known, we have a double allegory.

granted by Charles VI., and, preventing the representation of the *Cléopatre* by public actors, forced Jodelle to have it performed by his friends." No trade-union of actors, however, could check the growth of classical taste. The *Agamemnon* of Toutain, taken from Seneca, the dramatist whose rushlight was to be too often preferred by French artists to the full splendour of Attic tragedy, was published in 1557; and in 1580 were published the eight tragedies of Robert Garnier, which closely follow the plots of Seneca or Euripides, contain long speeches, relate events chiefly by messengers, and employ the chorus between every act.

Between the writers of any particular age, says Shelley, in the preface to his *Revolt of Islam,* "there must be a resemblance which does not depend upon their own will. They cannot escape from subjection to a common influence which arises out of an infinite combination of circumstances belonging to the times in which they live; though each is in a degree the author of the very influence by which his being is thus pervaded." The symmetry of form and analysis of individual character in the plays of Euripides and Sophocles exactly suited the time-spirit of Paris after the Wars of Religion had centralised culture in the courts of Louis XIII. and the " Grand Monarch." It has been said that the famous line of Corneille's *Médée* (1635)—

"Que vous reste-t-il contre tant d'ennemis?
—Moi!"

was the *cogito, ergo sum* of French tragedy, and struck its keynote—that of individual character.* If such study of character had been extended to all sorts and conditions of men and women in French society, if it had not been fettered by proprieties of Parisian etiquette and classical

* Cf. *Histoire de France,* H. Martin, liv. xiii. p. 552.

taste, France would have possessed a truly national drama. As it was, however, the Parisian tragedy failed to truthfully reflect even the life of Paris, much less that of France in general. On the one hand, the characters and social life of the classical theatre are *Gallicised;* in *Andromaque* the stigmas of slavery are wiped out, in *Iphigénie* Achilles is gifted with Parisian gallantry, in *Phèdre* the centre of interest is shifted from the hero of Euripides to a heroine more in accordance with Parisian sentiment.* On the other, the Parisian theatre was divorced from the provincial life of France and condemned to rapidly exhaust its narrowly restricted supplies of thought and sentiment; hence even the wit of Molière, confined within a narrow circle of individuality, tends to run into types—*Le Misanthrope, Le Grondeur*—rather than to create a living personality like that of Falstaff. Macaulay, comparing Bunyan and Shelley as writers who have "given to the abstract the interest of the concrete," observed that "there can be no stronger sign of a mind destitute of the poetical faculty than the tendency so common among writers of the French school to turn images into abstractions, no stronger sign of a mind truly poetical than a disposition to reverse this abstracting process and to make individuals out of generalities." But neither Macaulay nor the French dramatists seem to have known that individuality depends for life and variety on the range of social evolution which the artist has within his ken—a range which may be limited not only by the degree of evolution actually reached in the given group, but also by the proprieties of an *élite* circle or the restrictions of classical imitation.

§ 94. For a time it looked as if courtly and classical

---

* Cf. Géruzez, *His. de la Litt. Fran.*, vol. ii. pp. 246, *sqq.;* A. W. Schlegel, *Lect. on Dram. Art.*, lect. xviii.

associations were destined to produce a stationary state of national literature throughout Europe, and all inspiration was to be lost by men who had not learned that the form of literature cannot live apart from the spirit; that style consists not in mere arrangement of words, but in the harmony of thought and speech, and that this harmony is fullest where social life is most widely sympathetic, while at the same time individual life is most profoundly deep. In the masterpieces of Dryden and Pope, an age of refined but shallow individualism leaves its marks in character-portraits not to be surpassed for clearness of outline and boldness of touch; but, as Emerson has said, "to believe that what is true for you in your private heart is true for all men—that is genius," and for such belief the Paris of Boileau offered as little scope as the London of Johnson. From the middle of the seventeenth to the middle of the eighteenth centuries, personal satire, that witness to weak social sympathies, rules the literatures of London and Paris. Before the belief of which Emerson speaks could become possible a new resurrection of the social spirit had to take place— Boileau and the court had to be replaced by Rousseau and the Revolution. In the towns corporate feelings had been chilled in France and England by the shadow of the individualising central monarchy; but now the manifest disbelief of courtly individualism in itself, as well as new commercial and industrial activities, were arousing sentiments of personal equality and corporate union. It would be clearly impossible within our limits to describe the many causes which contributed to create democratic individualism side by side with industrial socialism—the great conflicting spirits in whom we live and move and have our being. Suffice it to say that in place of monarchical individualism now grown effete, in place of feudal individualism ousted by central force, in place of the narrow socialism of the medieval *communes*, came a conflict between personal and social action and thought on a scale which the world has never before witnessed. Since the close of the eighteenth century vast movements of men in masses have strengthened more and more the social spirit, have deepened more and more, by repulsion where in no other way, the sense of individuality. How this return to corporate life, how this deepening of individuality, have affected and are affecting literature, it would be a life-task to illustrate and explain; we shall here offer only some striking examples of their influences.

In Germany the literary centralism and courtly proprieties of Paris had found from the first a hazardous dominion. Without any definite national centre, and containing marked social contrasts in its local governments, cities, and feudal nobility, Germany could not easily fall in with the stereotyped literary ideas of Paris and her recognition of individual life within a very special and narrow circle as the only proper domain for the literary artist. Besides, what evidence was there, after all, that the models of Parisian taste were really classical? The countrymen of Sachs were not long in putting this question and answering it for themselves in a manner fatal to Parisian pretensions. Hence Lessing's endeavour to establish a truly German drama by criticism such as that of his *Dramaturgie*, and by creation such as that of his *Minna von Barnhelm*, " the first truly national drama that appeared on the German stage." Ten years later (1773) appeared *Götz von Berlichingen*, which displayed German independence not only in a disregard of French dramatic rules, but also in finding materials for a national drama in the old days of the *Ritterthum*.

Contemporary life and national history were thus alike expanding the horizon of the literary artist beyond Parisian limits. Types of individuality, of social life, not admissible within the purlieus of the Parisian theatre, were receiving attention; nay, the very idea of the stage as a great moral agent (Schiller's favourite idea) showed the rise of a social spirit totally at variance with Parisian taste. We might illustrate the rise of this new spirit in such type-characters as Saladin the Mussulman, Nathan the Jew, and the Christian Knight-Templar in Lessing's *Nathan ;* but we prefer to turn to the work of a greater than Lessing.

Johann Wolfgang Goethe, born at Frankfurt am Main on the 28th of August, 1749, was no believer in social Utopias such as the author of the *Contrat Social* might imagine in his *State of Nature;* but none the less was his a real voice from the new social spirit of European life. If the instruments to which he looked for the propagation of new doctrines—brotherhoods of men of high character and training as described in *Wilhelm Meister*—remind us of the bard-clans which appear at the rude beginnings of literary culture, his appreciation of *Hans Sachs' Poetical Mission,** and his abstract or allegorical personages in *Faust,* display deep sympathy with that corporate side of human life which since the days of the Mysteries had been almost ignored in literature. The "Prologue for the Theatre," in this latter famous piece, which, especially in the often unread Second Part, contains all the elements of the early European drama—sacred personages, allegory, mixture of comedy and tragedy, disregard of the unities—con-

* In this poem Goethe admirably hits off the allegorical spirit of Sachs, by introducing the symbolical personages Industry (a maiden with a wreath of corn upon her head), and the aged woman who bears indifferently the names Historia, Mythologia, Fabula.

2 B

trasts individual and collective life in a manner which would seem to mark this contrast as the primary thought in Goethe's mind. "Speak not to me," says the Poet to the Manager, " of that motley multitude at whose very aspect one's spirit takes flight; veil from me that undulating throng which sucks us, against our will, into the whirlpool." " You can only subdue the mass by mass," responds the Manager; " each eventually picks out something for himself. . . . Consider you have soft wood to split; and only look whom you are writing for." But the Poet is not ready to subject himself to *Das Gemeine;* "the Poet, forsooth, is to sport away the highest right which Nature bestows upon him. By what stirs he every heart? Is it not the harmony—which bursts from out his breast, and sucks the world back again into his heart?" A mysterious union of individual with social being, almost worthy of an Oriental philosopher-poet; but Goethe's Mystery-play is indeed throughout the great mystery of individual contrasted with social life, the mikrocosm contrasted with that makrocosm of corporate unity at whose sign Faust, thrilled with rapture, sees "Nature herself working in his soul's presence." On which side is Goethe? Is he for the individual mikrocosm, or for the group—the makrocosm? " It is a great pleasure to transport one's self into the spirit of the times," says Wagner. " What you term the spirit of the times," Faust replies, "is at bottom only your own spirit in which the times are reflected." This looks like individualism of Byron's type. But "before the gate" moves a world of social types—mechanics, servant-girls, students, the townsmen, the beggar, the soldier—"under the gay quickening glance of the Spring;" and as the "motley crowd" presses out of the town, "from the damp rooms of mean houses, from the bondage of mechanical drudgery, from the confinement of gables and roofs, from the stifling narrowness of streets," Faust, in the gladness of a truly social spirit, cries, " Here is the heaven of the multitude ; big and little are huzzaing joyously ; here I am a man." Not so Mephistopheles—"the devil is an egoist; " not so the wretched pedant Wagner, who is an enemy to coarseness of every sort," and hates to see " people run riot as if the devil were driving them, and call it merriment, call it singing." Yes, the dominant spirit of *Faust* is social ; and in the Second Part especially the signs of corporate and impersonal being come thick upon us— in a symbolisation of social progress, in allegorical personages such as the four grey women, Want and Guilt, Care and Need. But perhaps the true intent of Goethe is not to take sides with either the individual or the social spirit, but to reconcile their pretensions in an ideal of practical culture.

Before the eyes of Victor Hugo some such reconciliation seems likewise to loom forth as a grand ideal. His best work, like that of Goethe, is impersonal in tone ; his ideals are such as an age of social sympathies might suggest—Justice, Liberty, Progress. If Hugo is weak in individual portraiture, it is because there rises before his mind the vast figure of " Humanity " in which the countless differences of individual being disappear. " If his perception of individual character is ordinarily not very exact, some compensation for this lies in his abundant sympathy with that common manhood and womanhood which is more precious than personal idiosyncrasies." * In *Les Chants du Crépuscule*, for example, " the individual appears, but his individuality is important less for its own sake than because it reflects

* Dowden, *Studies in Literature*, 1789-1877, p. 437.

the common spiritual characteristics of the period." Above all, in *La Légende des Siècles* we have (as Hugo himself tells us in his preface) "an effort to express Humanity in a kind of cyclic work, to paint it successively and simultaneously under all the aspects—of history, fable, philosophy, religion, science—which unite in one immense movement of ascent towards the light; to show in a kind of mirror, dark and clear, that grand figure, one and multiple, gloomy and radiant—Man." Contrast this picture of the human race "considered as a grand collective individual accomplishing epoch after epoch a series of acts on the earth," with the picture of the world's past and future offered by a Miracle-play; contrast the profound depths of personality in *Faust* with the personages of a Morality-play; what an expansion of social sympathies, what an immense deepening of individual consciousness!

It would be easy to multiply examples of the social spirit as the grand maker of modern literature—the *Prometheus* of Shelley, the *Ahasuerus* of Edgar Quinet. It would be easy to illustrate the union of this social spirit with a spirit profoundly individual alike in the novels of George Eliot and the poetry of Walt Whitman. But our contrast of *Faust* with the medieval drama reminds us that, besides expanded sympathies and deepened personality, this social evolution of Europe was leaving other marks on its national literatures in new aspects of Nature and animal life. The splendid descriptions of Nature in *Faust*—Spring budding as old Winter flies to the bleak mountains, the green-girt cottages shimmering in the setting sun, the sunrise at the opening of the Second Part—contrast strikingly with the few bald allusions to Nature in the Mysteries and Moralities. Byron calls his *Heaven and Earth* and his

Cain "Mysteries;" but not only is his intense individualism, reflected in that of Cain as of Manfred, utterly at variance with the impersonal character of the early spectacles, and even fatal to any dramatic capacity by its inability to project sympathy beyond self, but the descriptions of Nature in these so-called "Mysteries" distinguish them alike from the rude drama of allegory and the mature drama of personal character. In the old impersonal drama of England, France, Germany, we have few touches of Nature even so slight as the *Gossip's Song* —" the flood comes flitting in full fast "—in the Chester Plays.* In the personal drama, that of Shakspere himself, for example, we have only splendid glimpses of Nature—the "oak whose antique root peeps out upon the brook that brawls along this wood," or "yon gray lines that fret the clouds are messengers of day"—as if Shakspere felt the open introduction of Nature to be as unsuited to his drama as that of the impersonal "many-headed monster." Byron's lone Japhet among the rocky wilds of the Caucasus lamenting the wave that shall engulf the rugged majesty that looks eternal, Byron's painfully individualised Cain watching with Lucifer the myriad lights of worlds sweep by in the blue wilderness of space as "leaves along the limped streams of Eden," are almost equally removed from the Mysteries and the mature drama. How is it that we find Nature socialised on a vast scale in *Faust?* How is it that we find the individual and Nature thus darkly face to face in Byron? It is to these questions that we now propose to turn.

* Edition of Thomas Wright, p. 53.

CHAPTER III.

NATURE IN NATIONAL LITERATURE.

§ 95. In the earliest poetry of Europe, poetry which reflects the stormy local life out of which national union was to slowly grow, man is too busy with his tribal wars and his conflict with rugged Nature to sing of the mountains or the forests with any sense of pleasure. In *Beowulf*, Grendel's shadow, dark and deadly, "roams all night the misty moors." When the cruiser "foamy-necked" across the "wild swan's path" has reached the glittering cliffs, the Weders thank God "for making easy to them the watery way." For the Scôp knows nothing of the glad waters of the dark blue sea or the moonlit lakes of later poesy; he fears the sunset when "dusky night, the shadowing helmet of all creatures, lowering beneath the clouds comes gliding on;" he fears "the haunted waters of the Nixes' mere," and gladly sees the dawn of " God's bright beacon " in the east.

Nor is this want of sympathy with Nature confined to the poetry of the Sea-Robbers. "We find no description of scenery either in the *Nibelungen* or the *Gudrun* even where the occasion might lead us to look for it. In the otherwise circumstantial account of the chase during which Siegfried is murdered, the only natural features mentioned are the blooming heather and the cool fountain under the linden tree." In *Gudrun*, indeed, as Wilhelm Grimm goes on to say, we have such slight descriptive touches as the morning star rising over the sea glistening in the early dawn; but, as in the Homeric pictures of the island of the Cyclops and the gardens of Alkinous, such descriptions of Nature are completely subordinated to human interests. Had we any truly primitive reliques of Celtic or Teutonic poetry, we might find in them Nature-myths, such as those of Hymir and Odin and the Jötuns, in which some Carlyle would descry for us vast reflections of man's primitive personality supposed to be colossal—"huge Brobdingnag genius needing only to be tamed down into Shaksperes, Dantes, Goethes," as if the diverse personalities of these three master-singers could not only be lumped together, but might be treated as the personality of a clansman "tamed down." But Christianity, while absorbing the folk-lore of its converts, humanised and, so to speak, denaturalised it. Combating the sentiments of clan life —Blood-revenge and the like—Christianity was also compelled to combat pagan worships of Nature and the songs in which they were voiced. Inheriting largely from the municipal life of Greece and Rome feelings of man's superiority to Nature, disdainful of material existence as corrupt and perishable, and now brought into direct conflict with the pagan worship of Nature, the new faith could not be expected to perpetuate such poetry of Nature. Moreover, each successive wave of barbaric conquest contributed to make these sentiments of Nature a kind of savage jungle in which the deities of the pagans figured in wild confusion as dragons and monsters more readily convertible into the devils of the faithful than the lovely forms of classical mythology. Finally, the degradation of those clansmen whose communal property these sentiments of Nature would have been, must have aided in dethroning the divinities of Nature; and when the free clans had sunk into the serfdom of feudal villages, it was less likely than ever that their old songs should attract the attention of the monks.* If new sympathies with Nature were to arise, clearly they must find their source in a material life more hopeful than that of feudal serfs, a life in which men might again become in some degree joyous pagans pleased with the odours of earth-flowers, and not for ever peering through their short-lived beauty into the unknown and eternal.

Such a life of material pleasure was now only possible in the feudal castle; and here, accordingly, the return to paganism took place. But this feudal paganism was something widely different from either the classical or the tribal. A coarsely objective individualism, almost equally removed from the individualism of the Alexandrian age, aware of its own pettiness in the presence of vast masses of men, and from the clan merger of individual in social being, had now assumed a gigantic and almost grotesque significance in the person of the seigneur. It might be anticipated that before the eyes of this feudal personage Nature, if she attracted attention at all, would assume a dress curiously contrasting with that which she had worn for the poets of Alexandria or the bards of the clan.

§ 96. Feudal song neither humanises Nature, as the Alexandrian had done, nor spiritualises her life—worships in her neither the life of man nor that of God. It would seem as if Christian associations, without doing much to lessen the prodigious self-importance of the seigneur, had been able to drive from his halls the

* On the monks as subduers of Nature's marshes and forests see Montalembert's *Monks of the West*. Their conflict with Nature seems rather to have confirmed their contempt for the material world than created any sympathy with Nature's life.

awe of Nature's lasting majesty or the true love of her beauty. In the *Chansons de Geste* and the songs of *Minnesingers* the life of the wandering minstrel could not but leave traces of Nature's influences; but these are seen merely in general allusions, and if among the trampling of horses and the baying of hounds, among the sights and sounds of the chase or the hawking party, we catch a glimpse of " gentle May," or the "dew glistening on the heather-bells," or hear the song of the nightingale, it is only because the feudal scene needs the addition of some such prettiness. These feudal singers reverse the practice of that prose-poet Bernardin de Saint-Pierre, who makes his narratives only frames for his pictures of Nature; they offer us hardly any pictures of Nature, little but scattered images (such as the "fading leaves of autumn" or "the fields bared in winter's snow"), which are so frequently and mechanically repeated as to suggest anything but lively sympathy with Nature. The flower and the leaf are but emblems of war and love to them; as sings Bertran de Born—

> " Bien me sourit le doux printemps,
> Qui fait venir fleurs et feuillages;
> Et bien me plait lorsque j'entends
> Des oiseaux le gentil ramage.
> Mais j'aime mieux quand sur le pré
> Je vois l'étendard arboré,
> Flottant comme un signal de guerre;
> Quand j'entends par monts et par vaux
> Courir chevaliers et chevaux
> Et sous leurs pas frémir la terre."

German critics have asked whether contact with Southern Italy, with Asia Minor and Palestine by the Crusades, enriched the feudal poetry of Germany with new imagery drawn from more sunny climes, and have decided in the negative. The question suggests one reason for the weak and stereotyped sentiments of Nature in feudal poetry. Modern science has gifted the literary artist with thoughts of Nature's unity, in which all individual and social distinctions lose themselves—are "made one with Nature;" but the narrowly local associations of feudal life prevented even the coarsest sense of Nature's unity. Only local aspects of Nature—those of their own neighbourhood—could have presented any charm for the seigneur and his retainers; and even these, far from being gilded with any halo like the local divinities of Hellas, were spoiled by associations of villeinage. The fields were for the serfs to till; the forest glades were beautiful only as the haunts of the deer. The *Chanson de Roland* might offer many an opportunity for descriptions of the Pyrenees, but what pleasure would a glowing picture of the Valley of Roncevaux have afforded the audience of a castle hall? Would they, who cared for Nature even round their walls only as the purveyor of the chase, have listened to descriptions, however beautiful, of a place they had never seen? No; the feudal minstrel suited his lyre to the common feelings of his feudal audiences; and, if he sang of Nature at all, only introduced her general features, without aiming at truth of local description or even variety of expression, and even these general touches as mere adjuncts of feudal life— "the greyhounds glancing through the groves," and "bowmen bickering on the bent."

Still feudal life and the poetry it created are by no means to be overlooked in the development of our European sentiments of Nature. Such images of Nature as are scattered through feudal songs, though only taken to throw into greater relief the charms of a mistress or the pleasures of the chase, are at least in the main truthful. It was something to have freed Nature from the load of tangled myths under which early barbarism had buried her. It was something to have risen above Christian anathemas of the material world even so far as to find the figures of lord and lady, horse and hound and hawk, more beautiful among the flowers of May and the singing birds. Nature is plainly assuming forms more friendly than were known to the kinsmen of Beowulf when they gladly saw "the Father loosen the bonds of frost," or "drove their roaring vessels over the mists of the floods." But this feudal sentiment of Nature is narrow in the extreme, socially and physically. "Among the Troubadours," says M. Fauriel, "we shall seek in vain for the least picture, false or true, of the country-folks' condition. These Theocriti of the castle know nothing of labourers, herdsmen, flocks, the fields, the harvest, the vintage; they have the air of never having seen brook and river, forest and mountain, village and hut. For them the pastoral world is reduced to lonely shepherdesses guarding some sheep, or not guarding them at all; and the adventures of this pastoral world are limited to conversations of these shepherdesses with the Troubadours who, riding by, never fail to see them and quickly dismount to offer their gallant addresses." How shall the life of Nature be observed from a broader and loftier platform than that of the feudal castle? How shall her immense variety of forms oust the stereotyped Nature-language of feudal song? What social expansion, what individual deepening of man's spirit, shall reveal in Nature sights and sounds not known before?

§ 97. Between the twelfth and sixteenth centuries we may watch three great influences at work in creating new ideas of Nature in Europe—the rise of the towns, the progress of geographical discovery, and the Renaissance. At first, indeed, the rise of the towns did not rouse any lively sympathies with Nature. The armed burghers of the *Commune*, seeing few but enemies beyond their walls, viewed the scenery of the country with much the same feelings as those of the old Greek town-republics. But, in spite of confining men's interest within the city walls at first, the towns of Europe were destined to expand directly and indirectly our modern sentiments of Nature. Their commerce, bringing back knowledge of new climates, animals, vegetation, gave currency to new ideas, new contrasts, of Nature; and the various types of character developed within their walls diversified the human standpoints from which Nature might be perceived. The soul of the free burgher, filled with new sights and sounds, was soon capable of adding much to the songs of feudalism. At the court of the monarch burgher and feudal elements could find a quiet union. Here, then, we might have expected to find a true poetry of Nature springing up. But the Latin and Greek Renaissances were to make our European poetry of Nature an exotic cared of courts before it became a home-growth of democratic taste.

The fantastic geography of the *Divina Commedia* has too little to do with the world of Nature to admit truthful and sympathetic pictures of her forms. The individualism of Dante's town-born muse leaves as few signs of Nature's handiwork as the town-drama of Athens. Here and there we meet descriptive touches—"il tremolar di marina," *
"la divina foresta spessa e viva;" † but even in the pine-forests on the shore of Chiassi we hear echoes from Vergil—

"Tal, qual di ramo in ramo si raccoglie
Per la pineta in sul lito di Chiassi,
Quand' Eolo Scirocco fuor discioglie."

If we turn to Petrarch expecting to find natural de-

* *Il Purgatorio*, i. 117.   † *Ibid.*, xxviii. 2,

scription as a fitting frame for human love-scenes, we shall be disappointed; for, though we may admire the Italian stylist's sonnet on the effects of the Valley of Vaucluse upon his feelings after Laura's death, he sympathises rather with city life and classical reminiscences than with the splendid life of Nature round about him. "I miss with astonishment," says Humboldt,* "any expression of feeling connected with the aspects of Nature in the letters of Petrarch, either when, in 1345, he attempted the ascent of Mont Ventour from Vaucluse, longing to catch a glimpse of his native land, or when he visited the gulf of Baiæ, or the banks of the Rhine to Cologne. His mind was occupied by classical remembrances of Cicero and the Roman poets, or by the emotions of his ascetic melancholy, rather than by surrounding Nature."

This was while the Greek revival had scarcely yet begun; no wonder that when the models which Rome had essayed to copy were unveiled before the eyes of Western scholars, their faces were averted from all sights and sounds of Nature save such as their classical gods— for gods indeed the classical artists now became—had stamped with approval. The beauties of the physical world exist only for him who can see them; and when the exquisite but delusive mirage of classical associations stole over the face of Western Europe, men of culture came to see Nature—nay, even social and individual life —through mists in which nothing loomed out clearly save the phantom men and manners of Athens and Rome. "For long the only forests or seas, gardens or fields, frequented by poets, were to be found in the descriptions of Vergil and Homer. In France, at least down to the time of Bernardin de Saint-Pierre and Chateaubriand, the only voyages made by men of letters, the only storms

* *Cosmos*, Poetic Descriptions of Nature, note 82.

and shipwrecks with which they were acquainted, were those of Ulysses and Æneas."* Even in Chaucer we find the conventional garden of the Italian or Provençal muse rather than the landscape of England. Not only does Chaucer know nothing of Nature in the Wordsworthian sense—for his allegories and types bespeak an age in which there was no profound individualism capable of feeling "the silence and the calm of mute insensate things"—but his merely animal enjoyment of her beauty prefers colourless generalities to local truth; he would, perhaps, have shrunk as little from transplanting Italian scenery into England as from making Duke Theseus an English noble, just as Shakspere sets the London guilds in Athens, and places lions in the forest of Arden.†

Just when the resurrection of Greek thought was beginning to send forth scholars bound hand and foot in the grave-clothes of antiquity, while mental freedom, fostered by growing towns and decaying feudalism, sought to clothe itself in classical dress so as to escape the censure of Christian dogma—an excuse for much of the Renaissance pedantry—voyages of discovery in the East and West spread new ideas of Nature's handiwork in distant climes. From the letters of Columbus and his ship's journal we may feel the overpowering amazement with which the navigator gazed on impenetrable forests, "where one could scarcely distinguish which were the flowers and leaves belonging to each stem," palms "more beautiful and loftier than date trees," "rose-coloured flamingoes fishing at the mouths of rivers in the early dawn." "Once," he tells us, "I came into a deeply enclosed harbour, and saw high mountains which no

* Victor de Laprade, *Le Sent. de la Nat. Chez les Mod.*, p. 57.
† Cf. M. Browne, *Chaucer's England*, vol. i. pp. 210, *sqq.*; vol. ii. pp. 224, *sqq.*

human eye had seen before, mountains with lovely waters streaming down. Firs and pines and trees of various form, and beautiful flowers, adorned the heights. Ascending the river which poured itself into the bay, I was astonished at the cool shade, the crystal-clear water, the number of singing birds. It seemed as if I never could quit a spot so delightful—as if a thousand tongues would fail to describe it—as if the spell-bound hand would refuse to write."

Here were materials for Chateaubriands and Lamartines, yet, excepting the great national epic of Portugal,* the influences of the new discoveries on literature as distinct from science were not very remarkable. It has been observed that Camoens, like Lucretius, gives us a picture of the water-spout; and no doubt his "cloud of woven vapour whirling round and round and sending down a thin tube to the sea" is at least as graphic as the Roman's "column reaching down from heaven to ocean." But, though Camoens tauntingly bids the learned "try to explain the wonderful things hidden from the world," the spirit of Lucretius was abroad. Before the poet's life closed (1579) Bacon was eighteen years of age; and that "experience," which against "so-called science" he had praised as "the sailor's only guide," was on its way

* "The *Æneid*," says Hallam (*Lit.*, vol. ii. p. 205), "reflects the glory of Rome as from a mirror; the *Lusiad* is directly and exclusively what its name ('The Portuguese,' *Os Lusiadas*) denotes, the praise of the Lusitanian people. Their past history chimes in, by means of episodes, with the great event of Gama's voyage to India." Having made an exception in favour of the *Lusiad*, we must remind the reader that ocean and Indian scenery by no means banish conventional personification of Nature under classical figures. Venus and the Nereids save the fleet; Bacchus delivers a speech to the assembled gods of the sea; and Neptune in true Vergilian fashion bids Æolus let loose the winds on the Portuguese fleet. But contrast the absence of scenery in Ariosto and Tasso, and we shall admit with M. Laprade that the *Lusiad* "est le plus ancien monument de notre poésie chrétienne où la nature tienne une grande place et joue un rôle indépendant" (*Le Sent. de la Nat. Chez les Mod.*, p. 73).

to be systematised. Independent inquiry readily sought an outlet in studies which at first wore the look of being unconnected with dogma; and, in spite of Bacon's imaginative style, the disciples of experience began to separate science from literature as if they possessed no bond in that imaginative element without which experience is a dead thing. Literature, too, just now becoming the toy of courts, without sorrow surrendered to science a study of Nature which would not only have limited the freedom of romance, but bred dissatisfaction with the scenic models of Theocritus and Vergil. It was through classical spectacles that the culture of the sixteenth and seventeenth centuries preferred to see Nature; and it was just in their sentiments of Nature that classical literatures, as already explained, were weakest. Moreover, such sentiments of nature as classical literature had possessed were likely to be gravely misinterpreted by Christian imitators. The pastoral elegy of Modern Europe is a striking evidence of this misinterpretation. The essence of the Greek pastoral elegy is the contrast of man's individual life with Nature's apparent eternity—a melancholy sentiment becoming the lips of a modern materialist, but in the author of *Lycidas*, the poetic champion of a faith before which the material universe is but as dust and ashes compared with the soul of the veriest wretch who wears the form of man, almost grotesquely out of place. Why should Nature lament the escape of a divinity greater than herself from its clay prison? The Greek chorus in the social life of the Hebrews speaking the Puritanism of England in *Samson Agonistes* is not a stranger union of incongruities than the poet of individual immortality repeating the materialism of the Greek in lamentations for Edward King. Plainly the individualism of the sixteenth and seventeenth centuries did not know whether it was of earth or the infinite ; and this confused judgment made it willing to look on Nature partially as a beautiful machine, its exquisite mechanism worthy of such word-pictures as *L'Allegro* and *Il Penseroso* contain, partially as a pagan god to be duly invoked only in good old pagan fashion, and partially as a perishable nullity destined to be "rolled together as a scroll"—in any case connected by no profoundly real links with man's social and individual life.

§ 98. "If we would copy Nature, it may be useful to take this idea along with us, that the pastoral is an image of what they call the golden age. So that we are not to describe our shepherds as shepherds at this day really are, but as they may be conceived then to have been, when the best of men followed the employment. To carry this resemblance yet farther, it would not be amiss to give these shepherds some skill in astronomy, as far as it may be useful to that sort of life." So thought and wrote Alexander Pope in his *Discourse on Pastoral Poetry*. Yet who would look for genuine sympathy with Nature from the poet of court intrigues, personal satire, well-bred criticism, and a mongrel Nature in which Sicilian muses sing on the banks of the Thames, and our Theocritean acquaintances, Daphnis and the rest, repeat the similes of the Greek in correct English couplets? Who could expect such sympathy from the disciple of a poet who in his *Passage du Rhin* is more troubled by the insertion of ugly names ("Quel vers ne tomberait au seul nom de Heusden ? ") than the description of Nature, and mistakes lifeless symbols like "Rhine, leaning with one hand propped upon his urn," or the classical Naiades, for the fresh inspiration of Nature ?

Yet it would be a mistake to suppose that the artificial poetry of courts did nothing for Nature but surround her with the extinct flocks of Pan, the long-withered fruits of Pomona, and the ancient charms of the elderly but ever-blushing Flora. It was in courtly literature that shallow individualism began to understand itself, and worked out to their bitterest disenchantment all the pleasures of which its "palace of art" was capable. The ferocious misanthropy of Swift is the spirit of this individualism in the act of violent suicide; the tame cynicism of Voltaire is this same spirit dying of old age, though wearing still the garlands of a vanished youth. Men, in the poetry of Allan Ramsay and Thomson, Klopstock, Saint Lambert, began to see that Nature without court dress was none the less beautiful; that there were myriads of her sights and sounds which the restricted and now effete individualism of courts had never freely experienced; that of "this fair volume which we World do name" they had been too long content with "coloured vellum, leaves of gold, fair dangling ribbons," or, at most, "some picture on the margin wrought." At first, indeed, simple truthfulness of description, such as may be found plentifully in Cowper's poems, marked the change from classical and courtly idealism into open-air freedom; but soon the sentiment of Nature was to become something infinitely deeper than any description, however accurate, however beautiful, could express.

Democratic revolution, with its vast masses of men in action, with its theoretic obliteration of all individual inequalities, and its consequent readiness to imagine human life as impersonal—a readiness to be increased by scientific ideas of physical laws likewise impersonal—now came to force into intense conflict ideas of individual and collective humanity. Individualism, feeling trampled underfoot in the rush of multitudes, turned to Nature in search of

"Jardins lumineux, plaines d'asphodèle
Que n'ont point foulés les humains."

One aspect of this newly roused individualism is to be seen in Byron and his imitators throughout Europe—an aspect which unites all the self-importance of a feudal seigneur with a real or affected despair of human happiness such as monastic asceticism alone can rival. Another aspect of it may be seen in Shelley's substitute of spiritual pantheism for individual immortality. In Shelley, personality knows its own weakness in the face of the physical world, knows its weakness as but one drop in the vast flood of humanity, and is willing to come down from feudal isolation, to mix in the democratic crowds, to merge itself in that spirit of Nature which knows neither personal nor social distinctions—

"He is made one with Nature. There is heard
His voice in all her music, from the moan
Of thunder to the song of night's sweet bird."

But this negation of self, expressing itself in abstractions as intensely realised as they are delicately beautiful, makes Shelley's sentiment of Nature less profound than that of Wordsworth. Neither in the presence of his fellow-men, whatever their myriad march, nor of Nature, how countless soever her worlds, can the indestructible personality of Wordsworth forget itself. His spirit, like that of Shelley, is divine; but it is no mere fragment of a vast divinity; backwards into the illimitable past, forwards into the illimitable future, now and for ever in the face of man and Nature, it dwells, has dwelt, shall dwell like a star apart in an individuality unmade, unmakable, unchangeable. Before this profound sense of personality, partially Platonic, partially Christian, but most of all awakened by the physical and social conditions of the poet's age, Nature assumes a depth of meaning which only beings of Wordsworthian mould may feel. Byron's descriptive powers, Shelley's musical communion with the sounds of

Nature, give place to a realisation of Nature's being all the more terribly significant because the observer refuses to reconcile its conflict with his own personality either by material or immaterial unity; and while the associations of his childhood, youth, and age become consecrated as the earthly dress of an eternal being—not the melancholy entirety of one made of such stuff as dreams are made of—Wordsworth fears not to be materialised by the companionship of Nature, because he has neither deified her being at the expense of his own, nor denied her divinity in order to make himself eternal.

§ 99. When, therefore, we ask, as we have already asked, why it is that in the "mysteries" of Goethe and Byron deep feelings of personality, deep sympathies with Nature, strikingly contrast with the impersonal allegories and absence of Nature in the early drama of Modern Europe, we find our answer in the social and individual evolution of European life—in the expansion of social life, in the deepening of individuality winning new senses of sight and hearing, as it were, for the lights and shades, the murmuring inarticulate voices of Nature—

"Voix fécondes, voix du silence
Dont les lieux déserts sont peuplés."

Social sympathies, individual consciousness, Nature's life, all on a scale of greatness never before approximated, seem to meet in a poet of that great Western Republic whose teeming population is indeed " not merely a nation, but a nation of nations." In America, says Walt Whitman, "there is something in the doings of man that corresponds with the broadcast doings of the day and night;" in America, more than in the old countries of Europe, far more than in the stationary East, there is "action magnificently moving in vast masses;" in America, too, this largeness of Nature and the nation of nations "were monstrous without a corresponding largeness and generosity of the spirit of the citizen." For Whitman the ideal individual of America—America's ideal man—is to absorb into his soul an almost boundless range of social life—all the sights and sounds of Nature and animals; "his spirit responds to his country's spirit; he incarnates its geography and natural life and rivers and lakes— Mississippi with annual freshets and changing chutes, the blue breadth over the inland sea of Virginia and Maryland, the growths of pine and cedar and cypress and hickory, forests coated with transparent ice, and icicles hanging from the boughs and crackling in the wind." *

There is a strange magnificence in this democratic individualism, so prodigious in its width and depth—in the social sympathies, in the personal consciousness of equality, in the fellowship with Nature's mighty life, of these democratic "comrades, there in the fragrant pines and the cedars dusk and dim." Far indeed have they passed from the comradeship of the clan, far from the citizenship of the city commonwealth, far from the castes of the East, far from the *communes* and seigneurs of the West; yet they feel not wholly disunited with the "garnered clusters of ages, that men and women like them grew up and travelled their course and passed on."

* Preface to *Leaves of Grass.*

CONCLUSION.

§ 100. HERE, at an effort perhaps uncouth, certainly in form but rudely rhythmical, to gather into song all that Nature on a scale stupendous, social life in forms most various, individuality most profound because realised as distinct from all groups and all Nature's wonders, we close our task. Very imperfectly have we essayed to follow the effects of social and individual evolution on literature from the rudest beginnings of song down to the poetry of the great Western Republic. We have but glanced at the progress of prose in place of those metrical forms which in the absence of writing supplied supports for the memory; the influence of conversation public and private—its character largely depending on the forms of social communion in which men meet—on such progress in the East and West; the influence of individualised thinking, of philosophy, in fact, upon the form and spirit of prose in Athens and Rome and Modern Europe. We have omitted the varying aspects of animal life as reflected in the literatures of different countries and climates. We have omitted the comparison of satire in different social conditions, though we willingly allow that "there is no outward expression, be it in literature, sculpture, painting, or any other art, which more openly tells of a nation's character and exhibits it to all eyes than caricature"—not that all satire is caricature, but, like caricature, it is a negative index to an ideal consciously or unconsciously upheld. In fine, want of room has also forced us to omit the development of criticism as itself illustrating the influences of social and individual evolution on literary ideals. To reduce the immense study which we have named Comparative Literature within the compass of a handy volume without losing completeness and minuteness of detail, it would be needful to separate the descriptive from the scientific treatment of literature. But to devote an introductory work like the present to the scientific treatment alone, would not only cut away many interesting illustrations, but convey an altogether false impression of the study as bare and uninviting. If, in spite of our willingness to sacrifice completeness to attractiveness, our readers should carry away this unpleasant impression, the fault is certainly in the writer and not in his subject.

Another word of apology may be also needed. It will be clear to any reader of this book that its author is far from regarding literature as the mere toy of stylists, far from advocating the "moral indifference" of art. In his eyes literature is a very serious thing, which can become morally indifferent only in ages of moral indifference. "Let the world go its way, and the kings and the peoples strive, and the priests and philosophers wrangle; at least to make a perfect verse is to be out of time, master of all change, and free of every creed."* Such was Gautier's view; but it is stamped false by the whole history of literary development. Whether men like it or not, their literary efforts at ideal beauty in prose or verse must involve ideals of human conduct. Action, speech, and thought are too subtly interwoven to allow their artistic severance aught but fancied truth; if it were otherwise, literature might indeed have been

* Dowden, *Studies in Literature*, 1789-1877, p. 401.

the product of a Cloud-cuckoo-town in which historical science and morality would be equally out of place. But, it may be said, your science cuts at the roots of moral conduct by treating the individual as made by conditions over which he has no control. Far from it. Our science traces a growth of social and individual freedom so far as the conditions of human life have hitherto allowed them to grow together. Nothing is really gained for morality or religion by assuming that the life with which they deal is unlimited, unconditioned; nay, such limitless pretensions have hitherto proved very fatal to morality by fostering suicidal extremes of social and individual thinking. How are these suicidal extremes to be best kept in check? By insisting on the individual and social, physical, and the physiological limits within which man moves and has moved; by answering the admirers of universal shadows, in which morality itself becomes shadowy, in the words of the Hebrew prophet: "Who hath heard such a thing? What hath seen such things? Shall a land bring forth in a day? or a people be born in a moment?"

INDEX.

The numbers refer to the pages.

A

'Abd Yaghûth, 143, 146
Abu Tammâm, 133
Academy, French, 343, 344
Accius, 231
Achilles, shield of, 105, 122
Adonis, 106, 109
Æschines, 204
Æschylus, *Persians* of, 33; character-drawing of, 60; his drama reflects early social life of Athens, 206 *sqq.*; his moral teaching, 211; 190, 327, 333, 364
Agathon, 212, 363
Alcæus, 104
Alcman, 255
Alexandrian, Library, 173; life, 260, 261; as treated by Shakspere, 30
Al-Harîrî, 13, 183, 237
Allegorical personages, 216, 218, 221, 224, 226, 354 *sqq.*, 369 *sqq.*
Ambarvalia, 115 *sqq.*
Ancestor worship, Chinese, 297
Antar, 139, 147
Apollo, Delian, hymn to, 109, 110
Apollonius Rhodius, 255, 261
Arabs, early poetry of, 97, 133 *sqq.*; materialism of, 137; chivalry of, 139; language of, 237
Aramaic language and thought, 278

Aranyakas, 298
Aratus, 254, 261
Archilochus, 181, 263
Argo, story of the, 99 *note*
Ariosto, 311, 363
Aristophanes, Hades of, 189 *sqq.*; criticises Euripides and Æschylus, 209-211; individualism of, 212; chorus of, 214; character-types of, 215 *sqq.*, 247; 258, 333
Aristotle, 10, 16, 34, 171, 246, 248, 252 *sqq.*, 266
Arnold, Matthew, 41, 79, 229 *note*, 260, 324, 343, 344
Arrow-dance, 119
Art, and historical truth, 177 *sqq.*; want of, in early Athens, 206; supposed indifferentism of, 391
Arval Brothers, song of the, 114 *sqq.*
Aryans, Indian, primitive type of, 289 *sqq.*
Asiatic Society of Bengal, Journal of, 134, 140, 148, 150
Atellanæ, Fabulæ, 196, 221, 222
Athenæus, 105
Athens; old village life of Attica, 172, 181; literary beginnings of, 183 *sqq.*; contrasted with Rome, 173
Authorship, impersonal, 103, 111, 113, 114, 127, 129, 205, 352 *sqq.*
Autos Sacramentales, 34, 218

B

Babylonian influences on Hebrew mind, 276
Bacchylides, 112
Bacon, 75, 383, 384
Bayard, 139
Bazin, M., 15, 31, 45, 121, 319, 321 note, 322
Beast-epic, 167
Bedouin character, 148, 149
Benû Sheybân, 151
Beowulf, 131, 143, 189, 347, 374, 379
Bergk, 106
Berith, 108, 235, 277
Berkeley, 59
Bhanrs, 311
Bhavabhúti, 16, 313
Biography, 23, 265
Bion, 118 note, 239, 256, 324
Blackie, Professor, 267
Bleek, Dr., 167
Boileau, 13, 80, 367, 385
Bolingbroke, 80
Born, Bertran de, 377
Bráhmanas, 298
Bráhmans, rise of, 289
Brandt, Sebastian, 355
Brooke, Stopford, 13
Brown, Dr., 97
Browning, Robert, 131
Brucheium, 253
Buchheim, Dr., 39
Buddha, 276, 302 *sqq.*
Builinas, 85
Bunyan, 366
Burckhardt, 137
Burnouf, M., 118
Byron, 53, 370, 372, 373, 387

C

Calderon, 34, 216, 218
Callimachus, 261, 263
Calsabigi, 343, 344
Calverley, 259
Camoens, 383, 384
Campbell, 40
Carlyle, 27, 28, 154, 375
Caste, 56, 289; musician-castes, 111; priest-castes, literature of, 160,

193; origin of Indian, 293 *sqq.*; 355
Cato, 195
Cattle, in early social life, 289
Catullus, 101, 118 note, 261
Celtic, fosterage, 129; genealogical poems, 158
Centaur, the, 213
Centralism, literary, 343 *sqq.*, 364
Chæremon, 212, 213, 363
Chamberlain, Basil Hall, 199 *sqq.*, 325 *sqq.*
Chansons de Geste, 46, 134, 347, 377, 378
Chateaubriand, 89, 243, 381
Chaucer, character-types of, 69, 229 note, 355; Italian influences in, 79; metres of, 225; his treatment of Nature, 382
Chinese, lyric, 12; prose-verse, 13; theatre, 15, 199, 207, 251, 313, 318 *sqq.*; drama, introduced to European scholars, 75; symbolic dance, 121; criticism, 121, 122, 211; want of "epic" poetry, 159, 220, 309; sentiment of Nature, 240, 296; odes contrasted with Indian hymns, 295 *sqq.*; drama, European authorities on, 321 note
Chœrilus, 204
Chorodidaskalos, 112
Chorus, 34, 60, 362; Japanese, 199, 200; prominence of, in Attic drama, 202 *sqq.*, 205; how related to social life, 205 *sqq.*, 208 *sqq.*; in comedy, 213 *sqq.*; choral song, of Dacotahs, 102; Spartan, 106; of Elis, 107; of marriage, 108, 109; choral dance-song, 123
Christianity, 66, 286, 287
Cicero, 195, 252, 261, 263
City Commonwealth, and Nature, 54; Athens, the type of, 172; definition of, 175; drama in, 198 *sqq.*
Clan, ethics of, 61, 63, 64; nature of, 90, 92, 94 *sqq.*; group at roots of literary growth, 94, 97; choral song of, 110; life-view of, 130; personal poetry of, 131, 132; spirit in Rome and Athens, 197; devotion of, 150; sentiment of

INDEX. 395

Nature, 162 *sqq.*; liability, 97; song, 101 *sqq.*; 58, 65, 113
Cleon, 217
Clergy, Christian, in ancient Rome, 32
Clough, A. H., 49 *note*
Coleridge, S. T., 11, 26, 27, 34, 42, 43, 86
Columbus, 382, 383
Comedy, Attic, rise of, 214 *sqq.*; steps into the shoes of tragedy, 218; later, 247 *sqq.*
Communism, Platonic, 246; Hebrew, 270
Comparative method, nature of, 73; in study of literature, 82; development of, in modern Europe, 75, 76, 93
Conington, Professor, 189
Coriolanus, 27, 29, 32
Corneille, 344, 365
Courts, influence of, on literature, 82
Cowper, 386
Criticism, Chinese, 15; Indian, 16, 313; Chinese and Indian contrasted, 45, 319; critic and artist, 178, 179

D

Dance, symbolic, 102, 120 *sqq.*; 104, 117, 119, 127
Daniel, book of, 276, 277
Dante, 28; individualism of, 69, 361, 380; *De Eloquio Vulgari*, 74; 272, 333, 287
Dásas, 289
Davis, Sir J. F., 45, 254, 319, 321 *note*
Demetrius Phalereus, 253
Demogeot, 79
Demosthenes, 182, 204, 244
De Retz, 258
Description, graphic, 328
Didactic poetry, 19 *note*; purpose of Chinese drama, 331
Diocletian, edict of, 267
Dionysius, 195
Dissen, 258
Djeláwy, 138

Domitian, 261
Donaldson, 9
Dowden, Professor, 69, 371, 391
Drama, an index to social life, 31, 212, 227, 310, 358, 364, 366; Indian, and Nature, 55, 314 *sqq.*; elements of, in choral song, 109, 110; in symbolic dance, 120, 121; Victor Hugo on, 153; beginnings of Roman, 196; Athenian and Japanese, compared, 199, 204; origin of Attic, 202; development of personality reflected in, 203 *sqq.*; Roman and Indian contrasted, 232; Greek and Indian contrasted, 309; Indian and Chinese, contrasted, 331, 334; historical, 356, 357; Menander's, compared with Indian and Chinese, 251; Indian, 304 *sqq.*; Chinese, origin of, 318; dramatic form in ancient Indian hymn, 290, 292, 304
Dryden, 26, 80, 367

E

Earle, 250
Egyptian paradise, 145
Eiresiône, 107
Eliot, George, 372
Embatéria, 110
Emerson, 367
Empedocles, 14, 256
Ennius, 231
"Epic," definition of, 42; derivation of, 44; poetry of medieval France, 101; Victor Hugo on, 153; beginnings of, 158, 159; Roman want of materials for, 195 220; Indian, 305 *sqq.*; 312, 313; no Chinese, 309
Epigram, 266
Epitaphios, 109
Eponyms, 166
Essenes, 246, 283
Euêmerus, 231
Eumolpids, 111
Euripides, his chorus, 60, 210; *Ion* of, 180; individualism in his plays, 209 *sqq.*, 230, 231; criti-

cised by Aristophanes, 217; 190, 203, 206, 362, 365
Ewald, 275
Ezekiel, on inherited guilt, 64, 65, 230, 269, 280; socialism of, 131, 270; 180, 187, 270 *sqq.*; 274, 275, 278, 284, 287, 303
Ezra, 276, 282

F

Faerie Queene, 15
Family, Shakspere's Roman, 32; development of, at Rome, 192 *sqq.*; effect of Roman, on drama, 228; effect of Chinese, on drama, 332
Fauriel, M., 379
Feudalism. 340, 376 *sqq.*
Finite, philosophy of the, 392
Flach, Dr. Hans, 104, 110
Fosterage, literary, 129
France, influence of, on England, 80
Freeman, 339
Future life and clan age, 96

G

Garnier, 365
Gautier, 391
Gefolge. 67, 97, 139
Géruzez, 43, 366
Ghosts on Chinese stage, 333
Gibbon, 93
Gobineau, 312
Goethe, 11, 19, 49, 68, 78, 135, 177, 303, 327, 334, 341, 368, 369 *sqq.*, 388
Grammatical criticism, 237
Gray, 14, 123
"Great-man theory," 85
Greek, metres in English and German, 49; Alexandrian, 42; contempt for comparative inquiry, 74
Grimm, Jacob, 167
Grimm, Wilhelm, 375
Grosier, 25
Group, social expansion of, 77, 81, 90, 235, 244; nature of, 91
Gubernatis, 167
Gudrun, 374

Guilds and literature, 353, 355
Guizot, 131, 132, 304
Gymnopædia, 103

H

Hades, growth of the conception of, 187 *sqq.*; of Ezekiel, 271 *sqq.*
Hallam, 4, 5, 42, 383
Hamáseh, 133, 134, 138, 150, 151
Hamlet, 28
Hase, Dr. Karl, 358 *sqq.*
Hebrew, dance-song, 124, 125; communism, 246; and Alexandrian Greeks, 276 *sqq.*; Hellenised, 279, 282; woman, 25; literature contrasted with Greek, 98
Hegel, 276
Heine, 267
Henriade, 43
Herder, 276, 345
Hesiod, 54, 66, 109, 255
Hexameter, origin of, 106
Hogarth, 345
Homer, women of, 25; Nature in, 54; Homeric poems imply advanced social evolution, 99; social life in, 100; question of authorship, 159, 160; and Peisistratids, 182; compared with Indian "epics," 308, 309
Homéridæ, 50, 112
Horace, *Carmen Sæculare*, 115; 262, 264
Hueffer, 101
Hugo, Victor, 11, 34, 50, 68, 78, 152, 155, 371
Humanitas, 230
Humboldt, 162, 267 *note*, 381
Humenaios, 108
Hunter, 289
Huzailian poems, 133

I

Ialemus song, 106
Ibn Khaldoun, 148
Idyll, nature of, 240, 259; home of, 257, 258
"Ignorance," age of, 78
Igor, song of, 84

INDEX.

Imagination, nature of, 242
Imitation literature, 83, 222, 224 *note.*
Impersonal poetry, 68, 69
Indian, "epics," 159; criticism, 16, 226; sentiment of nature, 240; drama, 55, 251
Individualism, in modern "lyric," 40; in growth of prose, 51; apparently prominent in early poetry, 62, 63, 347 *sqq.*; Christian, 66; in criticism, 68; development of, 72, 81, 86, 182, 185 *sqq.*, 192, 203 *sqq.*, 215 *sqq.*, 219 *sqq.*, 230, 244 *sqq.*, 256, 354 *sqq.*; in Homeric poems, 99; historical development of inverted, 154, 155; affecting ideas of Nature, 165 *sqq.*; in Hades, 187 *sqq.*; extreme, effect of, on drama, 213, 362, 370; in Athens, England, Spain, compared, 218, 249, 250; Greek, incapable of being hastily Romanised, 223; in satire, 262; in Imperial Rome, 264 *sqq.*; and self-culture, 268; Hebrew, 273, 277, 285; Indian, 303, 307; in East and West, contrasted, 328, 335; growth of modern European, 349 *sqq.*, 361; in Shaksperian drama, 364; narrowed artificially, 366, 367, 386; united with social spirit, 370 *sqq.*; feudal, 376; democratic, 386, 389
Inherited guilt, in Athenian drama, 61; how treated by Greek and Hebrew individualism, 64, 282; derived from clan life, 96, 184; in modern Europe, 360
Ionian festivals, 180
Isæus, 248
Isokrates, 38, 172, 245
Italian, influences on English literature, 79; drama, 362 *sqq.*
Izár, 135

J

Japanese lyric drama, 199 *sqq.*, 325 *sqq.*, 224
Játra, 311, 312
Jebb, 13, 49

Jeremiah, 275, 303
Jerusalem, 285
Job, book of, 149
Jodelle, 364, 365
Johnson, 43, 323, 367
Jones, Sir William, 76
Josephus, 283, 284
Julien, M. Stanislas, 321 *note,* 325
Juvenal, 25

K

Kálidása, 313, 318
Kantemir, 84
Kasida, 46
Khalaf-el-Ahmar, 134
Khomse, 137
Khorovod, 103, 203
Kingsley, 21, 22
Klopstock, 386
Körner, 40
Kosegarten, 133

L

La Bruyère, 250
Lamb, Charles, 3
Lamentations, Book of, 275 *note.*
Language, and translation, 48; deterioration of Hebrew, 236; Latin, nature of, 267; of Indian and Chinese dramas, compared, 334, 335
Laprade, Victor de, 19, 162, 240, 382, 383
Latifundia, 257, 258
Laveleye, 62, 95
Lebid, 147, 167
Legge, Dr., 122, 295, 296
Lermontoff, 327
Lessing, 276, 368, 369
Library, Alexandrian, 253
Linus Hymn, 105, 106
Literary tricks, Athenian and Chinese, 254; Hebrew, 275
Literate class, rise of Hebrew, 274
Literatura, 5
Literature, indefinite meaning of, causes of, 17; provisional definition of, 19; science of, 20; contrasted with specialised knowledge, 77, 78; Hebrew and Greek

contrasted, 98; differentiation in development of, 127, 128; popular, want of at Rome, 193 *sqq.*; in India, 302; attempt to sever, from practical life, 250; national, 399 *sqq.*; problems of, 346
Lityerses, 106
Livius Andronicus, 222
Livy, 196
Locke, 75
Lomonossoff, 84
London, influence of, on English literature, 345, 367
Longfellow, 49 *note*
Lowth, 45
Lucan, 265, 267
Lucretius, 239, 383
Lusiad, 383 *note*
Luther, 39, 359
Lyall, 134, 140, 147, 150
Lycidas, 260, 384
"Lyric," definition of, 38; varieties of, 39, 40; Dorian and Æolian, 101; personal and impersonal, 104, 105; Hugo on, 153; of early contrasted with modern life, 155; under the tyrants, 182, 183; lyric poetry and Nature, 255

M

Macaulay, 26, 42, 89, 93, 195, 242, 344, 366
Magdâni, 237
Mahábhárata, 159, 305 *sqq.*, 316
Mahaffy, Professor, on status of Greek women, 25, 248, 249; on culture-influence of the tyrants, 182; on the chorus of Æschylus, 207
Maine, Sir Henry, 62, 72, 95, 100, 120, 129, 132, 340
Malachi, 277, 278
Málatí and Mádhava, 16, 226
Manu, code, 245
Marlow, 356
Martial, 266
Marzûki, 133
Mâshâl, 142
Masks, Athenian and Japanese dramatic, 201, 202

Menander, 203, 214, 231, 250 *sqq.*; philosophy of, 251; sentiment of Nature in, 252, 255
Menshim, 141
Metres, development of, 46; influences of language-structure on, 48; Arab, 134
Microcosmography, 250 *note.*
Mictlan, 145
Miletus, development of literature in, 183, 194
Milton, 218, 246, 324, 325, 364 *note,* 384, 385
Mimes, 221, 222
Mimnermus, 182, 256
Mir, 103, 122, 283
Miracle-plays and mysteries, 34, 58, 61, 351 *sqq.,* 356, 364, 388; contrasted and compared with *Faust,* 370, 372
Mo'allaqah, of Zuheyr, 140; of Lebid, 147, 167
Modernised poetry, 47
Molière, his characters, 26, 366; 194, 247, 250
Mommsen, 193, 262
Monks and literature, 348, 376
Montesquieu, 70, 156–158, 162, 345
Morrison, 16
Moschus, 118 *note,* 239, 256, 324
Müller, K. O., 6, 9, 103, 104, 106, 109, 112, 122, 123, 181, 202, 204, 207, 213, 216, 246
Müller, Max, 114, 290
Music and early literature, 105, 110, 112
Myths, 166 *sqq.*; Roman, 195, 239; Greek, 238, 239
Nábis, 112, 125, 126, 275, 277
Nævius, 223
Nasse, 62
National literature, 80, 81, 339 *sqq.*
Nature, how treated in Athens and Rome, 54; Indian reverence for, 55, 290, 308, 309, 313 *sqq.*; in clan poetry, 163, *sqq.*; individualised, 165; in world-literature 238 *sqq.*; socialised or individualised, 240; sentiment of, in Homeric poems, 255; sentiment of, and social life, 53 *sqq.,* 257, 267, 336, 380; humanised, 260 *sqq.*;

INDEX.   399

in Chinese plays, 320 *sqq.*; in *Faust* contrasted with Mystery-plays, 372, 373; Christianity and, 375; feudalised, 377; Hellenised, 381 *sqq.*; Milton's treatment of, 384, 385; sentiment of, in Byron, Shelley, Wordsworth, compared, 387, 388
Nehemiah, 282
Nibelungenlied, 347, 374
Niebuhr, 195
Nirvana, 304

O

Odyssey, Hades of, 63, 187; 123, 222, 255
Officia and early drama, 354
Omar, Khalif, 173
Orestes, 31
Osann, Professor, 253
Overbury, 250
Ovid, 261, 267

P

Pacuvius, 231
Painting, Roman, 267 *note*
Palgrave, 14, 38
Paradise Lost, 42, 43
Parallelism, Arabic, Chinese, Hebrew, 45, 51
Parasite, Indian, 316
Paris, influence of, on French literature, 345, 365, 366, 369
Parthenia, 103
Passion-plays, Persian, 31
Pastoral, poetry, its Sicilian home, 257, 258; elegy, 324, 384, 385; drama, 363
Patria potestas, 129, 173, 197
" People, the," rise of, 67
Percy, *Reliques*, 97, 161 *note*
Periclean Age, unhistorically treated, 171
Personal poetry, 130, 158, 159
Personality, objective in clan age, 152; various types of, 156, 375; how these affect aspects of Nature, 165, 373
Peruvian dances, 118

Pessimism, Hebrew, 282, 284
Petrarch, 380, 381
Pherecydes, 180
Philomon, 214
Phrynichus, 204
Pindar, 14, 40, 107, 110, 112, 122, 187 *sqq.*, 258; contrasted with Ezekiel, 271, 272
Pi-pa-ki, 319, 321 *note*, 331
Plato, 14, 37, 59, 122, 186, 191, 244 *sqq.*, 252, 279, 280, 281 *note*, 387
Platonius, 215
Plautus, 26; *Pænulus* of, 33, 226; his drama and social life at Rome, 196, 227; 221, 224; metre of, 225; names of his characters, 229 *note*; his *Captivi*, 249
Pliny, 266
Plutarch, 105, 106
Poetry, didactic, 19
Pope, 79, 323, 367; his treatment of Nature, 385
Prâkrit, 301, 334
Prémare, 75
Prometheus, 209 *note*
Propertius, 261
" Prophets, sons of the," 112
Prose, development of, 46, 51, 82, 128, 183, 195, 237, 244, 246, 252, 264, 266, 300; checked in India, 299, 301; *Aristotelized*, 51; rhythmical, 52 *note*, 181 *note*
Ptolemy Soter, 253
Purânas, 299
Pyrrhic, 119, 122

Q

Quinet, Edgar, 372
Quintilian, 252, 262
Qôheleth, 272 *sqq.*; 279, 284, 303
Qur'ân, 8, 29, 128, 137, 238, 275

R

Rabelais, 355
Racine, uses chorus, 218
Ragnar Lodbrok, 143 *sqq.*
Ralston, 103
Râmâyana, 159, 305 *sqq.*

Ramsay, Allan, 386
Rása, 311, 312
Rdwy, 128
Raymi, 118, 125
Realism, medieval, 59, 350; dramatic, meaning of, 357
Recitation in early literature, 181, 305
Reformation, 75
Renaissance, 74, 382
Renan, 161 *note*, 194
Reuchlin, 76
Réville, Professor, 117
Rig-Veda, 39, 113, 289, 304
Roman, women, 25; poetry of Nature, 54; want of "epic" inspiration, 159; literature, indebtedness of, to Alexandrian, 261
"Romantic" school, 11, 35
Rothschild, Baron, 353
Rousseau, 153, 154, 367, 369
Rucellai, 362
Rümelin, 364
Ruskin, 46, 52 *note*, 229 *note*, 267 *note*
Russia, imitation literature of, 83, 84; choral songs of, 103

S

Sachs, Hans, 355, 358 *sqq.*, 368, 369
Saint Lambert, 386
Saint-Pierre, 377, 381
Saint Simon, 265
Sallust, 265
Samson Agonistes, 218, 384
Sanskrit, 76, 237, 299, 310, 311
Sappho, 101, 104
Satire, 262, 367, 390; Chinese dramatic, 324 *note*
Saturnian metre, 194, 222, 223, 225
Savigny, 132
Saxon poetry and blood-revenge, 97
Scandinavian paradise, 145
Scephrus, 106
Schiller, 54, 327, 369
Schlegel, A. W., 11, 34, 43, 92, 342, 343, 366

Schoolcraft, 102, 106, 119
Schopenhauer, 256
Schultens, 135
Science and literature, 252
Scóp, 39, 163
Scott, Sir Walter, 57, 60, 136
Seneca, 362, 365
Serapeum, 253
Shakspere, his characters, 26, 229 *note*; his conceits and puns, 28; his "histories," 30; survivals from ruder drama in, 124, 221, 363; foreign associations on his stage, 33; his treatment of "the people," 69; 315, 327, 330, 333, 356, 373, 382
Sheól, 63, 145, 188, 271
Shelley, on translation, 47; on imagination and sympathy, 243; 266, 309, 327, 365, 366, 372, 387
Shih King, 12, 39, 114, 159, 294 *sqq.*
Sidney, 364
Simcox, 222
Simmias, 254
Simonides of Amorgos, 24, 181
Simonides of Keos, 107, 111, 273, 274
Singing personage in Chinese plays, 199, 319, 320
Sismondi, 4
Slane, Baron de, 29
Slaves, in Hades, 192; influence of Attic, 248; as affecting the sentiment of Nature, 257, 258; at Rome, 263
Smith, Adam, 149
Social, studies, peculiar difficulties of, 92; spirit, 368, 372
Socrates, 37, 186, 216, 217, 279
Solon, 181, 182, 192, 194
Sophists, 37, 186, 217, 245
Sophocles, 10, 60, 184, 198, 207 *sqq.*, 258, 326, 327, 364, 365.
Soumarokoff, 84
Sounds and ideas, 44
Spain, influence of, on England, 79
Speech, public, illustrating growth of Greek literature, 77
Spenser, 15, 78, 86, 109

Stage, Japanese, 200; Athenian, 205
Stanley, Dean, 275, 278
Stoicism, 268
Style, true nature of, 367
Suetonius, 265
Suidas, 237
Sûktas, 113
Sutras, 113, 298
Swift, 263, 386
Swinburne, 111, 219 *note*
Symonds, J. A., 8, 179
Syrinx, the, 254, 276

Tyndall, 77
Tyrrell, Professor, on the prologues of Plautus, 225
Tyrtæus, 110

U

Umm Aufa, 140
"Unities," the, 35, 37, 205, 313, 329 *sqq.*, 363
Upanishads, 298

T

Tacitus, 264 *sqq.*, 274
Talmud, 271
Targûms, 236
Tasso, 363
Tazya, 312
Tekya, 31
Ten Brink, 8
Ten Broeck, 119
Terence, 196, 221, 224, 227, 230
Terpander, 111
Teuffel, 219, 222, 237
Thâr, 63, 137, 184
Theocritus, 55, 165, 239, 254, 255 *sqq.*, 258 *sqq.*, 261, 324, 363, 385
Theognis, 177
Theophrastus, 249
Thespis, 203
Thomson, 386
Thrênos, 109, 110
Thucydides, 172, 266
Thymele, 205
Tibullus, 115
Tobit, 278
Tocqueville, 343
Toutain, 365
Towns, modern European, rise of, 67, 68, 341, 348 *sqq.*, 380; drama in, 81, 198, 353, 359; Arab, and culture, 148, 150
Tragedy, Attic, decline of, 213
Translation, 44
Trissino, 362
Tylor, 36

V

Valmiki, 305
Veda, 113, 114, 288, 293, 298
Vega, Lope de, 313
Vergil, 54, 239, 260, 261, 264, 267, 272, 333
Verse, prevalence of, in early literature explained, 160
Vicarious punishment, origin of, 96
Vidûshaka, 219, 316, 334
Village communities, 55, 62, 103, 172, 202, 203, 270, 277, 283, 335, 348
Villeinage, 378
Vita, 316
Voltaire, 43, 75, 80, 93, 220, 344, 386
Von Maurer, 62

W

Weber, 300, 301
Wehrgeld, 143, 184, 188
Whitman, 32, 69, 71, 364, 372, 388, 389
Williams, Monier, 290, 304, 305
Wilson, H. H., 114, 310, 311, 314, 334
Wisdom, Book of, 280 *sqq.*, 284
Women, 25, 32, 193, 248
Wordsworth, J., 117
Wordsworth, W., 49, 165, 382, 387, 388

2 D

World-literature, marks of, 236; place of, in literary evolution, 240, 241; 288, 342

Writing, influence of, on literature, 128, 161

X

Xenophon. 186
Xuthus, 180

Y

Yahvism, 112, 120, 208, 278, 288
Youen anthology of plays, 319, 321

Z

Zechariah, 278
Zenodotus, 254
Zuheyr, 140

THE END.

www.ingramcontent.com/pod-product-compliance
Lightning Source LLC
Chambersburg PA
CBHW022113290426

44112CB00008B/663